Women, Class, and Society in Early Christianity

Women, Class, and Society in Early Christianity

MODELS FROM LUKE-ACTS

JAMES MALCOLM ARLANDSON

HENDRICKSON
PUBLISHERS

ISBN 1–56563–181–1

First Printing — April 1997

Library of Congress Cataloging-in-Publication Data

Arlandson, James Malcolm, 1956–
　　Women, class, and society in early Christianity: models from
　Luke–Acts / James Malcolm Arlandson.
　　Includes bibliographical references and indexes.
　　ISBN 1–56563–181–1 (cloth)
　　1. Bible. N.T. Luke—Criticism, interpretation, etc. 2. Bible.
N.T. Acts—Criticism, interpretation, etc. 3. Women in the Bible.
4. Women in Christianity—History—Early church, ca. 30–600.
5. Sociology, Biblical. 6. Social classes—Rome. 7. Rome—Social
life and customs. I. Title.
BS2589.6.W65A75 1996
226.4′0830542—dc21　　　　　　　　　　　　　　　　　96–48298
　　　　　　　　　　　　　　　　　　　　　　　　　　　　　　　CIP

In Memoriam

Ella Leone (Lee) Ryland Arlandson
October 30, 1917 – September 21, 1994

TABLE OF CONTENTS

ACKNOWLEDGMENTS

This book is the product of an idea that occurred to me in 1988 when I was reading Luke–Acts, my favorite portion of Scripture. I noticed for the first time, so it seemed, Luke 2:34, which speaks of Jesus being destined for the falling and rising of many in Israel. Why did Luke insert that enticing concept in the extended introduction that makes up the first two chapters of his Gospel? What does it mean to fall and rise? How would Jesus cause this? Answering these questions provided the motivation and framework for the doctoral studies I was about to embark on.

This doctoral program took many twists and turns, and I appreciate every one of them, for they broadened my horizon beyond just New Testament scholarship. Traveling that long road, I accumulated a debt of gratitude to several persons. First, the dissertation committee guided me through the whole process, especially the chairman, Jean-Pierre Barricelli. He convinced me that a comparatist approach is better than a confined, single-discipline one. The other three members, S. Scott Bartchy, Douglass Parrott, and Jerry Camery-Hoggatt, kept me from straying too far from New Testament scholarship, since, after all, my focus was Luke–Acts. Peter Pettit, who had just finished his Ph.D. in Old Testament (early Judaism) at Claremont Graduate School, made sure my use of the rabbinic literature was within the bounds of scholarship in that area. It goes almost without saying that all errata and missteps are my own responsibility, not theirs.

When this book was a dissertation, I thanked Harvey and Alice Hettinga and Austin and Judy Miller for their support, which took many forms. I will always be grateful to them. Yet, I am sure they would not mind giving place to my mother, whose unexpected departure from this life into the next is still felt by me. She was an accomplished author in her own right, with sixty-nine publications to her credit. Hers was not a scholarly path but one for the enjoyment of children and adults. I can still hear her typewriter clacking out a children's book or an article on the old West. Whatever desire I may have to write springs from her own gifts and talents as I observed her during my formative, growing-up years. I dedicate this book to her. Thank you for everything.

ABBREVIATIONS

BOOKS AND PERIODICALS

AB	Anchor Bible
ABD	*The Anchor Bible Dictionary*, ed. D. Freedman et al.
AER	*American Ecclesiatical Review*
ATR	*Anglican Theological Review*
BA	*Biblical Archaeologist*
BARev	*Biblical Archeology Review*
Behr	Behr, C., ed., Aelius Aristides, *The Complete Works: Orations*
Bib	*Biblica*
BLit	*Bibel und Liturgie*
BJS	Brown Judaic Studies
BN	*Biblische Notizen*
BT	*The Bible Translator*
BTB	*Biblical Theology Bulletin*
BVC	*Bible et vie chrétienne*
BZ	*Biblische Zeitschrift*
CAGN	*Collected Ancient Greek Novels*, ed. B. Reardon
CBQ	*Catholic Biblical Quarterly*
ConNT	Coniectanea neotestamentica
CRINT	Compendia rerum iudaicarum ad Novum Testamentum
CurTM	*Currents in Theology and Mission*
Danby	Danby, H., trans., *The Mishnah*
EstBib	*Estudios biblicos*
ETL	*Ephemerides theologicae lovanienses*
ETR	*Etudes théologiques et religieuses*
EvQ	*Evangelical Quarterly*
EvT	*Evangelische Theologie*
ExpT	*Expository Times*
FoiVie	*Foi et Vie*
GR	*Greece and Rome*
GRBS	*Greek, Roman, and Byzantine Studies*
Greg	*Gregorianum*

HeyJ	*Heythrop Journal*
HTR	*Harvard Theological Review*
ICC	International Critical Commentary
IESS	*International Encyclopedia of the Social Sciences*, ed. D. L. Sills
Int	*Interpretation*
JAAR	*Journal of the American Academy of Religion*
JBL	*Journal of Biblical Literature*
JESHO	*Journal of the Economic and Social History of the Orient*
JFSR	*Journal of Feminist Studies in Religion*
JJS	*Journal of Jewish Studies*
JR	*Journal of Religion*
JRH	*Journal of Religious History*
JRS	*Journal of Roman Studies*
JSNT	*Journal for the Study of the New Testament*
JSOT	*Journal for the Study of the Old Testament*
JSOTSup	Journal for the Study of the Old Testament, Supplement Series
LCL	Loeb Classical Library
MMAR	Memoirs of the American Academy in Rome
Neusner	J. Neusner, trans., *The Mishnah* and *The Tosephta*
NovT	*Novum Testamentum*
NovTSup	Novum Testamentum, Supplements
NRT	*La nouvelle revue théologique*
NTS	New Testament Studies
OTP	*Old Testament Pseudepigrapha*, ed. J. H. Charlesworth
QD	Quaestiones Disputatae
RB	*Revue biblique*
REG	*Revue des études grecques*
RHE	*Revue d'histoire ecclésiastique.*
RSR	*Recherches de science religieuse*
RThom	*Revue thomiste*
SBL	Society of Biblical Literature
SBLDS	Society of Biblical Literature Dissertation Series
SBLSP	Society of Biblical Literature Seminar Papers
ScEs	*Science et esprit*
SJT	*Scottish Journal of Theology*
ST	*Studia Theologica*
StLukeJ	*St. Luke's Journal of Theology*
TAPA	*Transactions of the American Philological Association*
TBT	*The Bible Today*
TD	*Theology Digest*
TPQ	*Theologisch-Praktische Quartalschrift*
TS	*Theological Studies*
TT	*Theology Today*
ZNW	*Zeitschrift für die neutestamentliche Wissenschaft*

ANCIENT WRITERS

Aelius Aristides
    Or.   *Orationes*
Cato
    Agr.   *De agri cultura*
Chariton   *Chaereas and Callirhoe*
Cicero
    Flacc.   *Pro Flacco*
    Ver.   *In Verrem*
Dio Chrysostom
    Or.   *Orationes*
Josephus
    Ag. Ap.   *Against Apion (Contra Apion)*
    Ant.   *Jewish Antiquities (Antiquitates Judaicae)*
    J.W.   *The Jewish War (Bellum Judaicum)*
    Life   *The Life (Vita)*
Longus   *Daphnis and Chloe*
Lucian
    Alex.   *Alexander (Alexander the False Prophet)*
    Cat.   *Cataplus (The Downward Journey,* or *The Tyrant)*
    D.Meretr.   *Dialogi Meretricii (Dialogues of the Courtesans)*
    Fug.   *Fugitivi (The Runaways)*
    Gall.   *Gallus (The Dream,* or *The Cock)*
    Nec.   *Necyomantia (Menippus,* or *Descent into Hades)*
    Sat.   *Saturnalia*
    Somn.   *Somnium sive Vita Luciani (The Dream,* or *Lucian's Career)*
Paus.   Pausanius, *Description of Greece*
Phaed.   Phaedrus, *Fabulae (Fables)*
Philo
    Contempl.   *De vita contemplativa*
    Prob.   *Quod omnis probus liber sit*
Plutarch
    Mor.   *Moralia (Essays)*
Strabo   *Geography*

BIBLICAL BOOKS

Genesis   Gen
Exodus   Exod
Leviticus   Lev
Numbers   Num
Deuteronomy   Deut
Joshua   Josh

Judges	Judg
Ruth	Ruth
1–2 Samuel	1–2 Sam
1–2 Kings	1–2 Kgs
1–2 Chronicles	1–2 Chron
Ezra	Ezra
Nehemiah	Neh
Esther	Esth
Job	Job
Psalms	Ps/Pss
Proverbs	Prov
Ecclesiastes (or Qoheleth)	Eccl (or Qoh)
Canticles (or Song of Solomon)	Cant (or Song Sol)
Isaiah	Isa
Jeremiah	Jer
Lamentations	Lam
Ezekiel	Ezek
Daniel	Dan
Hosea	Hos
Joel	Joel
Amos	Amos
Obadiah	Obad
Jonah	Jonah
Micah	Mic
Nahum	Nah
Habakkuk	Hab
Zephaniah	Zeph
Haggai	Hag
Zechariah	Zech
Malachi	Mal
Matthew	Matt
Mark	Mark
Luke	Luke
John	John
Acts	Acts
Romans	Rom
1–2 Corinthians	1–2 Cor
Galatians	Gal
Ephesians	Eph
Philippians	Phil
Colossians	Col
1–2 Thessalonians	1–2 Thess
1–2 Timothy	1–2 Tim
Titus	Titus
Philemon	Phlm
Hebrews	Heb

James	Jas
1–2 Peter	1–2 Pet
1–3 John	1–3 John
Jude	Jude
Revelation	Rev

JEWISH WRITINGS

b.	Babylonian Talmud
m.	Mishnah
t.	Tosepta
B. Meṣiᶜa	*Baba Meṣiᶜa*
B. Qam.	*Baba Qamma*
Ketub.	*Ketubot*
Meg.	*Megillah*
Qidd.	*Qiddušin*
Šebu.	*Šebuᶜot*
Tem.	*Temura*
Yebam.	*Yebumot*

LIST OF FIGURES

Therefore we must support the cause
of order and in no wise suffer a
woman to worst us. Better to fall from
power, if we must, by a man's hand;
then we could not be called weaker
than a woman.[1]

1

INTRODUCTION

Nearly every ancient literary work employed a preface or prologue to
reveal its main themes, plots, and characters. Invoking the Muses,
Homer foretold of the anger of Achilles and the wandering of Odysseus. Historians from tale-bearing Herodotus and austere Thucydides
to Josephus and the Roman historians disclosed their subjects and
goals in prefaces. Usually through a main character the dramatists let
the audience know in the prologue which myth cycles they were
dealing with. The Greek novelists, such as Xenophon of Ephesus,
Chariton, and Achilles Tatius, revealed their main characters and
plots in the first few paragraphs. Living under the weight of such an
august and widespread tradition, Luke in his dual work, Luke–Acts,
also makes use of two prefaces, one in each volume.[2]

---

[1] Sophocles, *Antigone* (lines 677–80), trans. R. Jebb, in *Greek Drama* (ed.
M. Hadas; New York: Bantam, 1982) 96. For a brief discussion of this passage,
see J. Arlandson, " 'The Fall and Rise of Many': A Socio-narratological
Analysis of Women in Luke–Acts" (diss., University of California, Riverside,
1994) 19 n. 1.

[2] Luke shows evidence of being familiar with some of the literary traditions through his prefaces and speeches and through scenes such as riots,
travels, storms at sea, and shipwrecks, all of which occur in histories and
novels. D. E. Aune, *The New Testament in Its Literary Environment* (Library

For many decades scholars have seen the value of studying the first four verses in Luke and the first five or so verses in Acts to glean Luke's strategies and purposes, among other things. But they have also moved beyond these verses and have seen the paradigmatic value of the entire first two chapters of the Gospel as disclosing recurrent themes.[3] The term "paradigmatic" here means that the events and words occurring briefly in chapters 1 and 2 serve as proleptic and foreshadowing clues for understanding the rest of Luke–Acts.

One of Luke's main themes is revealed through the words of Simeon in 2:34. It is proleptic, since its content recurs throughout Luke–Acts.

> Then Simeon blessed them and said to his mother Mary, "This child is destined for the falling and the rising of many in Israel, and to be a sign that will be opposed."

In addition, Luke has already cued the audience to people's fall and rise through Mary's song (1:51–53).

> [51] He has shown great strength with his arm;
>   he has scattered the proud in the thoughts of their hearts.
> [52] He has brought down the powerful from their thrones,
>   and lifted up the lowly;
> [53] he has filled the hungry with good things,
>   and sent the rich away empty.

Simeon's prophecy reinforces Mary's song and puts Luke's strategy into a succinct description. In 2:35 the word διαλογισμός, *dialo-*

---

of Early Christianity 8; Philadelphia: Westminster, 1987) 77–117, has a thorough analysis of the subject. I use the name Luke without prejudice towards the complex issue of his identity. W. V. Whitney, "Women in Luke: An Application of a Reader-Response Hermeneutic" (diss., Southern Baptist Theological Seminary; Ann Arbor, Mich.: University Microfilms International, 1990) 39, wisely states, "If the quest for the historical Jesus has turned into a less-than-rewarding enterprise, then the quest for the historical Luke has been even less rewarding." On the dates of Luke–Acts, J. A. Fitzmyer, *The Gospel according to Luke* (2 vols.; AB 28, 28a; New York: Doubleday, 1981–85) 1.57, is probably correct when he postulates 80–85 C.E. But I do not oppose earlier dates, such as those for which C. J. Hemer, *The Book of Acts in the Setting of Hellenistic Historiography* (ed. Conrad H. Gempf; Tübingen: J. C. B. Mohr [Paul Siebeck], 1989) 365–414, strongly argues: Acts in 62, Luke after 70. In either case my argument will not be affected. For geographical location, I again agree with Fitzmyer: "It is really anyone's guess. The only thing that seems certain is that it was not written in Palestine" (*Luke* 1.57). My assumption is that it was somewhere in the Greek East—Asia Minor or northern Syria.

[3] H. H. Oliver, "The Lucan Birth Stories and the Purpose of Luke–Acts," *NTS* 10 (1964) 202–26; and P. S. Minear, "Luke's Use of the Birth Stories," in *Studies in Luke–Acts* (ed. L. E. Keck and J. L. Martyn; Philadelphia: Fortress, 1980) 111–30.

gismos (inner thoughts), in the rest of Simeon's sentence, echoes διάνοια, *dianoia* (thoughts) in 1:51, which further supports the parallelism.[4] Both passages heighten the expectations of the audience that the newborn Jesus, surrounded as he is with supernatural visitations and songs, will make many fall or rise when they meet him.[5]

When Luke included Simeon's announcement in 2:34, who were the "many" that Luke had in mind? In 1:51–53 the δυνάσται, *dynastai*, are humbled, the πλουτοῦντοι, *ploutountoi*, are rejected, the πεινῶντες, *peinōntes*, are filled, and the ταπεινοί, *tapeinoi*, are raised up. Further designations occur when Luke has Jesus reading from Isa 61:1–2 (Luke 4:18–19). These words also reveal the people's social condition: πτωχοί, *ptōchoi*, αἰχμάλωτοι, *aichmalōtoi*, τυφλοί, *typhloi*, and τεθραυσμένοι, *tethrausmenoi*. The words in 1:51–53 and 4:18–19, though not specific sociological categories, are pregnant with social meaning. However one interprets Luke's words about falling and rising, the interpretation has to include at the very least the social location of the characters in Luke–Acts.

Luke's preferred mode of communication is through stories. As he introduces the characters within these stories, he always applies to the characters epithets, titles, or occupational descriptions, such as "synagogue ruler," "centurion," "silversmith," "purple-seller," and so forth. Why are they important for his stories? What do they mean in his society? It seems that Luke is blending, therefore, a social strategy with a narrative strategy. He locates the characters socially and then exploits their location to fulfill his storytelling. In Luke–Acts the social always undergirds the literary, and the literary always assumes the social.

From the beginning of modern biblical scholarship in the nineteenth and into the twentieth centuries, scholars have widely recognized that Luke favors the poor and needy.[6] In particular, he devotes considerable attention to the plight of women, though, as we shall

---

[4] R. C. Tannehill, *The Narrative Unity of Luke–Acts* (2 vols.; Philadelphia: Fortress, 1986–90) 1.32.

[5] J. O. York, *The Last Shall Be First: The Rhetoric of Reversal in Luke* (JSNTSup 46; Sheffield: JSOT, 1991) 10–38, has a thorough survey of scholarship on reversals. Elsewhere in his book he demonstrates quite convincingly that it is a far-reaching theme in Luke (but he does not analyze Acts). His only passage about women is the sinful woman and Simon the Pharisee (Luke 7:36–50). Thus, his work can only be referred to occasionally. There is much he does not discuss concerning women.

[6] For further study see W. Pilgrim, *Good News to the Poor: Wealth and Poverty in Luke–Acts* (Minneapolis: Augsburg, 1981); and D. P. Seccombe, *Possessions and the Poor in Luke–Acts* (Linz: Studien zum Neuen Testament und seiner Umwelt, 1983).

see, not all of them are poor and needy. His nativity narrative, when
compared with Matthew's, is usually cited as prima facie evidence
for his concern. What has been missing so far is the linking of an
analysis of women in Luke–Acts with Simeon's prophecy of the
falling and rising motion not only as a literary strategy but also as a
sociological strategy.

The main argument of this study is that only certain women are
portrayed in needy conditions and then are exalted while, in the
same pericope or story line, wealthy, powerful, and privileged men
fall, thereby fulfilling Luke 2:34; women who come from the lowest
levels in Greco-Roman culture not only rise from their ambiguous or
troubled circumstances when they confront the kingdom of God, its
chief representative, Jesus, and his emissaries, the disciples, but they
are also exalted even if men in the same passage fall out of favor
when they resist the kingdom and have to be rejected by it. Powerful
and wealthy women, however, or even women who, though not
necessarily powerful and wealthy, are productive and contributing
members of society, are excluded from Luke's theme of women rising
while men fall. Several scholars have noted that Luke pairs women
with men in a positive light, and some pairings in a negative light,
but no one, to my knowledge, connects the pairing with the falling
and rising movement.[7] Women serve as test cases for "the rise of
many," and men, serving as their foils, are the test cases for "the fall
of many."

Since the social undergirds the narratives in Luke–Acts, the
primary methodologies for this book are sociology[8] and narratology.
Both terms, however, can be polyvalent. As is true for any discipline,
they have a variety of angles by which the same data are examined.
The sociological method, introduced in chapter 2, entails dividing
the women into classes according to those outlined by G. E. Lenski in
his book *Power and Prestige*,[9] even though his classifications have

---

[7] See M. R. D'Angelo, "Women in Luke Acts: A Redactional View," *JBL*
109 (1990) 441–61, for her study of pairing, along with a bibliography. Since
her analysis is the most recent and thorough, I will rely on it.

[8] For a summary of the objections against, and strong apologies for,
sociology, see B. Holmberg, *Sociology and the New Testament: An Appraisal*
(Philadelphia: Fortress, 1990) 6–17; J. G. Gager, *Kingdom and Community: The
Social World of Early Christianity* (Englewood Cliffs, N.J.: Prentice Hall, 1975)
2–14; and P. F. Esler, *Community and Gospel in Luke–Acts: The Social and
Political Motivations of Lucan Theology* (New York: Cambridge, 1987) 12–16.

[9] G. E. Lenski, *Power and Prestige: A Theory of Social Stratification* (New
York: McGraw-Hill, 1966) 189–296. His workable and proven theory will be
explained in ch. 2. Some scholars have already made productive and practical
use of it. See A. Saldarini, *Pharisees, Scribes, and Sadducees in Palestinian*

been heavily adapted. And to locate persons in their class, three concepts will be used for which W. G. Runciman has argued: class (or wealth), status, and power.[10] The narratological method, introduced in chapter 5, is limited to a specific and narrow form and designed to track the falling and rising movement in six of Luke's stories about women. By analyzing this vertical movement in the way proposed in that chapter, we will discover that Luke profoundly understands the social hierarchy in his culture and exploits the hierarchy to tell his stories.

Society: A Sociological Approach (Wilmington, Del.: Michael Glazier, 1988); D. C. Duling, "Matthew's Plurisignificant 'Son of David' in Social Science Perspective: Kinship, Kingship, Magic, and Miracle," *BTB* 22 (1992) 99–116; and D. A. Fiensy, *The Social History of Palestine in the Herodian Period: The Land Is Mine* (Studies in the Bible and Early Christianity 20; Lewiston, N.Y.: Edwin Mellen, 1991). H. C. Kee, *Knowing the Truth: A Sociological Approach to New Testament Interpretation* (Minneapolis: Fortress, 1989) 41–42, approves of Lenski's theory. For a definition of class, I have adopted that of G. E. M. de Ste. Croix, *The Class Struggle in the Ancient Greek World* (2d ed.; Ithaca: Cornell, 1989) 43–44, who writes from a Marxist perspective:

> *class* (a particular class) is a group of persons in a community identified by their position in the whole system of social production, defined above all according to their relationship (primarily in terms of the degree of ownership or control) to the conditions of production (that is to say, the means and labour of production) and to other classes. Legal position (constitutional rights . . .) is one of the factors that may help to determine class: its share in doing so will depend on how far it affects the type and degree of exploitation practised or suffered—the condition of being a slave in the ancient Greek world, for example, was likely (though far from certain) to result in a more intense degree of exploitation than being a citizen or even a free foreigner. The individuals constituting a given class may or may not be wholly or partly conscious of their own identity and common interests as a class, and they may or may not feel antagonism towards members of other classes as such.

I have adopted Ste. Croix's definition because, though a Marxist, he is a classicist. Lenski, who is not a classicist, has to depend on classicists when describing the Roman Empire as an advanced agrarian society, though Lenski's definition of class (*Power,* 74) would certainly not contradict Ste. Croix's.

[10] W.G. Runciman, "Class, Status, and Power," in *Social Stratification,* ed. J. A. Jackson (New York: Cambridge, 1968) 25–61. For further discussion, see Arlandson, " 'Fall and Rise,' " 21–22 nn. 12–13. There I discuss the concerns of R. Rohrbaugh, "Methodological Concerns in the Debate over Social Class Status of Early Christians," *JAAR* 52 (1983) 519–46; and of classics historians, including M. I. Finley, *The Ancient Economy* (2d ed.; London: Hogarth) 41–50; and R. MacMullen, *Roman Social Relations: 50 B.C. to A.D. 284* (New Haven: Yale) 88–97.

One of the extraordinary features of NT scholarship as it pertains to women is the neglect of class structure, except for a few passing comments in a few works. (It is tempting to trace this oversight to NT scholars living in a Western, post-Enlightenment culture with its emphasis on *égalité* and *fraternité,* but further discussion would exceed the scope of our study.) Too often scholars view women in Greco-Roman societies as homogeneous, thereby making their surveys imprecise. This study represents a departure from that common view because the ancients, female or male, did not see themselves in that way. The advantage of analyzing women's lives according to their class is profound. For example, it may turn out that a wealthy female landowner enjoyed more favorable legal rights, stronger political power, and higher status than a male peasant or artisan. The question is not, How did women fare in the Mediterranean world?— as if their experience were uniform. Rather, we should ask, How did women fare in their own class? How was their daily life according to, say, their access to wealth and political power?[11]

Two results occur when scholarship overlooks class structure and women's location in the structure. First, such scholarship reinforces the widespread modern-day belief that all women were universally and uniformly oppressed throughout the ancient Mediterranean world, especially in Palestine; second, it reinforces the neglect of the underclasses. And after concluding that women were uniformly oppressed, scholars usually take the easy next step: the message of the kingdom of God is so unique compared with its historical setting that it alone liberates all women equally from their uniform oppression. While I side with the viewpoint that the gospel liberates—and chapters 4 and 5 will support that claim—it does not liberate in exactly the same way for women in different classes. A survey of representative scholarship should illustrate the problems that arise when class structure is ignored or touched on only lightly.

E. and F. Stagg's book, *Woman in the World of Jesus* (1978),[12] has an overview of women in the Jewish, Greek, and Roman worlds.[13] They base their findings exclusively on literary references. Only

---

[11] A. Cameron, " 'Neither Male nor Female'," *GR* 27 (1980) 60–68, was urging NT scholars to avoid facile generalizations about women. For a discussion of feminist hermeneutics, see K. E. Corley, *Private Women, Public Meals: Social Conflict in the Synoptic Tradition* (Peabody, Mass.: Hendrickson, 1993) 3–11. See also T. Ilan, *Jewish Women in Greco-Roman Palestine* (Peabody, Mass.: Hendrickson, 1995) 1–21, for a survey of feminist NT hermeneutics. Others have covered a history of feminist NT hermeneutics, so I defer to them.

[12] E. Stagg and F. Stagg, *Woman in the World of Jesus* (Philadelphia: Westminster, 1978).

[13] Ibid., 15–100.

rarely does this not pose a problem. References to women may be found in widely ranging authors, from educated Philo in Alexandria and the elite authors in Athens, such as Aeschylus, Sophocles, Xenophon, Plato, and Aristotle, to the elite writers in Rome, such as Plautus, Cicero, Catullus, and Ovid. One may ask just how profoundly the thinking of these elite, educated men influenced the rural people in "the world of Jesus" (or even how their writings reflect rural life there). One can quote Plato's voluminous works, for example, to prove or disprove just about anything.[14] With these intellectuals as their source, the Staggs, not surprisingly, overlook the underclasses and how they really lived. For the Jewish world, however, the Staggs have an easier task because, for example, the Dead Sea Scrolls represent very well the views of the group—or groups—that produced them, since the group was so controlled. That is, it was small, limited in geography, and relatively confined within itself. In the present study, the literature of the Greco-Roman era is cited, but references to it will be very selective and critical.

L. Swidler's *Women in Judaism* (1976) and *Biblical Affirmations of Women* (1979) include a brief survey of women in the Greco-Roman and Jewish world.[15] In both books he sees the value of distinguishing between social classes, but he rarely follows this otherwise good counsel.[16] When he departs from the Greco-Roman world and enters the Jewish world (mostly in Palestine, and rightly so), he usually does not deal with even the rich and the poor and how Jewish law and custom applied to them. In one example, however, Swidler correctly states, on the issue of women appearing in public, that the restrictions varied with the rural and city environments and the upper and lower classes.[17] Women in the country and among the lower classes were freer than women in the city and in the upper classes. Though one may argue that wealthy women were freer than anyone because, it will be shown, money and power went hand in hand, Swidler's effort is commendable. But apart from this exception and a few others, he does not systematically work out how the teachings of the rabbis—his main emphasis—should be weighed and sifted with class structure, historical realia, and economic hardships. Our limited purpose in the following chapters does not allow us to

---

[14] Finley, *Ancient Economy,* 37–38.

[15] L. Swidler, *Women in Judaism: The Status of Women in Formative Judaism* (Metuchen, N.J.: 1976); and *Biblical Affirmations of Women* (Philadelphia: Westminster, 1979). *Women in Judaism* deals with Hebrew sources, but it eventually elucidates the NT.

[16] Swidler, *Women in Judaism,* 13; and *Biblical Affirmations,* 20.

[17] Swidler, *Women in Judaism,* 118–19.

analyze the teachings of the sages systematically; but whenever they are cited, attention will be paid to how the teachings and rulings may be applied to social classes.

E. Schüssler Fiorenza, in her landmark book *In Memory of Her* (1983), states that "women's actual socioreligious status must be determined by the degree of their economic autonomy and social roles rather than by ideological or prescriptive statements."[18] Her theory is valid, but I cannot find where she even partially works it out, especially in a way similar to the one proposed in this study. In particular, some questions arise about the Sophia-God and her community of women equals.[19] Though the poor, needy, and oppressed are admitted into this community,[20] it remains unclear who its leaders are and what degree of economic autonomy they enjoy. In Greco-Roman religions aristocratic women occupied positions of power. In the Christian communities, if Mary, the mother of John Mark (Acts 12:12), and Lydia (Acts 16:14–15, 40) are cited as examples,[21] then was not their economic independence very great? And if "feminist historians, therefore, seek a theoretical framework that can maintain the dialectical tension of women's historical existence as active participants in history as well as objects of patriarchal oppression,"[22] then how does one describe the oppression of the wealthy compared with the oppression of the poor? What are the differences between wealthy women's active participation in history versus the participation of, say, unclean and degraded women? Schüssler Fiorenza's work leaves much undone. Even so, her book, which merits respect as seminal—and her articles, for that matter—will be amply referred to, if only to debate her conclusions.

Although J. Fitzmyer, *The Gospel according to Luke* (1981–85), and R. Tannehill, *The Narrative Unity of Luke–Acts* (1986–90), do not treat of women as their main emphasis, their impressive volumes have been selected because they represent scholarship's typical view

---

[18] E. Schüssler Fiorenza, *In Memory of Her: A Feminist Theological Reconstruction of Christian Origins* (New York: Crossroad, 1983) 109 and passim. The quotation is italicized in her book.

[19] See ibid., 130–40, for a discussion of this innovative idea.

[20] Ibid., 123–43, passim.

[21] Ibid., 166 (Mary), 178 (Lydia). Schüssler Fiorenza wrongly deduces that Lydia was not wealthy (178). She acknowledges that wealthy and prominent women assumed positions of leadership in Acts, that this is a one-sided picture, and that the records of other women are lost (167).

[22] Ibid., 85–86. On pp. 285–315, she discusses wealth, patriarchy, and women's involvement in the church around the Mediterranean and during later centuries, but there is no systematic discussion of women and the church in Luke–Acts in the context of class structure.

of women when they are not distinguished according to classes. Fitzmyer mixes ordinary women in with "those beyond the pale of respectable society."[23] Tannehill also blends sick and degraded women (e.g., the woman bent double [Luke 13:10–17], ordinary women such as Mary and Martha [10:38–42],[24] and the wealthy Joanna [8:3]) with "the excluded" and "the poor."[25] In chapters 2 and 3 it will become evident that the women in Luke's day would never have seen themselves so indiscriminately.

B. Witherington says that he saw the need for a thorough exegesis of women in the ministry of Jesus,[26] so his book, *Women in the Ministry of Jesus* (1984), spans the Synoptics and the Fourth Gospel, as well as a few passages in Acts that serve as guides for further study. He proposes broad categories, such as "Women in the Parables of Jesus" or "Women and the Deeds of Jesus," and then does an exegesis of the pericopes that fit into these categories. Generally, his purpose is to reconstruct Jesus' attitude towards women as opposed to the typical attitudes in Palestine. Though he sees that some cultural views of women were positive,[27] he concludes that Jesus did indeed have reformational ideas because the Jewish world was, for the most part, conservative and even oppressive towards women.[28] In his introductory survey on women and their roles in Palestine, however, the discussion of economic issues (to cite only these) fluctuates between such topics as property rights and the ketubah with little attention paid to the wealth of these two entities according to women who belong to this or that class. Thus, he raises more questions than he answers. What happens to a woman who was so poor going into her marriage that she only brought the clothing on her back with her ketubah? Knowing that a woman usually retained the price of her ketubah upon divorce,[29] would her husband seek a divorce more easily than if she had brought in a handsome ketubah? How many

---

[23] Fitzmyer, *Luke,* 1.191–92.

[24] I tentatively argue in ch. 4 that Mary and Martha may have been fairly well-off landowners.

[25] Tannehill, *Narrative Unity,* 1.131–39, esp. 139.

[26] B. Witherington, *Women in the Ministry of Jesus* (New York: Cambridge, 1984) 1.

[27] Ibid., 10.

[28] Ibid., 125–31.

[29] Swidler, *Women in Judaism,* 158–59, gives a few exceptions from a few rabbis. L. J. Archer, *Her Price Is beyond Rubies: The Jewish Woman in Graeco-Roman Palestine* (JSOTSup 60; Sheffield: Sheffield Academic, 1990) 171–88, has a thorough discussion of the *ketubah.* Essentially the *ketubah* is the marriage contract and includes any settlement due to the wife if she should be divorced.

peasants had property large enough for its inheritance to play a significant economic role except for the oldest son? How did rabbinic laws in the Mishnah apply to widows with little or no property?

In Witherington's book *Women in the Earliest Churches* (1988),[30] he looks at women in the early Christian communities, mostly through the Pauline letters, along with a brief review of Luke's Gospel and a survey of Acts. In the first chapter the cultural background includes the larger Mediterranean world. But a quick glance at his bibliography shows that he ranges from classical Athens to Egypt and Rome, with a few works on the status of women in the larger Roman Empire. A glance at the chapter reveals a similar pattern: he moves from classical Athens and Sparta, to ancient Corinth in Pindar's time and then Hellenistic times, over to Egypt, and finally to Rome in the first centuries B.C.E. and C.E. A sociological analysis demands a greater control over the data. For the Greek East, Witherington rightly acknowledges that the plight of upper-class women was improving, especially in Asia Minor, but unfortunately his discussion is limited mostly to them.[31] What about the underclasses? Did the benefits of the wealthy trickle down to commoners? What was life like for them? Taken together, Witherington's two books serve as occasionally valuable cross-references. But his methods, the amount of data, and the reconstruction and interpretation of them differ from the present study.

W. Whitney's dissertation, "Women in Luke" (1990), is an application of a particular reader-response hermeneutic that incorporates a feminist perspective. It is based on an article written by Patricinio Schweikert. Put briefly, when we the readers approach a text, we must consider our own location in time (the twentieth century), the setting of the original audience (men and women in the first-century Mediterranean), and the author (a male in the same time and place as his audience). Luke has a high view of women, but he is writing in a society, Whitney argues, that does not view women highly.[32] Luke is caught between his own view and the larger society's view. The discrepancy should show up in his Gospel and create dissonance within the ancient and modern readers who are informed of women's status in Luke's period. This feminist hermeneutic takes into account the problem of a text that liberates but is time- and culture-bound in a patriarchal society. Thus, a work swings between two poles, which

---

[30] B. Witherington, *Women in the Earliest Churches* (New York: Cambridge, 1988). His third book, *Women and the Genesis of Christianity* (ed. A. Witherington; New York: Cambridge, 1990), is virtually a reworking of the same material with little added.

[31] *Women in the Earliest Churches,* 15–16.

[32] Whitney, "Women," 66.

Schweikert and Whitney call continuity/legitimation (C/L) and dis-
continuity/revolution (D/R). C/L in the text reflects the dominant
view of the original setting, a male-dominated society. It would be
unrealistic to expect a literary work not to have some continuity
with, and even legitimation of, its culture. But in some sense a text
appears discontinuous and revolutionary (D/R) by challenging the
status quo of its culture.

For example, women in Luke's time were considered nothing more
than "baby-makers," says Whitney, a particularly mundane and sexist
role for women in the ancient world[33] and probably a way of keeping
women from interacting with society.[34] Mary is depicted as subjected
to these ordinary customs and mores of the day, which would place
childbirth on the C/L end of the continuum. But when God breaks in on
the scene, he lifts the mundane to sublime heights, which constitutes
D/R. Whitney does an exegesis of every passage in which women are
mentioned in the Gospel and comments on how Luke supports the
culture of his day (C/L) but breaks from it with the supernatural (D/R).

Though Whitney's overall goal is valid and admirable, a prob-
lom emerges when he has to conclude that women were universally
and uniformly "repressed" and "oppressed" in Palestinian and
Greco-Roman society.[35] He has the strongest motivation to draw this
conclusion because he needs to show how Luke makes a break (D/R)
from the norm (C/L). But what if, according to Luke, Mary was not
merely a "baby-maker" nor oppressed socially? What if Luke grants
her a religious lineage and Joseph a royal one? Not every woman in
Luke–Acts was oppressed in the same way and to the same degree.

R. Kraemer's book *Her Share of the Blessings* (1992)[36] deserves
attention as well, since she surveys women in a variety of religions.
Her remarkable book extends from the Brauron girls in Attica to
John Chrysostom. Her three chapters (10–12) on the NT and early
Christianity cut across chronological layers, mixing Luke–Acts with
other Christian documents. Therefore, her treatment of Luke–Acts is
necessarily very slim. The material does not include a systematic
analysis of the social hierarchy. In her analysis of women's religious
offices in Greco-Roman paganism, she quite rightly emphasizes
that the offices were held by wealthy, powerful, and prestigious

---

[33] Ibid., 136, 159, 312.

[34] Ibid., 148. If anything, a woman's having a baby gave her freer interaction in society.

[35] Ibid., 60–66.

[36] R. S. Kraemer, *Her Share of the Blessings: Women's Religions among
Pagans, Jews, and Christians in the Greco-Roman World* (New York: Oxford,
1992).

women.[37] But since the inscriptions and literary references on this subject almost exclusively emanate from this level, Kraemer confines most of her discussion to them.

A bright light in this array of scholarship is K. Corley's book, *Private Women, Public Meals*,[38] in which she analyzes the meal settings in the Synoptic Gospels. Its second chapter contains her long survey of the dinner setting in the Greco-Roman world and of women's place at it. She begins by dividing the women into four classes: aristocrats, freedwomen, free women, and slaves. This is very useful for her subsequent examination of public meals and symposia because she can now determine the kinds of women who were excluded or included and avoid the easy generalization contained in the word "woman." A major weakness emerges in her study, however, as it touches on the present work: Corley's choice of classes is too vague and broad. It will become evident in our chapters 2 and 3 that her choice does not at all account for women who are in many other classes in Greco-Roman society. For example, a free woman might be a wealthy purple-merchant, an artisan, or a common day laborer—three "professions" that belong to three different classes according to the present study. Ancient sources, while mentioning Corley's four classes, assume social locations that outnumber her four. The present survey will attempt to fill out the picture of women in various classes a lot more. This criticism notwithstanding, her effort to divide women into classes brings precision to her analysis.

In light of NT scholarship's neglect of social hierarchy as it relates to women, it seems, then, that the time is ripe for an attempt to apply a theory of classes to Luke–Acts. This becomes all the more necessary when we realize that Luke is concerned about hierarchy. The first two chapters of his Gospel assume an understanding of it. And beyond these two chapters Luke leaves all sorts of hints and clues about the social location of his characters, with such descriptions as synagogue ruler, centurion, jailer, purple-seller, and so forth. What did they mean in his time and, hence, in his stories? Why mention them at all? Since the social undergirds the literary and the literary assumes the social, it seems appropriate to blend two methodologies, sociology and narratology, if they are narrowly defined.

The format of this study goes from the general to the specific by following four groups.[39]

---

[37] Ibid., 80–92.

[38] see note 10 above.

[39] The word "group" here is defined very loosely. It is not as if the persons in the Greco-Roman world and the characters in Luke–Acts realize that they belong together.

(1) Chapters 2 and 3 survey women in Greco-Roman society according to the classes outlined by Lenski, although Lenski's ideas are modified.

(2) The end of chapter 3 shows that all the men and women of Luke–Acts, the second group, easily fit within the classes described in chapters 2 and 3.

(3) Chapter 4 discusses the third group, women who in Luke–Acts are among the upper classes or among those who, even if not located there, are productive, contributing members of society.

(4) Chapter 5 analyzes the target group, women who are the lowest members in society: only they will rise at the expense of wealthy, powerful, and prestigious men, according to Luke.

Finally, chapter 6 draws conclusions to our findings.

Yet Clytaemnestra treated him as
she did not because she was a woman,
but because she was a wicked woman;
and there is no more reason for not
being kind to a woman than to a man.[1]

2

WOMEN AND CLASS IN THE ROMAN EMPIRE, I

An analysis of the women in Luke–Acts according to the theme of falling and rising must begin with a description[2] of the social classes of the Greco-Roman world and of women's location in them. And to facilitate this description, one goal serves as guide: to tell the story of the lives of women in the first century and in the Greek East. This chapter and chapter 3 present the first of the four groups of women mentioned in chapter 1, as we move closer to our target group—those women whom Luke exalts and esteems at all costs, even at the expense of men.

---

[1] Dio Chrysostom, *Or.* 74.19, trans. Crosby, LCL 5.229. For a discussion of this passage, see Arlandson, " 'Fall and Rise,' " 78 n. 1.

[2] I adopt the terminology used by Ste. Croix, *Class Struggle,* 91–96. As he attempts to clarify Finley's use of status as a tool for analyzing ancient society, he sees status as valid only for a *description* of society, not for an *explanation* why society behaves as it does. Omitting the debate over status, I readily admit that in chs. 2 and 3 I adopt the approach of a description of women in Greco-Roman culture, not an explanation. That is, I describe women in their various classes (e.g., that they lived this way, that they usually were behind the men in their own class, that they had these political rights but not those, etc.); my *explanation* is reserved for chs. 4 and 5, where I offer for Luke's portrayal of women possible reasons and causes that are based on my description of women in chs. 2 and 3.

In this survey, information about men in their respective classes will be included. It is a common complaint today that the ancient documents were written from a male viewpoint and thereby skewed from representing "how things really were."[3] Even a cursory reading of the sources cannot contradict this complaint. In the ancient world, however, the lives of women were invariably tied to the lives of men.[4] If it turns out, for instance, that women were excluded from official, legislative powers, then in order to determine what this means, male power structures will have to be discussed. But we need studiously to avoid—or, at most, treat of lightly in most instances, though not all—those passages in which elite male authors consciously wax eloquent about women. In these ramblings the men almost always suppress women. Instead, the focus will be on offhanded references about women. Used judiciously, these passages hold out the greatest hope of being reliable for describing women's involvement in any area of life in the first century.

The chronological and geographical limitations of this descriptive survey should be clarified. While staying mostly within the first century of our era, this study will appeal to earlier and later data if they reflect daily life in the first century.[5] For example, inscriptions of female political officeholders in Asia Minor not only from the first but from the second and third centuries C.E. will be included because they are a culmination of a general trend beginning as far back as the Hellenistic period.[6]

---

[3] See R. Van Bremen, "Women and Wealth," in *Images of Women in Antiquity* (ed. A. Cameron and A. Kuhrt; London: Croom Helm, 1983) 234; Stagg, *Woman,* 55–100; and Witherington, *Women in the Earliest Churches,* 5–23, for a survey of some of the literary references.

[4] For further discussion, see Arlandson, " 'Fall and Rise,' " 78 n. 4.

[5] One of the striking facts about classics historians is their use of data ranging from the Hellenistic to the late Roman periods in order to illuminate a point in, say, the first century. All of the historians are aware of the differences time and location can cause, but they judiciously make use of any datum they can. I hope to be as judicious. In most aspects of life in the Greco-Roman world, the transition between the first and second centuries is not a magical threshold differing radically from the 80s, the assumed date of Luke–Acts, especially in Asia Minor, where prosperity grew steadily for some centuries before and after the first century. I will try, however, to avoid data that differ from those in our period of study, as one might expect to find, say, in Palestine after the fall of Jerusalem. Whenever I use second-century authors as resources, such as Lucian (ca. 120–190), Aristides (118–ca. 180), and Pausanius (ca. 120–180), I am choosing only information that can apply to other centuries in the ancient world. See Ilan, *Jewish Women,* 22–43, for a discussion of how to use ancient sources.

[6] D. Magie, *Roman Rule in Asia Minor to the End of the Third Century after Christ* (2 vols.; Princeton: Princeton, 1950) 1.649, 2.1518 n. 50.

When Luke composed his dual work, he used the countryside of Palestine for most of the background of the Gospel, and Jerusalem and the cities of Asia Minor, Greece, Achaia, Macedonia, and Thrace for most of the background of Acts.[7] His plan will be followed, with one further geographical limitation: besides Jerusalem, the cities in Asia Minor are chosen over those in the other regions. The cities in Asia Minor are given priority because it is assumed that Luke possibly wrote in Asia Minor. And according to Luke, Paul and his team preached in more cities in Asia Minor than in other eastern regions. But just as data from earlier or later periods are used, so data from other regions are included when they shed light on urban and rural life in Asia Minor and Palestine. Some things in the Roman Empire did not change from one region to the next, such as farming technology, the amount of crops six acres could produce, and the hard life of the poverty-stricken, unskilled urban laborer and other occupations.[8]

A MACROSOCIAL MODEL FOR SOCIAL CLASS

Determining class structure in modern societies is a tenuous enterprise. The articles and books on the subject are many, even quite unmanageable, indicating that this area of the social sciences is still open to debate. And if modern, observable societies are difficult to classify, then a fortiori Greco-Roman society is difficult. These difficulties emerge because of the barrier of time and because the surviving evidence is scarce and mostly emanates, with exceptions, from the economically and politically powerful. Any attempt at understanding the Greco-Roman world and its class structure should proceed with caution. Therefore, the reader will notice the frequent use of qualifiers, such as "probably," "likely," and "perhaps," throughout these two chapters.

---

[7] The distinctions between urban and rural people are vast and many. It is to our advantage to examine at least two of the three societies—urban, rural, and semirural—since the ancients viewed them as separate and since the issue will touch on the idea of status. Strabo 13.1.25, trans. Jones, LCL 6.47, says, "there is a certain difference among these of the rustics [ἀγροίκων, agroikōn], the semi-rustics [μεσαγροίκων, mesagroikōn], and the city-dwellers [πολιτικῶν, politikōn]." I do not see the need to discuss fully the semirural. See, however, ch. 3, "Landowners," pp. 70–71.

[8] "The occupations of Palestinian Jews were the same, on average, as those in other Mediterranean countries" (E. P. Sanders, *Judaism: Practice and Belief, 63 BCE–66 CE* [Philadelphia: Trinity, 1992] 119). For further discussion of these chronological and geographical limitations, see Arlandson, " 'Fall and Rise,' " 80 n. 9.

One of the major hindrances to a consensus over classes is the difficulty of finding the criteria for measuring a person's social location. This volume gives the works of Runciman and Lenski special weight and priority. These two sociologists provide our macro-sociological framework for a more detailed inquiry of the daily lives of women. Runciman eliminates some of the confusion, for our purposes at least, when he keeps a multidimensional approach to stratification yet limits the dimensions to three: class, status, and power. He allows some freedom for the detailed filling out of these three interdependent criteria.

By "class" Runciman means wealth, access to the markets and the means of production, or the lack thereof.[9] The more specific word "wealth," with an emphasis on occupation—or access to wealth—and social condition (or lack thereof for widows and beggars), will be used in our survey instead of "class" in order to avoid confusion. The phrase "access to wealth," though nebulous, must be kept in addition to "occupation" because it can hardly be maintained that a wealthy landowner who engaged in politics had an occupation. That said, however, the emphasis will be placed on occupation and social condition as a means of discussing wealth because the Greco-Roman world, the NT, and Luke–Acts saw people in this way, as the title, epithet, or occupational description next to their name indicates: proconsul, purple-seller, landowner (all of whom manipulated a lot of wealth); tent-maker, widow, farmer, day laborer (all of whom had very little control over wealth). A person's occupation or means of creating capital (or lack thereof) will be understood in these two chapters as one of the factors considered in determining a person's social location. So "class" will serve as the genus, and "wealth" or "occupation" will serve as two of the species of "class."

Runciman joins status with esteem, prestige, privilege, birth, etc.[10] Status is necessary as a criterion because in a few cases a person's wealth did not match his or her status. The ubiquitous and protean slave is usually cited as the prime example of a person who, attached to a wealthy household, may have access to fabulous wealth but no status. In contrast, the freeholder of a farm of few acres may possess higher status but is struggling to survive economically.[11] Still, status is a notoriously subjective concept, with few objective indicators in the ancient world.[12] So it will be referred to only when there is enough information.

---

[9] Runciman, "Class," 30, 38.
[10] Ibid., 30, 43–48.
[11] Finley, *Ancient Economy*, 62–63.
[12] For a further discussion of objective status and subjective status, see S. M. Lipset, "Social Stratification" *IESS*, 15.310–15.

Finally, power is linked with a person's ability to bring about his or her wishes or, conversely, the ability to avoid the control of others.[13] This definition is a little too broad, so it is narrowed down to political power. In the ancient world money and political power went hand in hand, despite the rare exceptions: some men were so wealthy that they could avoid holding public office and all the expense it entailed.[14] Power should play a part in a theory about stratification because sometimes wealth followed behind power, as when the military machine of Rome was conquering Asia Minor and Palestine. And at other times power followed wealth and status, as in a case of daughters who inherit their father's wealth and legal status in the shipping business and grow up to wield the power needed to guard the same wealth or access to the market their father had.[15]

As it turns out, this trilogy of interdependent criteria for locating a person socially receives independent confirmation from two sources: the first-century essayist and biographer Plutarch (before 50–after 120 C.E., Boeotia), and the orator Dio Chrysostom (ca. 40–120 C.E., Bithynia), who traveled extensively through the Greek East and beyond. They often wrote about proper social attitudes.

In the context of the assembly and other formal meetings, Plutarch notes that politicians were profoundly aware of these three concepts in order to rank the value of a man's proposal.

> So, too, in an assemblage or a formal meeting they may be observed to begin a subject of discussion, and later to give ground as though before their betters, and to shift over with the utmost readiness to the other side, if the man opposing them be a person of power [δυνατός, *dynatos*], wealth [πλούσιος, *plousios*] or repute [ἔνδοξος, *endoxos*].[16]

In another essay Plutarch counsels his readers to adopt good cheer with their wealth, reputation, and power.

> And wealth [πλοῦτος, *ploutos*] is pleasanter, and repute [δόξα, *doxa*] and power [δύναμις, *dynamis*] more resplendent, if with them goes the gladness which springs from the heart.[17]

And in one of Plutarch's essays about philosophers and men in power, he sees the three criteria almost as commodities that can be manipulated for achieving social esteem.

---

[13] Runciman, "Class," 48–53.

[14] P. Garnsey, *Social Status and Legal Privilege in the Roman Empire* (Oxford: Clarendon, 1970) 257.

[15] A. H. M. Jones, *The Greek City* (New York: Oxford, 1940) 180.

[16] Plutarch, *Mor.* 58C-D, trans. Babbitt, LCL 1.313.

[17] Ibid., 100D, trans. Babbitt, LCL 2.95.

But the man of sense, if he is engaged in active political life, will ask for so much reputation [δόξης, *doxēs*] as will inspire confidence and thereby give him power [δύναμιν, *dynamin*] for affairs. . . . But even he [who has withdrawn from public life] does not despise reputation [δόξαν, *doxan*] among the right-minded and estimable; but wealth [πλοῦτον, *plouton*], reputation [δόξαν] as a leader, or power [δύναμιν] in his friendships he does not pursue, however neither does he avoid these qualities if they are associated with a temperate character.[18]

Dio likens the philosopher to a physician who has to be severe in his treatment of the sick when the illness becomes advanced. For this reason the philosopher never gains wealth (χρήματα, *chrēmata*) or power (δύναμις). Instead, he receives hatred, abuse, and reviling—a bad reputation, in effect.[19]

When class tension erupted in Tarsus between the wealthy, those in the assembly, and the so-called linen-workers, who were outside the constitution because they did not have enough money to buy a political voice, Dio cites examples of entire cities engaged in strife and enmity, notably Athens and Sparta after the Persian Wars, so that he can show and thereby curtail destructive civic strife. Dio describes the process at the time when Athens began to lose control of its empire. "The first thing of all to happen was to lose their commendation [ἔπαινον, *epainon*] and good repute [εὐφημίαν, *euphēmian*], and next to lose their power [ἰσχύν, *ischyn*] and wealth [χρήματα]."[20] These three criteria are valid for socially locating not only Athens and Sparta in macropolitics but also individuals in micropolitics.

In all of these passages from Plutarch and Dio, ἔνδοξος, δόξα, εὐφημία, and ἔπαινος, can signify more than reputation. They can mean opinion, estimation, honor, and glory, as these touch on the public's view of a person. All of these definitions are aligned with the notion of social status mentioned earlier.

Plutarch's and Dio's choice of criteria confirms, rather than determines or controls, the choice of the criteria in the present study (and Runciman's study). Plutarch and Dio should not be regarded as infallible guides in such matters, as if they were modern sociologists. On the other hand, they were keen observers of social relations and should not be lightly dismissed. These three criteria do not always occur with such convenience in the same context in ancient literature, but they recur throughout. Plutarch and Dio, out of their keen

---

[18] Ibid., 778A, trans. Fowler, LCL 10.39.
[19] Dio Chrysostom, *Or.* 32.19, LCL 3.191.
[20] Dio Chrysostom, *Or.* 34.50, trans. Crosby, LCL 3.383. For a discussion of the civic strife between the wealthy, the assemblymen, and the linen workers, see *Or.* 34.21–23 and, in the present work, ch. 3, "Artisans," p. 85.

observation of social relations, summarized them and reduced them to their simplest forms.

In *Power and Prestige* Lenski first examines sociological issues common to all societies, then chronologically surveys the developments of societies. He begins with hunting-and-gathering societies, shifts to surveying simple and advanced horticultural societies, then agrarian societies, and ends with industrial societies. Our interest is focused on the agrarian societies, of which, he says, the Roman Empire is a prime example because of its advancement in production and general technology (mainly through the plow), compared to horticultural societies, and in military technology.[21]

As Lenski adumbrates the well-known story of the growth of the empire, two salient features stand out. First, advancements in military technology inevitably led to expanding borders, which in turn led to a social cleavage between the rulers and the ruled.[22] As borders expanded, the government became more and more centralized, culminating in the emergence of the emperors. The major source of revenue, the land, fell into fewer and fewer hands. Land should be considered the major source of revenue because it was the almost exclusive domain in which production took place. (The huge manufacturing conglomerates and financial institutions found today did not exist.) Confirming Lenski's assessment of this bifurcation, R. MacMullen, in an extraordinarily lucid statement, compresses five centuries of Roman ascendancy into three words: "fewer have more."[23] And the opposite is equally true: more have less. Thus, Rome deliberately became the patron to all other local governments in the provinces, such as the decurion councils in the major cities of Asia Minor, and engendered and fostered a social cleavage.

Second, the centralized rulers had to develop policies by which they could maintain their vast empire, so they sent legates and representatives and their helpers or retainers to various urban centers in order to keep the peace and to make sure the revenues were collected. When Rome sent its representatives to urban centers and permitted local governments to exercise real power, the cities and larger towns augmented their permanence, wealth, and prestige, which had been missing in many of the advanced horticultural societies.[24] A prominent classics historian summarizes the prosperity of Roman Asia Minor in these terms:

---

[21] Lenski, *Power,* 192–94, 198.
[22] Ibid., 194.
[23] MacMullen, *Roman Social Relations,* 38.
[24] Lenski, *Power,* 198.

If the period of Augustus and the Julio-Claudians gives the impression of a gradual and sound recovery from a time of great distress, that of the Flavians and Antonines creates one of widespread and general prosperity. If the first saw a good beginning of the Greco-Roman municipal forms and Hellenic culture . . . the next saw the continuation and culmination of the movement, which reached its maximum strength for the pre-Diocletian period with Marcus Aurelius.[25]

Thus, because of the "widespread and general prosperity" of the urban centers, a diversity of vocations and occupations developed: bureaucrats, scholars, scribes, soldiers, merchants, servants, numerous "guilds" of artisans, laborers, the working poor, and even beggars.[26] This development of numerous occupations prompts a description of class structure and women's place in it.

By means of a graph Lenski illustrates class structure in agrarian societies. In the present study his graph is adapted and modified according to other scholars' analyses of it[27] and according to other studies of the Greco-Roman period. Before presenting our adaptation (fig. 1), its limitation and purposes should be mentioned.[28]

As cognitive perception of landscape can take place from the air at several thousand meters, so one can view societies from a distance. A model that represents a view from a long distance does not "simulate an exact appearance of things that are perceived." Instead, it simplifies "only important representative aspects of complex social structures, behavior and relations."[29] So our adaptation of Lenski's model is not intended to be a detailed representation of Greco-Roman culture; rather, it is only a bird's-eye view.

With that limitation in mind, it serves four functions: (1) It will help us to see the interrelations of groups within the Roman Empire at a more general and abstract level. In this survey some specific cases of persons within groups are examined as the groups interact with each other in a struggle over limited economic, reputational, and political resources, but this is done only with (2) the purpose of illustrating the lives of women in the larger society. (3) Following Lenski, our diagram clarifies a misconception about stratification in agrarian societies. Classes are not "layers superimposed on each

---

[25] T. R. S. Broughton, "Roman Asia Minor," in *An Economic Survey of Ancient Rome* (ed. F. Tenney; Baltimore: John Hopkins, 1938; reprint, Paterson, N.J.: Pagent Books, 1959) 4.794.

[26] Lenski, *Power,* 201.

[27] Duling, "Matthew's," 99–106; Fiensy, *Social,* 155–76.

[28] Duling, "Matthew's," 99–100, commenting on Lenski's graph or model, has a fine survey of the purpose and limitations of his own version of the graph. I base my discussion on his.

[29] Ibid., 99.

other"; they touch a range in the supply of the three limited resources of wealth, power, and status and overlap each other to some degree. There is a continuum of the three resources, not "a series of separate and distinct strata in the geological sense." Many of the borders, far from being sharp, are unclear or, for lack of information, unknown. (4) Classes are not best depicted in a pyramid that "ignores the depressed classes at the very bottom of the social order and mini- mizes the degree of inequality."[30] Thus, Lenski's model has the advantage of distinguishing two subsocieties at the very bottom from the bulk of the population. The graphs of Lenski and others who follow him are, however, inadequate because they draw the graphs in the shape of a diamond, which implies that the social gap be- tween the rich and poor was more gradual than it really was. In Greco-Roman society the difference between the elite and "all the rest" was very wide, as shown in our adaptation of his model.

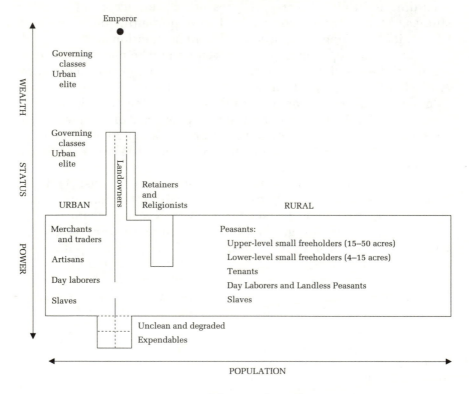

Figure 1

---

[30] Lenski, *Power,* 285.

A few general comments on the physical outlay of the graph are required. Its shape resembles L. Summarizing his own survey of class structure in the Roman Empire, MacMullen says that " 'verticality' is key to the understanding of it."[31] This can easily be applied to our model. The vast majority of people lived just a little above or at poverty level with little or no status and power—somewhere in the widest portion of the graph[32]—while a very small minority benefited from great wealth, status, and power. Very few lived in between. Indeed, Lenski claims that the page length limits his graph because it should have "a spire far higher and far slenderer."[33] In our graph the page width also limits it because the population in the widest portion was far more numerous than the model is able to show. The right side of the L, representing the rural sphere, is longer than the left side, representing the urban sphere, because most Mediterraneans lived outside the large metropoleis and in small towns and villages.

Inside the model, lines block off various domains—e.g., between rural and urban, and retainers and peasants—because not many people crossed over into new careers and jobs. Aelius Aristides (117–ca. 180 C.E.), who lived in Smyrna but owned estates in Mysia, observes,

> Those who were yesterday shoemakers and carpenters are not today infantry and cavalrymen, nor as on the stage is one transformed into a soldier who was just now a farmer. Nor as in a poor home where the same people do the cooking and keep the house and make the beds, have you mixed your occupations.[34]

A few persons did cross boundaries, however, such as wealthy merchants and proconsuls' faithful assistants (retainers), all of whom could accumulate enough wealth to acquire land, and the day laborers who migrated from the city to the country or back again, depending on where jobs were found. In these cases there are gaps in the boundaries. The lines above the unclean and degraded and the expendables are very porous because if social mobility existed at all, then it was almost exclusively downward.

Finally, two words appear to be anachronistic, "retainers" and "expendables." All the others listed in the model can be found in

---

[31] MacMullen, *Roman Social Relations,* 94.

[32] Placing poverty in the widest portion of the model can be exasperatingly vague, but not much information exists to offer more precision. In this study "poverty" is defined as the condition of a person who barely subsists from day to day, earns only enough money to feed himself and his family and to take care of a few basic needs, and lives without hope of setting aside some resources to improve his lot in life.

[33] Lenski, *Power,* 285.

[34] Aristides, *Or.* 26.71, Behr 2.81.

Greco-Roman literature either directly, such as "slaves," or through synonyms. It will become clear that the words "retainers" and "expendables" are merely tools to describe historical reality: the first describes a class that the rulers employed to carry out their will and policies; the second, argues Lenski, describes people, found in every agrarian society, "for whom the other members of society had little or no need."[35] Anyone vaguely familiar with the Gospels should recognize that they acknowledge the existence of expendables. Jesus ministered to them, and chapters 4 and 5 will argue that the women whom Luke exalts at the *expense* of powerful, honorable, and wealthy men come from the *expend*ables and the unclean and degraded.

Governing Classes and Urban Elite.   Situated below the emperor were two classes or orders (*ordines*) of aristocrats who comprised the nobility of Rome—the senators and, below them, the equestrians. The rationale for drawing a thin line between the emperor and the rest of the model is that the senators numbered only about two one-thousandths of one percent of the very roughly fifty million inhabitants of the empire. The equestrians numbered less than one-tenth of one percent.[36] To be a senator, one needed property, the principal source of wealth, of which the minimum value was 250,000 times a day's wage, a denarius; equestrians needed somewhat half of that amount.[37]

As Rome expanded, so did the desire of these two *ordines* for accumulating wealth. They sent persons from their orders to make sure the peace was kept and taxes collected. Generally, persons sent out from the senators held offices as legates and proconsuls in the larger provinces, while equestrians went to the smaller provinces and were made prefects and procurators.[38] For example, the legate of Syria, Quirinius in Luke 2:2 (C.E. 6–9), and the governors of the small province of Judea conformed to this hierarchy: the first came from the senatorial order, the second from the equestrian.[39] And the senate, after Octavian consented, appointed Herod as a client king.[40]

---

[35] Lenski, *Power,* 281.

[36] MacMullen, *Roman Social Relations,* 88–89. The estimate of fifty million is his.

[37] Ibid., 89.

[38] A. N. Sherwin-White, *Roman Society and Roman Law in the New Testament* (New York: Clarendon, 1963) 5. B. Levick, *Roman Colonies in Southern Asia Minor* (Oxford: Clarendon, 1967) 103–20, has a thorough discussion of the senators and equestrians and their rank and behavior in southern Asia Minor.

[39] E. M. Smallwood, *The Jews under Roman Rule* (Leiden: Brill, 1981) 144–45.

[40] E. Schürer, *The History of the Jewish People in the Age of Jesus Christ*

Conquering the Greek East, the Romans permitted the existence of two governmental bodies, the local council, called the βουλή, *boulē,* numbering several hundred[41] and consisting of βουλευταί, *bouleutai,* or *decuriones* (decurions), who were wealthy landowners, and the popular assembly, called the ἐκκλησία, *ekklēsia,* consisting of the δῆμος, *dēmos,* who were formally enrolled adult male free citizens. Theoretically, the assembly, often itself called the δῆμος, should have held the ultimate power because the Hellenistic polis was specially regarded for its democratic form of government.[42] Because of the presence of commoners in the assembly, it appears that the governing class slides down or coalesces with the widest portion in the graph. (Or perhaps a few commoners slide upwards.) This shows why it is necessary to understand stratification as an overlapping continuum and not as layers in the geological sense. Under Roman rule, however, the βουλή embodied the legislative and executive power because Rome was suspicious of ordinary citizens running affairs. It simply would not do that a "dangerously irresponsible"[43] and "bizarre amalgam of very diverse elements"[44] should hold such powers. So Rome transferred the government over to the propertied class, which would stand to lose more if political unrest or upheaval erupted.[45] It is almost as if the assembly were allowed to exist in order to placate the masses and to perpetuate the half-truth or even the illusion that they had a decisive voice in important political decisions and that they carried substantive political clout.[46] The

---

(175 B.C.–A.D. 135) (3 vols.; rev. and enl. G. Vermes, F. Millar, and M. Black; Edinburgh: T. & T. Clark, 1979) 1.281.

[41] A. H. M. Jones, *Roman Economy: Studies in Ancient Economic and Administrative History* (ed. P. A. Brunt; Oxford: Basil Blackwell, 1974) 12. Broughton, "Roman Asia Minor," 814, offers the following list of the sizes of councils: Prusa, Bithynia—100; Oenoanda, Lycia—500; Halicarnassus—100; Thyatira, Lydia—500–650; Ephesus—450.

[42] Magie, *Roman Rule,* 1.57.

[43] Jones, *The Greek City,* 164.

[44] V. Chapot, *Province romaine d'Asie* (Paris: 1904; reprint, Rome: "L'Erma" di Bretschneider, 1967) 206, my translation.

[45] Ste. Croix, *Class Struggle,* 532–33; Jones, *The Greek City,* 164; Magie, *Roman Rule,* 1.57–58; Levick, *Roman Colonies,* 78–79; Chapot, *Province romaine,* 94–216; and I. Lévy, "Etudes sur la vie municipales de l'Asie Mineure sous les Antonins," *REG* 8 (1895) 205–31. Lévy's time period is late, but she traces the shift of power from the assembly to the council to long before the Antonines. Josephus, *J.W.* 1.167–71, LCL 2.79, and *Ant.* 14.89–93, LCL 7.495, records that Gabinius, governor of Syria (57–55 B.C.E.), divided Palestine into five unions and reconstituted the civil administration under an aristocracy.

[46] See Dio Chrysostom, *Or.* 34, LCL 3.337ff.; *Or.* 48, LCL 4.275ff.

"chief political function [of the δῆμος] appears from the inscriptions to have consisted in acclaiming its benefactors in the theatre."[47]

Since the senate in Rome and the councils in cities throughout the empire seated only a few hundred men, other elites did not necessarily occupy political positions, though many may have served as decurions for a season. Their principal source of wealth was land, the major area of production in the Roman Empire.[48] And because land was their source of wealth, they can also be known by another designation, "landowners."[49] In the thinnest and upper section of the graph, they occupy the middle strip proceeding upward out of the peasants, with the merchants and traders on one side and the retainers and religionists on the other. Many landowners, however, were not part of the aristocracy; their land varied in size, so they can be found up and down this middle strip. Some lived in small villages and were rustics but still wealthy. In order for landowners to live comfortably in the city, they had to own at least one estate of medium size (50–315 acres).[50] In any case, this class of landowners has been included in the present study because often ancient literature cites cases of the wealthy who were landowners yet whose political involvement is not explicitly stated or made clear. But as noted, it is likely that those in the upper echelon of landholdings occupied political offices at times or at least influenced politics whenever this was to their advantage.

The monetary qualification for a councilship varied in some regions. In Pliny's hometown of Comum it was 25,000 denarii,[51] but in municipalities of Africa 5,000 denarii sufficed.[52] Some owned

---

[47] Levick, *Roman Colonies* 78–79.
[48] Ste. Croix, *Class Struggle,* 120–33.
[49] Ibid., 114–20. For a discussion, see ch. 3, "Landowners," pp. 168–73.
[50] Fiensy, *Social,* 23–24, calculates three estate sizes that apply not only to Palestine but also throughout the empire, since farming technology and the proceeds from the crops did not vary by much:

(1) small holdings (10–80 *iugera* [6–50 acres])
(2) medium-sized estates (80–500 *iugera* [50–315 acres])
(3) large estates (over 500 *iugera* [315 acres])

His estimate is based on a comparison with estates around Pompeii. The estates averaged 63 acres, though some landowners probably owned more than one estate.
[51] J. Gagé, *Les classes sociales dans l'Empire romain* (2d ed.; Paris: Payot, 1971) 163.
[52] G. Alföldy, *Römische Sozialgeschichte* (Wiesbaden: Franz Steiner, 1975) 113, cited in D. C. Verner, *The Household of God: The Social World of the Pastoral Epistles* (Chico, Calif: Scholar's, 1983) 51.

enough to reach the equestrian order.[53] For our purposes the requirement that they had to own property valued minimally at 25,000 denarii
is adopted, since Augustus made this amount legal.[54] In Asia Minor the
assembly elected men to the council, but this democratic practice was
also stripped of its power because of the property qualification of the
candidates; it ended up electing the wealthy landowners.[55] A requirement placed firmly on the shoulders of a βουλευτής, *bouleutēs,* or
decurion, to ensure his election was a hefty contribution to public
works.[56] This requirement bifurcated the economic and social distance between councilmen and assemblymen; but the requirement
could be a severe burden, and its only recompense in most cases was
that the decurions enjoyed the esteem of being in the "little Senate."[57] "They sat in special seats at the games and in the theatre; they
dined at public expense; they used public water free of charge . . . ;
they wore distinctive dress; high-sounding epithets were applied to
the order as a whole."[58] Honor and prestige were very important to
the aristocrats, and they spent money to prove the point.[59]

The aristocrats' quest for honor and prestige was not limited to
seeking these only from their peers; they desired that the masses as
well should ascribe them honor. Aelius Aristides writes,

> Those who think that they should be superior [κρείττους, *kreittous*]
> should calculate that if they willingly destroy their inferiors [ἥττους,
> *hēttous*], they injure their own source of pride [φιλοτιμία, *philoti-*
> *mia*]—for the existence of inferiors is an advantage [κέρδος, *kerdos*] to
> superiors since they will be able to point out those over whom they are
> superior.[60]

Besides the class tension exhibited in this passage, the source of
pride for the superior (whom Aristides later clarifies as property
owners) is the inferior. From an aristocrat's viewpoint, the logic is
impeccable. As dark colors serve as a contrast for bright colors, so the
inferior serve as a contrast for the superior.

On the other side, the poor have an able representative to
express their views, Lucian the satirist (ca. 120–90 C.E., Syria). Even
though Lucian was not poor (nor was he an aristocrat), his satirical

---

[53] Garnsey, *Status,* 240.
[54] MacMullen, *Roman Social Relations,* 90; Gagé, *Classes,* 163.
[55] Jones, *Roman Economy,* 12–13; Magie, *Roman Rule,* 1.649.
[56] Jones, *Roman Economy,* 14.
[57] Gagé, *Classes,* 40.
[58] Garnsey, *Status,* 244.
[59] See Josephus, *Ant.* 16.153, LCL 8.269; MacMullen, *Roman Social Relations,* 57–62, 76–77.
[60] Aristides, *Or.* 24.34, Behr 2.52.

wit means that he observed social relations and commented on them from a variety of viewpoints. In one of Lucian's dialogues a lowly priest complains to the has-been and ineffective deity, Cronus, about economic injustice. As the situation stands now, says Lucian's fictitious priest, the difference between the poor (οἱ πένητες, *hoi penētes*) and the rich (οἱ πλούσιοι, *hoi plousioi*) is the difference between "an ant and a camel."[61]

> We should be less distressed about it, you may be sure, if we did not see the rich living in such bliss, who, though they have such gold, such silver in their safes, though they have all that clothing and own slaves and carriage-horses and tenements and farms, each and all in large numbers, not only have never shared them with us but never deign to notice ordinary people [τοὺς πολλούς, *tous pollous*].[62]

The rich and the poor do not constitute classes as such but are the generic designations for all sorts of persons who either have access to wealth or who do not. Throughout this dialogue Lucian mixes in "ordinary" persons with the poor yet sometimes distinguishes between them. This may not be just comedic imprecision; it shows the overlap between the two. As to the economic injustice, one of Cronus's remedies is that the poor should ignore and despise the rich, look the other way, and stop gaping at them and doing them obeisance as the rich pass by in their carriages, dressed in purple clothing, wearing emerald rings. Adopting this novel behavior, the poor would force the rich to treat them with respect or at least take notice of them, since the source of pride for the rich are the poor.[63]

An interpreter must always cautiously use comics and satirists in the ancient world because they exaggerate or twist the facts to suit their purposes. (Of course, "objective" historians in antiquity were not above twisting the facts or putting spins on them, either.) But Lucian's description of the economic bifurcation (an ant and a camel) and the subsequent tension between the poor and the rich can be confirmed with other ancient sources. Epictetus (55–135 C.E., Phrygia) says that the distance between the decurions and the people was comparable to that between a general and a rank-and-file soldier, and a magistrate and a private individual.[64]

---

[61] Lucian, *Sat.* 19, LCL 6.115–17.

[62] Ibid., 20, trans. Kilburn, LCL 6.117–19.

[63] Ibid., 29–30, LCL 6.127–29.

[64] Epictetus, 3.24.99: τίνα με θέλεις εἶνει; ἄρχοντα ἢ ἰδιώτην, βουλευτὴν ἢ δημότην, στρατιώτην ἢ στρατηγόν; *tina me theleis einai; archonta ē idiōtēn, bouleutēn ē dēmotēn, stratiōtēn ē stratēgon;* cited in Garnsey, *Status*, 244.

There is an inscription of a lavish foundation of 300,000 denarii for children and monetary gifts to various citizens from a woman named Menodora at Sillyum in Pisidia. The donations to the citizens follow a hierarchical order, so they offer a glimpse of how the eastern peoples viewed the ruling elite.

> The council [*sic*, γερουσία, *gerousia*][65] and the people [δῆμος] honoured the priestess of all the gods and hierophant for life and one of the ten chief citizens, [δεκάπρωτον, *dekaprōton*] Menodora, daughter of Megacles, *demiourgos* and gymnasiarch for the provision of oil, who gave on behalf of Megacles, her son, 300,000 silver *denarii* for the maintenance of children and further gave both in her own gymnasiarchy and in the office of her son, as *demiourgos,* and in the gymnasiarchy of her daughter, to each councillor 85 *denarii,* to each member of the body of elders[66] 80 *denarii,* to each member of the assembly 77 *denarii.*[67]

The councilors come first, followed by the elders and assemblymen. Not every city had a council of elders, and it seems to have had more prestige than political clout. But that the elders usually had no real power but only prestige and yet were listed above the assemblymen may reveal just how far below councilors the assembly members were. Indeed, in another version of the inscription both the elders and assemblymen receive 20 denarii each.[68] Conspicuous by their absence are the poor. The children are not destitute. This is confirmed not only in the above description, which does not explicitly state that these are poor children, but also in other inscriptions about donations from the rich. In these inscriptions, not often do the rich establish funds for poor children.[69]

---

[65] In another inscription the Greek reads, βουλή. See P. Paris, *Quatenus Feminae Res Publicas in Asia Minore, Romanis Imperantibus, Attigerint* (Paris: Ernest Thorin, 1891) 141.

[66] For a discussion of elders see Jones, *The Greek City,* 225–26; Magie, *Roman Rule,* 1.63.

[67] Broughton, "Roman Asia Minor," 784–85. I used the translation of A. R. Hands, *Charities and Social Aid in Greece and Rome* (Ithaca: Cornell, 1968) 192. For further discussion, see Arlandson, " 'Fall and Rise,' " 83 n. 52. R. MacMullen, "Woman in Public in the Roman Empire," *Historia* 29 (1980) 213, says that these proportions match up very well with inscriptions listing donations in the Latin West. It should be pointed out that Menodora gives the wives "of these" three denarii, thus conforming to a conservative viewpoint that always exists in any society at any time, as the viewpoint pertains to women. This fact will support our conclusion that women were behind the men in their own class.

[68] Broughton, "Roman Asia Minor," 785.

[69] Ste. Croix, *Class Struggle,* 196–97, correctly notes that the children are not destitute. Hands, *Charities,* passim, translates the other inscriptions.

Menodora has so much wealth and power that she can offer landowning councilors monetary gifts. This reveals that it was possible for wealthy women to have power and prestige even if they were not officially admitted into the ranks of the bodies politic, the council and the assembly. Menodora is evidently making this decision on her own. Her father is mentioned only to heighten her prestige. Also, she may be donating the money on behalf of her son and daughter, but her son should not be seen as a κύριος, *kyrios*, or male guardian. She holds very powerful offices: she was honored with a lifetime priesthood and is δημιουργός, *dēmiourgos*, and gymnasiarch (which are discussed momentarily). She is called "one of the ten chief citizens." It is possible that the word δεκάπρωτον should be translated "(a member of the) Finance Committee" because Menodora held the office of this same title and all of them were males.

As stated, so far no evidence has turned up that women participated directly in the council,[70] though it did in fact acclaim certain women, such as Plancia Magna of Perga, as benefactresses of the city (see below for Plancia Magna). And it is not clear whether women regularly attended the assembly. In the novel *Chaereas and Callirhoe*, Chariton (1st c. C.E., Caria) says that when it was discovered that Callirhoe's body was missing (she was actually alive and kidnapped by pirates), her father, Hermocrates, the "first man" of the city, called an assembly, which women attended, to investigate the matter.[71] And when Chaereas and Callirhoe returned home triumphantly, the crowd wanted to hear their story. With one voice the people demanded that the couple be ushered into the assembly, whose setting would facilitate hearing their story a little better. Chariton specifies that both men and women attended.[72] When Chaereas went in alone, all the women—who are mentioned first—and men shouted to invite Callirhoe into the meeting. This indicates that women played an active, not silent, role. Though Chariton is writing fiction, the context of the two passages does not seem so outlandish that women's participation in the assembly could not have even remotely taken place, because in terms of social

---

[70] Magie, *Roman Rule*, 1.649.

[71] Chariton, 3.4, *CAGN*, 41–42. The Greek reads, ἐκείνην τὴν ἐκκλησίαν ἂν ἤγαγον καὶ γυναῖκες , *eikeinēn tēn ekklēsian an ēgagon kai gynaikes* ("*that* assembly even women attended," or "*that* assembly women also attended"). The placement of καί, *kai,* and the use of ἐκείνην, *ekeinēn,* denote that this occasion was an exception.

[72] Ibid., 8.7, *CAGN*, 121–22. The Greek reads, λόγου δὲ θᾶττον ἐπληρώθη τὸ θέατρον ἀνδρῶν τε καὶ γυναικῶν, *logou de thatton eplērōthē to theatron andrōn te kai gynaikōn* ("more quickly than a word [can tell], the theater was filled with men and women"). Unlike the first example, the grammar does not suggest that this was an exception.

data Chariton strives to maintain verisimilitude (the supernatural elements are another matter). Until more evidence turns up or is discovered, however, it must be conceded that these two examples are probably exceptions because of the unusual circumstances surrounding the couple and because the assembly did not intend to vote on legislation.

One of the main functions of the council was the electing and appointing of magistrates, committees, and boards, all taken, not surprisingly, from the same economic class as the decurions. The number of the titles burgeoned, such as ἄρχοντες, *archontes* (magistrates), *duoviri* (two chief magistrates), στρατηγοί, *stratēgoi* (see below), πρυτάνεις, *prytaneis* (see below), βουλάρχοι, *boularchoi* (presiding officers of the council), ἀγορονόμοι, *agoronomoi* (controllers of the market), ἀστυνόμοι, *astynomoi* (city managers), gymnasiarchs, chief priests, etc. The requirement for these offices was that the holders carry out their duties not only without recompense (in most cases) but also at their own expense through acts of generosity. These munificent acts—very public—were called "liturgies," meaning "services to the city."[73] A gymnasiarch, for example, who had oversight of the cultural and educational center of the polis, might have to pay for the maintenance of the building or for the supply of oil, a sizable expense, used as a cleanser and lubricant for those who exercised in the facilities.[74] The upkeep of the building itself meant a heavy cost, since in some cities it housed, besides exercise rooms, hot and cold public baths, a lecture hall, a library, and rooms for general conversation.

Since the principal qualification for these political officeholders was wealth and the ready desire to spend it, women of means occupied the offices as well.[75] The following list includes the offices, the number of women who held them, the number of cities where these women held office, and the centuries when they held them, as far as all of these data are known.[76]

hipparch, ἵππαρχος, highest civic office (5 women in Cyzicus, Troas; 1st–3d C.E.)[77]

prytanis, πρύτανις, ruler (28 eponymous women in 8 cities; 1st–3d C.E.)[78]

---

[73] P. Veyne, *Bread and Circuses* (abr. Oswyn Murray; trans. Brian Pearce; London: Penguin, 1990) passim.

[74] Magie, *Roman Rule,* 1.62.

[75] Ibid., 1.649; Jones, *The Greek City,* 175.

[76] See Magie, *Roman Rule,* passim, for an explanation of the titles. P. Trebilco, *Jewish Communities in Asia Minor* (New York: Cambridge, 1991) 113–26; Paris, *Quatenus,* 68–77; O. Braunstein, *Die politische Wirksamkeit der griechischen Frau* (Leipzig: August Hoffmann, 1911).

[77] Trebilco, *Communities,* 123.

[78] Ibid., 120. Eponymous documents and records were dated according to the year or years that the officeholder was in power.

stephanēphoros, στεφανηφόρος, wreath bearer, related to a secular magistracy and a priesthood (37 women in 17 cities; 2d B.C.E.–3d C.E.)[79]

dekaprōtos, δεκάπρωτος, member of the finance committee (1 woman, Menodora, 3d C.E.)[80]

demiurge, δημιουργός, artificer (10 women in 6 cities; 2d B.C.E.–3d C.E.)[81]

archon, ἄρχων, civic magistrate, a general title (3 women in 3 cities)[82]

agonothete, ἀγωνοθέτης, sponsor of the contests (18 women in 14 cities; 1st–3d C.E.)[83]

panēguriarchēs, πανηγυριάρχης, sponsor of the sacrifices and banquets (1 woman in 1 city)[84]

gymnasiarch, γυμνασιάρχης or γυμνασίαρχος, ruler of the cultural and educational center (48 women in 23 cities; 1st–3d C.E.)[85]

timouchos, τιμοῦχος, honor holder, where there was no prytanis (1 woman)[86]

priestess, ἀρχιέρεια[87]

strategos, στρατηγός, member of magisterial board (1 woman in Aegiale)[88]

gerousiarchissa, γερουσιαρχίσσα, president of the council of elders (1 woman in Thessalonica; 3d C.E.)[89]

Lyciarch, Λυκιάρχης, presiding officer over the Federation of Lycia (2 women)[90]

---

[79] Magie, *Roman Rule*, 2.836 n. 23, defines the title; Trebilco, *Communities*, 121, provides the other data.

[80] Trebilco, *Communities*, 116–17.

[81] Ibid., 117.

[82] Paris, *Quatenus*, 75.

[83] Magie, *Roman Rule*, 1.653, gives the definition of sponsor of contests; Trebilco, *Communities*, 123, provides the other data. This office was perhaps the most important to the people, for obvious reasons.

[84] Paris, *Quatenus*, 51, and Magie, *Roman Rule*, 1.653, give the title; Trebilco, *Communities*, provides the other information.

[85] Trebilco, *Communities*, 118.

[86] Paris, *Quatenus*, 76.

[87] R. A. Kearsley, "Asiarchs, *Archiereis*, and the *Archiereiai* of Asia," *GRBS* 27 (1986) 183–92. Other priestesses are numerous.

[88] Trebilco, *Communities*, 124. Aegiale was on the island of Amorgos, just off the southwest coast of Asia Minor. Trebilco notes that this board "involved large responsibility and considerable power" (ibid.).

[89] MacMullen, "Woman," 215 n. 35. Trebilco, *Communities*, 123, notes that in Sebaste, Phrygia, in 99 C.E. three women were admitted into this council of elders.

[90] Trebilco, *Communities*, 124. A federation of cities consisted of cities in a province joined together to maintain the imperial cult and to discuss "matters of general interest concerning the administration of the province" (ibid.).

Pontarch, Ποντάρχης, presiding officer over the Federation of Pontus
(1 woman)[91]

Asiarch, Ἀσιάρχης, highest provincial office in Asia Minor
(1 woman)[92]

It would be misleading to conclude that these inscriptions
correspond to the maximum number of women who held office.
Rather, these records are those which have survived or have been
found so far. It is likely that they represent far more women who held
these offices, more so than the surviving records are able to show.
Coins with men's names on them, however, far outnumber coins with
women's names. The same is true with inscriptions. Thus, it is
probable that regardless of the many women who held political
office, the number of men was far greater. If women were numerically
equal with men, one would expect a more even male:female ratio in
the surviving inscriptions and coins.[93]

D. Magie conjectures that many duties were honorary and that
some offices were derived from the women's husbands.[94] But R. A.
Kearsley convincingly demonstrates through a careful analysis of
fifteen inscriptions from Ephesus of the title ἀρχιέρειαι, *archiereiai*
(chief priestesses) that these women often held this office independently of their husbands and not always honorifically.[95] Eight of
the fifteen mention the women's husbands, seven do not. When
Kearsley examines the eight more closely, one of them gives the
husband's name without a title behind it, but his wife's name has a
title. Yet from other inscriptions her husband held the office of
Asiarch. If her title were dependent on her husband's, one would
expect to see his title in her inscription. Another woman is described
twice as ἀρχιέρεια, *archiereia,* of Asia, while her husband bears the
title Asiarch with no sign of his repeating his term of office. So for
one term at least she bore her title alone.

Transferring Kearsley's analysis to the above list of offices
would exceed the necessary limits of our survey, but a cursory
glance at some of the inscriptions reveals that often a woman
is mentioned without her husband or other males, as seen with

---

[91] Ibid.

[92] Ibid.

[93] MacMullen, "Woman," 213.

[94] Magie, *Roman Rule,* 1.649.

[95] Kearsley, "Asiarchs," 183–92. Most of the inscriptions are dated from
the first to the second centuries, and some in the third. The argument that
follows can be found ibid., 187–88. Trebilco, *Communities,* 113–17, also
decisively argues that prominent Gentile women, independently of men and
not only honorifically, held various offices beyond just the religious ones.

Menodora.[96] So if the inscriptions of the chief priestesses resemble the inscriptions of other offices, and they do, then the question of dependence or independence is not a simple one. But the evidence points towards independence more often than scholarship has so far acknowledged.

On whether the offices were honorary, Magie apparently modifies his earlier conjecture because he goes on to say that indeed some of the women's political offices were not honorary and carried within them real power.[97] This is especially true with such positions as δεκάπρωτος, dekaprōtos, and στρατηγός, stratēgos, because the officeholders oversaw their city's finances and public policies. But MacMullen's comments on this matter are particularly perceptive and decisive. He says that even men's positions were often honorary.[98] More important, the emphasis should not be placed on how the men or women might have carried out their duties. It is unimaginable that a wealthy landowner, just appointed gymnasiarch, for example, would have walked to the local market, bought oil for the athletes, and hauled it back to the facilities. He delegated such tasks to assistants. All of these officeholders were content with broadcasting their benefactions on feastdays, sitting aloft in special thrones in the theater during civic festivities, and later on having their names and deeds inscribed in stone in the forum.

Plutarch expresses the views of most aristocrats against doing menial jobs:

> But the old man in public life who undertakes subordinate services, such as farming of taxes and the supervision of harbours and of the market place . . . seems to me, my friend, a pitiable and unenviable object, and to some people, perhaps, a burdensome and vulgar one.[99]

The "old man in public life" is a politician or part of the ruling class, and those jobs are beneath his dignity; they could be carried out by retainers hired by the city.

We have another example of how the elite delegated mundane tasks to their retainers. Dionysius, a major character in *Chaereas and Callirhoe*, the "first man" of Miletus, wanted to throw a feast in celebration of his upcoming wedding to Callirhoe.[100] He called his

---

[96] Paris, *Quatenus,* passim. Hands, *Charities,* 175–209, conveniently translates many inscriptions describing social aid and donations by the wealthy, many of whom include women.

[97] Magie, *Roman Rule,* 1.649.

[98] MacMullen, "Woman," 215.

[99] Plutarch, *Mor.* 794A, trans. Fowler, LCL 10.133.

[100] Chariton 3.2, *CAGN* 52.

slave Leonas and carefully instructed him to buy herds of cattle and imported grain and wine. Leonas scurried off to fulfill his master's wishes. The circumstance differs a little from that of political offices because Dionysius did not hold one, but this brief vignette illustrates very well how the elite must never transgress the boundary of dignity by doing menial chores.

By analogy, when a woman announced that she wanted to spend her money to build or improve a structure, the council and assembly cheered and gratefully acclaimed her as δημιουργός, while an architect was appointed to carry out her wishes. Plutarch describes the process after the money had been procured.

> Cities, as we know, when they give public notice of intent to let contracts for the building of temples or colossal statues, listen to the proposals of artists [τῶν τεχνιτῶν, *tōn technitōn*] competing for the commission and bringing in their estimates and models, and then choose the man who will do the same work with the least expense and better than the others and more quickly.[101]

Thus the wealthy and prestigious woman who had donated the money in the first place would not be seen on the job site with a papyrus blueprint furled under her arms, ordering workers what to do and where to go. So the question whether an office held by a man or woman was honorary or real is moot because once a woman or man spent her or his money, an act of political power and social prestige, then the title was added on as a token of appreciation.

Our goal is to tell the story of the life of women, so one of these female politicians will serve as a representative from among the governing orders, since her father was governor of Bithynia. Plancia Magna lived in Perga (or Perge), a town in Pamphylia, about ten miles from the southern coast.[102] Like so many prominent women, her existence is known only through inscriptional and numismatic evidence, which almost always contradicts the literary and philosophical writings about women. The latter writings generally portray the ideal woman as being strictly domestic. Plancia did not fit that mold. She moved into traditional male spheres.

She descended from the leading family of the city, the Plancii, who had come as traders from Italy at the end of the Republic and subsequently acquired land. She lived during the late first and early second centuries C.E. and married a prominent peregrine (non-Roman) named Iulius Cornutus Tertullus, who was a wealthy

---

[101] Plutarch, *Mor.* 498E, trans. Helmbold, LCL 6.367.
[102] For a brief list of the inscriptions, see Arlandson, " 'Fall and Rise,' " 85 n. 75.

landowner. Together they owned vast estates, some as far away as eastern and southern Galatia.

Euergetism (lit., "good-deed-ism"), allied with liturgies,[103] was expected of all wealthy citizens of Asia Minor. It consisted of donating time, energy, and money for the benefit of the city. Accordingly, Plancia Magna donated money for the construction of one of Perga's more opulent features, its southern main gate, which was two stories high and had elaborately sculpted designs. For this and other acts of largesse, the council, assembly, and elders erected two statues of her, on the bases of which they inscribed that she was the daughter of M. Plancius Varus and "daughter of the city." She was also identified as δημιουργός, as priestess of Artemis, as the first and only lifetime priestess of the mother of the gods, and as being pious and loving towards her homeland.

In Greek law it was sometimes necessary for a woman making legal decisions, such as donating money or inheriting property, to have a κύριος.[104] But scholars are divided over this subject. Some highlight women's independence, others see the guardian as necessary, still others consider him more shadow than substance.[105] The latter conclusion is tentatively preferable, with a slight modification. It seems that a guardian was necessary for most women in Asia Minor, but not always for the very wealthy. Plancia Magna and Menodora are two examples among many of such women who did not have one. As noted, other female officeholders did not need their husband's or another male's name in the inscriptions describing their benefactions to the city.[106] (Plancia Magna's and Menodora's fathers were mentioned only to elevate the women's prestige through birth.) Still, other women apparently needed one, as in the case of the very wealthy mother-in-law of a certain Amyntas, whose property was confiscated by a Roman merchant (see this chapter, "Landless Peasants," pp. 56–57). Thus, apparently for the wealthy the κύριος was either not necessary or a token shadow figure in most cases, and for

---

[103] See Veyne, *Bread,* 70–156, for a full discussion. Broughton, "Roman Asia Minor," 746–97, has an extraordinary list of donors and their donations—note the number of pages—many of whom are women.

[104] For excellent discussions of κύριος, see Van Bremen, "Women," 223–42; D. M. Schaps, *Economic Rights of Women in Ancient Greece* (Edinburgh: Edinburgh University, 1979) 48–60, esp. 48–52; and C. Vatin, *Recherches sur le mariage et la condition de la femme mariée à l'époque hellénistique* (Paris: E. de Boccard, 1970) 241–53.

[105] Van Bremen, "Women," 230–35, has a careful discussion of the views.

[106] M. T. Boatwright, "Plancia Magna of Perge: Women's Roles and Status in Roman Asia Minor," in *Women's History and Ancient History* (ed. S. B. Pomeroy; Chapel Hill: University of North Carolina, 1991) 254–55.

other women he was almost always needed. In the empire money could buy legal privileges, and women's wealth performed the same function. More money meant more freedom, which resulted in social boundaries becoming a little more porous. Social boundaries usually manifested physical boundaries—women were typified as being domestic—but wealth purchased for them access into the outside world. They crossed over traditional boundaries, often without a male guardian. In contrast, Jewish adult women did not need a male guardian "in legal actions mentioned in the law."[107] In this regard Jewish women appear to have been freer than Gentile women.

As to the ruling orders in Jerusalem, there is very little scholarly consensus over "who ran what."[108] According to one view, "the high-priestly aristocracy, supported by distinguished laymen"[109] and through the instrument of the Sanhedrin, a court of seventy-one men, ruled over Jerusalem and Judea. The Sanhedrin was a mixture of Sadducees, Pharisees, and some scribes. And since the Romans saw the Sanhedrin as the supreme tribunal for governmental matters, it carried moral weight throughout the Jewish world.[110]

According to another view, the hierarchy was as follows: priests (the high priest and chief priests), influential laity, magistrates, Sadducees, Pharisees, and scribes, followed by the institutions of the βουλή/γερουσία, the συνέδριον, *synedrion* (Sanhedrin), and the "common council," the latter of which was formed after the Jewish revolt in 66 C.E.[111] The essential point is that the city and surrounding region were controlled by a select, elite group of men, while the συνέδριον was an ad hoc court used only to adjudicate legal difficulties, such as the trial of Jesus. It never had lifetime members, nor was it a permanent institution, and certainly it was not a "representative national body."[112]

---

[107] Z. Falk, "Private Law," CRINT, 1.507.

[108] Sanders, *Judaism*, 458.

[109] Schürer, *History*, 2.210–18. Sanders, *Judaism*, 460, depicts scholars on this issue as "allies."

[110] Schürer, *History*, 2.218.

[111] J. S. McLaren, *Power and Politics in Palestine* (JSOTSup 63; Sheffield: Sheffield Academic, 1991) 188–225, esp. 199–225. Sanders, *Judaism*, 472, aligns himself with McLaren and claims M. Goodman, *The Ruling Class of Judaea* (New York: Cambridge, 1987), is in their group. But Sanders sees minor differences as well and (p. 490) would also counsel that the situation in first-century Palestine varied too often for us to reach firm conclusions. McLaren's thesis in these pages is not clearly written. On pp. 223–25 McLaren seems to indicate that the order is chief priests, influential laity, βουλή/γερουσία, magistrates, and then συνέδριον.

[112] McLaren, *Power*, 223.

As with the Gentile world, so the Jewish world knew of wealthy men and women who did not necessarily occupy official positions of power in the bodies politic; they were the urban elite who were landowners. Those who were merchants also may have owned land, a much stabler means of earning capital. These men and women might also be known as lay aristocrats, since they were not priests or other religionists.

The purpose of this glimpse at Jewish political institutions is not to resolve the discrepancy in scholarship but to make two observations. First, however the hierarchy might have existed, it was a plutocracy. The authors of *1 Enoch* (2d C. B.C.E.–1st C. C.E.), in an extraordinarily terse and incisive classification of the elite, denounce the "kings, governors, high officials and landlords" as enemies of God because they oppress children and God's elect.[113] When the polemics—obligatory in apocalyptic literature—are ignored, the authors' choice of words reveals that they clearly knew who lived among the upper classes and what their source of wealth was: the land and its monetary and in-kind fruit. In this passage landlords can be translated as "administrators or governors of the land" or, more literally, as "those who hold, possess or seize the land."[114] And many other ancient texts and documents concerning Jewish economic and social history support this passage in *1 Enoch*. Though most political leaders in Palestine derived their wealth from ownership of land, a few were merchants dealing in grain, wine, oil, and wood; others were bankers and tax farmers (retainers).[115] This is in sharp contrast to the Roman and Greek elite, who might invest in business and trading or even own a ship or two, but never be a merchant or trader or banker.[116] But as in the pagan world, it is likely that a wealthy Jewish merchant or banker owned land and relied heavily on retainers to carry out the day-to-day duties.

The second observation is that women appear to have been officially excluded from these positions of power in the βουλή or συνέδριον and from being priestesses or even judges in the towns. But they enjoyed a large degree of influence, taking another route.

Josephus (37/8–100 C.E.), not known for his philogyny, recounts stories of powerful women in the ruling families of Palestine. But his portrayal of them is ambiguous because the women are always ulti-

---

[113] *1 Enoch* 62–63, trans. and notes Isaac, *OTP* 1.43–44.
[114] *1 Enoch* 62.3 n. b, trans. and notes Isaac, *OTP* 1.43.
[115] J. Jeremias, *Jerusalem in the Time of Jesus* (3d ed.; trans. F. H. Cave and C. H. Cave; Philadelphia: Fortress, 1969) 95–96. Fiensy, *Social*, 50, questions Jeremias's assumptions, however. These men probably owned land.
[116] Ste. Croix, *Class Struggle*, 41, 125–29.

mately subjected to male rulers within the ruling families (usually not outside the families), or their power and status are dependent on men, or they work behind the scenes prodding the men to get their way. Salome Alexandra (142–69 B.C.E.) of the Hasmonean family will serve as a representative for every other woman in the ruling class in Palestine, since she was the sole ruler for nine years until her death and therefore had the greatest opportunity to exercise absolute power.

On his deathbed Alexander Jannaeus advised his wife Alexandra to yield a certain amount of power to the Pharisees, which she did.[117] She was made to promise that while she was on the throne, she would not take any action without their consent.[118] "And so, while she had the title of sovereign [ὄνομα τῆς βασιλείας, *onoma tēs basileias*], the Pharisees had the power [τὴν δὲ δύναμιν, *tēn de dynamin*]."[119] Nevertheless (μέντοι, *mentoi*), the queen took certain matters into her own hands. She looked after the welfare of the kingdom by recruiting a large force of mercenaries and making her own troops twice as numerous.[120] Josephus notes that Alexandra was a brilliant administrator in "larger affairs."[121] She took pity on some men who were being slaughtered by the Pharisees by ordering the men to guard fortresses outside the Pharisees' reach.[122] She ordered her son Aristobulus to march out to Damascus against Ptolemy, son of Mennaeus.[123] And she bribed the invading Tigranes, king of Armenia, who thereupon withdrew his army.[124] Though the bribes placated him, he also withdrew when he heard that Lucullus (a Roman consul in 74 B.C.E.) was ravaging Armenia and besieging the capital of Armenia. Josephus summarizes her life in equally split terms. "She was a woman who showed none of the weakness of her sex; for being one of those inordinately desirous of the power to rule, she showed by her deeds the ability to carry out her plans."[125] Yet she had no consideration for decency or justice. She created domestic strife,

---

[117] Josephus, *Ant.* 13.398–432, LCL 7.429–47. In Josephus, *J.W.* 1.110–12, LCL 2.53–55, the Pharisees are said to have taken over the administration slowly.

[118] Josephus, *Ant.* 13.403, LCL 7.429–31.

[119] Josephus, *Ant.* 13.409, trans. Marcus, LCL 7.433. Josephus, *J.W.* 1.112, LCL 2.55, says, "But if she ruled the nation, the Pharisees ruled her" (trans. St. J. Thackeray).

[120] Josephus, *Ant.* 13.409, LCL 7.437–39.

[121] Josephus, *J.W.* 1.112, LCL 2.55.

[122] Josephus, *Ant.* 13.410–18, LCL 7.433–39.

[123] Ibid., 13.418, LCL 7.437–39.

[124] Ibid., 13.419–21, LCL 7.439.

[125] Ibid., 13.430, trans. Marcus, LCL 7.445. Josephus, *J.W.* 1.108, LCL 2.53, says, "For this frail woman firmly held the reins of government, thanks to her reputation for piety" (trans. St. J. Thackeray).

disturbances, and misfortune that "arose from the public measures taken in her lifetime."[126] "Nevertheless, in spite of reigning in this manner, she kept the nation at peace."[127]

It is possible that the discrepancy in Josephus's account of the power struggle between this lone woman and the Pharisees finds its roots in different sources: "a Jewish-Pharisee source in defense of Salome or a Greek source hostile to the Jews (or a Jewish source aimed against the Pharisees)."[128] This theory may be true in this particular case, but it fails to explain the subordination of all the other women in the ruling families to men in those same families, according to Josephus. Is this subordination based only on his personal ideology? Or is it based on the ideology of his times? And if either one or a mixture of both is the basis, then does this ideology reflect historical reality? While it is accurate to claim that a wise ruler should consolidate her power by forming alliances, it is possible that Josephus is expressing only his own ideology when he describes the Pharisees as holding most of the de facto power.[129] The question of Josephus's and his culture's ideology confronting historical reality is complex and not quickly answered. But if we judge only from the ratio of male to female rulers, more men than women occupied positions of power sanctioned by Rome; this sanctioning by Rome counterbalances the claim that Josephus writes from his own ideology, and indicates that most women were behind the men in the ruling class, since the men resisted any attempt from women to usurp even the smallest degree of their power.

It is not clear whether women were involved in politics in cities and towns outside Jerusalem. In the fictional story of the heroine Judith, which was probably written in a Palestinian setting in the second or first centuries B.C.E., three magistrates (ἄρχοντες) of her hometown, Bethulia, whose precise location in Palestine is unknown, called the elders into an assembly (ἐκκλησία) to which all the young men *and women* ran in order to participate in the proceedings (Jdt 6:16). And when the Assyrians were besieging the town (the literary period of the story), men, women, and children "gathered around Uzziah [a magistrate] and the rulers [ἄρχοντας, *archontas*] of

---

[126] Josephus, *Ant.* 13.432, trans. Marcus, LCL 7.445–47.

[127] Ibid.

[128] J. Klausner, "Queen Salome Alexandra," in *The World History of the Jewish People,* vol. 6, *The Hellenistic Age* (ed. A. Schalit; 6 vols.; New Brunswick, N.J.: Rutgers, 1972) 6.243.

[129] Josephus, *Ag. Ap.* 2.199–204, LCL 1.373–75. B. Halpern Amaru "Portraits of Biblical Women in Josephus' *Antiquities,*" *JJS* 39 (1988) 143–170, notes that biblical women in Josephus are idealized and subservient.

the town and cried out with a loud voice" (7:23). This gathering, in which women participated, the author also calls an assembly. It is difficult to know whether all villages and small towns had the political structure of three magistrates, a council of elders, and an assembly of the populace, but it is clear that in this town women attended the panicked proceedings in the more democratic institution, the assembly.[130] Since, however, the context of the women's involvement in the assembly is emergency situations (as was seen in Chariton's novel), it is impossible to conclude with a high degree of certainty that their involvement reflects historical reality, even though the author seeks to maintain verisimilitude in at least the social data. Until more information is discovered or turns up, it should be conceded either that conclusions one way or the other cannot be reached or that women's involvement in the assembly was exceptional at best.

But fictional Judith's own story is another matter. Because she was extremely wealthy (cf. 8:7–8), it is easier to believe that she—if she was like some powerful and wealthy women in Asia Minor—carried enough political clout in her small town to summon the magistrates and elders to a meeting in order to rebuke them for their lack of trust in God and to reveal her heroic plans to rescue the town (vv. 9–27). She should be considered part of the lay aristocracy. It is no coincidence that her wealth and respect among all the citizens is mentioned just before her political move to call the meeting (vv. 7–8). Traditions that were ultimately fixed in the Mishnah a few centuries

---

[130] See Sanders, *Judaism,* 483–84, and Goodman, *Ruling,* 110–11, for a discussion of the assembly. Goodman correctly notes that Rome stripped the assembly of its power, but Sanders misses this point. Its residual power was, however, weaker than Goodman (and perhaps Sanders) admits, for in the examples from Josephus and others that Goodman cites, the rulers carried out their policies regardless of the assembly's opinion, or the rulers bullied the assembly: (1) In Josephus, *J.W.* 1.457–66, LCL 2.215–17, Herod returns from Rome after Caesar reconciles Herod's sons. Herod convenes an assembly and announces that his sons are the heirs to the throne. With Caesar's name being thrown around, opponents in the assembly would not assert their own opinion; indeed, they did not (cf. 1.466). (2) In Josephus, *J.W.* 1.437, LCL 2.207, Herod fears the popular support of Aristobulus, the last Hasmonean high priest. This is not unusual, for rulers often sought to control the nameless masses, fearing that if trouble erupted, Rome would intervene with penalties in hand. (3) The assembly in 1 Macc 14:25–49 appears to have slightly more power only because the events of this passage occur in 140 B.C.E., before Rome took over. (And even in this passage the power of the assembly is more problematic than Goodman cares to concede.) Thus, *pace* Goodman, it is not the assembly as such that Herod and other leaders feared but the masses and civic unrest. The assembly was much weaker than leaders appointed by Rome.

later give autonomous women such as Judith (whose husband apparently did not have a brother who would have married her in a levirate ceremony) a great deal of authority over their deceased husbands' and their own estates.[131] It may very well be that these later rabbinic rulings shed some light on Judith's situation, though caution must be exercised here because of the redactional and chronological problems that rabbinic literature poses. It is probable, anyway, that she was wealthier than the magistrates and elders (though the text does not say this explicitly) because she resembles a few historical women, such as Menodora in Asia Minor, who had more wealth than did many magistrates and members of the council. As noted, the juxtaposition of her wealth to her political power is calculated to lend credence to the idea that a woman in the highest levels could wield much power, especially in a town of this small a size.

Regardless of the ambiguity of these women's political power and status both in Josephus and the Book of Judith, a sample of their wealth is revealed in the settlement of Herod the Great's will.

> Jamneia, Azotus and Phasaelis were given over to his sister Salome along with five hundred thousand pieces of coined silver. He also provided for all his other relatives and left them wealthy through gifts of money and the assignment of revenues.[132]

> Caesar made her [Salome] a present of the royal palace in Ascalon. Altogether, then, she had a revenue of sixty talents yearly.[133]

> To each of his two unmarried daughters, beside what their father left them, Caesar made an additional gift of two hundred and fifty thousand pieces of coined silver, and gave them in marriage to the sons of Pheroras. He also gave to the children of the king the sum of fifteen hundred talents out of the amount left to him.[134]

As seen with the wealthy women of Asia Minor, women in Palestine with control over this much wealth exercised considerable power certainly in their own right and in their own circles,[135] and they lived far above ordinary citizens in Palestine.

---

[131] J. R. Wegner, *Chattel or Person? The Status of Women in the Mishnah* (New York: Oxford, 1988) 10–19, shows convincingly and easily that women were at their freest when they were not tied to men. Wegner discovers that when the rabbis try to protect patrilineage, they invariably treat women as chattel in relation to their husbands. When the husband dies and no levirate marriages are required, the rabbis treat women as persons and give them great power over wealth.

[132] Josephus, *Ant.* 17.189, trans. Marcus and Wikgren, LCL 8.459.

[133] Ibid., 17.321, trans. Marcus and Wikgren, LCL 8.521.

[134] Ibid., 17.322, trans. Marcus and Wikgren, LCL 8.521.

[135] G. Macurdy, *Vassal-Queens and Some Contemporary Women in the Roman Empire* (Baltimore: Johns Hopkins, 1937) 63–91.

That the ancients in Jewish society made such distinctions between the comfortable lifestyle of wealthy women and the misery of poor men and women is commonplace, but the distinction is illustrated most remarkably in a passage in the Tosephta.

> The sages awarded to the daughter of Naqdimon b. Gurion five hundred golden *denars* daily for a cup of spices, and she was only a sister-in-law awaiting levirate marriage. But she cursed [the settlement] and said, "So may you award for your own daughters!" Said R. Leazar b. R. Sadoq, "May I [not] see comfort, if I do not see her picking out pieces of barley from under the hoofs of horses in Akko. Concerning her I pronounced the following Scripture, *If you do not know, O most beautiful of women* (Song 1:8)."[136]

If her attitude did not reflect the real-life attitudes of others in the ancient world who were wealthy, the entire scene could be comical to a modern reader. Naqdimon lived before and during the first Jewish revolt in the first century C.E. and was one of the richest men in Jerusalem. The sum offered this daughter-in-law for a daily cup of spices or perfume is exorbitant by any standards. (Even if the sum could be proven to be misreported—and it cannot—a fraction of it would still make her very rich indeed.) In any case, she curses an award given on a daily basis that a laborer, not to mention a beggar, would never see in his or her lifetime. As the rabbis depart from the presence of this extremely wealthy and spoiled (so they believe) woman, they say, in effect, "If only you knew about the plight of the poor, O most beautiful of women, you would be more than satisfied with the ruling!"

The luxurious living quarters of these women (and men) also speak of their wealth. Mansions from the Herodian period have been excavated.[137] The mansion known as the Herodian House was 2,000+ sq. ft. Its rooms were arranged around a central courtyard that had a large reservoir partly vaulted over, a small cistern, and four ovens sunk in the floor. The western wall had three niches, used for storing household cookery. There was a fine set of red sigillata ware, beautifully designed, and a large group of amphorae bearing Latin inscriptions, indicating that the occupants drank wine imported from Italy. In other houses, wall paintings were discovered with warm colors, such as red, yellow, and brown, and also green, black, and other colors, commonly depicting floral

---

[136] *t. Ketub.* 5.9–10, Neusner 3.76. Following Peter Pettit, a friend and colleague, I adapted the translation only slightly.

[137] N. Avigad, "How the Wealthy Lived in Herodian Jerusalem," *BARev* 2 (1976) 1, 23–35.

motifs. Wood furniture did not survive, but a luxurious stone table did. There were coins of varying value and from various regions, and a menorah incised on a fragment of plaster. Besides their architectural and movable features, these mansions were situated in the Upper City of Jerusalem, whose location on a twin-peaked, high, broad hill served as a visual reminder of the social separation between the rich and the commoners. Not surprisingly, it was this area which the rebels and *sicarii* eventually overran at the beginning of the revolt in 66 C.E. and where they burned the archive building, which housed the records of debts.[138]

To sum up, the assessment of wealthy Jewish women's position in society is far from clear: (1) Appearing before a panel of judges, they did not need a male guardian. But other than in the context of legal actions, one could question how this freedom helped their daily lives. (2) The evidence that even ordinary women regularly participated in a small town's assembly is far from conclusive. More evidence is needed. (3) As stated, women were blocked from most official positions of power. But women of extreme wealth and power, such as the historical Alexandra Salome and the fictional lay aristocrat Judith, enjoyed a corresponding degree of freedom. Evidence in Josephus and elsewhere shows that even though wealthy women could control politics from behind the scenes or outside official leadership roles, they did not hold the ultimate reins of power. It only partially answers the question to assert that Jewish texts written by men squeeze women into molds and patterns that conform to domesticity and subservience to men. In real life, women were a step behind the men in the governing orders, if only in sheer numbers. That is, even if women were not restricted to the house or reduced to abject social, legal, and economic submission, women were still behind the men because far more men than women occupied positions of power—a patriarchy; therefore, not surprisingly, men crafted many real-life laws to their advantage. And when Rome sanctioned men as the rulers, women could only work behind the scenes with their wealth and power. (4) But despite all of this, in comparison with the masses, these women's wealth, status, and power combined to provide them with good food, luxurious clothing, spacious houses, respect from the poorer classes (at least face-to-face) and the better choices of wealthy young persons for their daughters and sons—which kept the money in the elite families.

At least seven facts emerge from the survey of the wealthy women of Asia Minor: (1) The council and the assembly were ruled

---

[138] Josephus, *J.W.* 2.425–29, LCL 2.491.

by men only. Until more information turns up, it has to be conceded that women were usually excluded from leadership roles. As with Jewish women, the evidence showing their regular participation in the assembly is far from conclusive. (2) But women of wealth such as Menodora or Plancia Magna could exercise their own form of power with their own money. From the little information that exists, they do not appear to have been stressed or hampered by this exclusion from the two political clubs. (3) Women were political officeholders, and the power resident in these positions was not always dependent on their husbands' status in society. The political offices were not more or less honorary than men's offices because, like men, women with money and a ready desire to spend it purchased their way into these positions and into making decisions on how or where the money would be spent. (4) These positions of power indicate their status. Money raised it to be very high indeed. That these women were acclaimed political officeholders at all is remarkable because many wealthy men never achieved this status. (5) Inscriptions reveal that some women with this much wealth, status, and power were free from the power of the κύριος, though more study is needed on this subject before firm conclusions can be drawn. (6) Women left the domestic sphere and moved into the outside world, earning for themselves more freedom without suffering loss of status. They made financial and political decisions. (7) Yet for all the political offices that women held, for all the wealth they possessed, and despite conclusion 2 above, women, on a percentage basis, were behind men in the control of wealth and power. (This conclusion takes into account the disparity between the references and inscriptions of women rulers and leaders and the actual number of such women.) To be sure, they were making inroads, but fewer women than men occupied political offices. As with Jewish women, fewer Asian women than men were proconsuls, procurators, prefects, or other leaders. Men, dominating the councils and assemblies, acclaimed women as officeholders, not the reverse. Fewer women than men had enough control of money to do acts of euergetism. In short, men still controlled society politically and economically despite the remarkable gains that women achieved in the prosperous Greek East.

Retainers and Religionists. It was a physical impossibility for the rulers to govern by themselves, so they employed the services of retainers, who were primarily urban. They were the power brokers between the rulers and the ruled and filled positions as clerks, subclerks, financial bureaucrats, tax farmers, rent collectors, judges, Roman lictors (similar to bodyguards and all-around assistants), personal estate managers, jailers, eirenarchs (chief peace officers), *sitōnēs* (commissioners for grain purchases), chiliarchs (commanders of a thousand soldiers), centurions (commanders of a hundred), doctors,[139] and scholars. Scholars, especially those of advanced studies, "regularly received freedom from municipal burdens and in some cases at least a salary from the city."[140] Teachers of less advanced studies had mixed status. Besides scholars for the city, those who attached themselves to wealthy families received a good salary, lived quite comfortably, and sometimes made enough money to enter politics.

The religionists were priests and priestesses. For Palestine this list of religionists may be added: the synagogue leaders, the Pharisees, the rabbis, many of the scribes, the priests, and the Levites. The religionists served as power brokers between God (or the gods) and humanity, but some were also retainers for the state.[141] That is, they interpreted God's (or the gods') will here on earth in order to decide spiritual or practical questions on how to live properly before the Deity (or deities).

In the model (see fig. 1), as the retainers and religionists move up to the governing classes, the line becomes dotted. This indicates that the boundary between the two sections is porous.[142] In some cases one can never be sure where the day-to-day power resides. For example, the γραμματεῖς, *grammateis,* in Asia Minor (the clerks for the council) and in Palestine (the scribes) might sometimes be numbered among the ruling class because of the power they wielded.[143]

Most priests in Asia Minor earned a comfortable living. From the Hellenistic period onwards, some temple priests were selected on the basis of wealth and heredity, but normally the people granted the offices to a citizen through annual elections for great services rendered to the city.[144] These great services also meant wealth. Priests

---

[139] Jones, *The Greek City,* 264, says that doctors received salaries from cities and wealthy patients (who surely were political leaders).

[140] Broughton, "Roman Asia Minor," 853.

[141] Sanders, *Judaism,* 182, observes that "priests and Levites were the employees of the nation for the purposes of maintaining the worship of God in the temple, and teaching and judging the people." The Pharisees, *pace* Saldarini, *Pharisees,* passim, were not retainers, even though a few were part of the government. As a sect, they did not represent the state. Retainers derived their wealth, status, and power as direct hangers-on to the governing elite. Pharisees did not depend on this elite for legitimation. Rather, they considered themselves power brokers between God and the people, thereby making them retainers for God.

[142] Lenski, *Power,* 244, observes that the boundaries are "fuzzy."

[143] For Palestine, see Saldarini, *Pharisees,* passim.

[144] Jones, *The Greek City,* 227–28.

were assimilated into the political offices and were selected from that group.[145] In his travels Strabo (64/3 B.C.E.–21 C.E.) observed that in the city of Mylasa (Caria) "the priestly offices are held by the most distinguished [οἱ ἐπιφανέστατοι, *hoi epiphanestatoi*] of the citizens and always for life."[146] Generally, the priests were immune from liturgies and were paid from the animal sacrifices and from the treasury in some cities. The position was very lucrative.[147] The high priest of Zeus at Venasa (Cappadocia) drew fifteen talents a year from the very productive (εὔκαρπον, *eukarpon*) land farmed by the "temple-slaves."[148] In Ephesus the council "had reduced Artemis to penury by the enormous salaries they granted her priests."[149] These high-level priests, then, are another example of the overlap between the religionists and the governing classes.

Many priests in Jerusalem were aristocratic as well because their power was consolidated by family connections and the political process, especially from the Persian period onwards.[150] That is, since the Torah prescribed that the temple and its functions be placed in the hands of the religious leaders whose qualification was based on family origins and since the temple was a collection and distribution center for wealth, the priestly class could control the political decisions and the flow of money. These elites should be considered as part of the governing class and not so much as retainers for God or the state.

The model, however, shows the wealth, power, and perhaps status of the entire group descending to the level of the merchants, artisans, day laborers, and peasants. Some male and female ἱερόδουλοι, *hierodouloi* (lit., "temple slaves") who farmed land belonging to pagan temples might have been priests and priestesses, but they do not appear to have accumulated wealth or to have enjoyed much status with the people, or their status was the same as the people's.[151]

---

[145] Ibid., 227.

[146] Strabo 14.2.23, trans. Jones, LCL 6.293.

[147] Jones, *The Greek City*, 228.

[148] Strabo 12.2.6, LCL 5.359. See Jones, *The Greek City*, 228, for a discussion. For other passages in Strabo about the wealth of priests in Asia Minor, see 12.2.3, LCL 5.351–53; 12.3.31, LCL 5.371–73; 12.3.37, LCL 5.441–43; 12.5.3, LCL 5.471–73.

[149] Jones, *The Greek City*, 228–29.

[150] M. Stern, "Aspects of Jewish Society: The Priesthood and Other Classes," in *The Jewish People in the First Century* (2 vols.; ed. S. Safrai and M. Stern; CRINT; Philadelphia: Fortress, 1976) 2.580–96.

[151] Strabo 12.2.3–4, LCL 5.351–53; 12.3.34–35, 37, LCL 5.435–39, 441–43. Broughton, "Roman Asia Minor," 642–48; Ste. Croix, *Class Struggle,* 153–54; and P. Debord, *Aspects sociaux et économiques de la vie religieuse dans l'Anatolie gréco-romaine* (Etudes Préliminaires aux Religions Orientales dans l'Empire Romain 48; Leiden: Brill, 1982) 83–89, all discuss the ἱερόδουλοι

The majority of priests, rabbis, and scribes in Palestine lived in "great poverty," eking out their livelihood as artisans or peasants or day laborers.[152] As noted, status is notoriously difficult to measure; and though the Jewish priests living in rural areas mostly worked at jobs similar to those of the people, they still kept their status by virtue of their ethnic purity and yearly religious functions.[153] Were it not for these two examples of Jewish priests and pagan ἱερόδουλοι, the portion of the model (fig. 1) representing retainers and religionists would not have extended so far down.

Women could be found among the retainers in Asia Minor. A woman held the office of γραμματεύς, *grammateus.*[154] Antiochis, a female physician living in Tlos, Lycia (Asia Minor), late in the first century C.E., was honored by the council and assembly for her "healing arts."[155] And in the second century a male doctor from Pergamum (the home of the famous Galen) built a tomb for his wife and fellow doctor, Panthia, with an inscription, part of which reads, "[you] raised high our common fame in healing—though you were a woman you were not behind me in skill."[156] In ca. 200 C.E. an unnamed freedwoman of Artemis, wife of Meidianus Plotinianus Varus, was a πραγματευτής, *pragmateutēs* (estate manager) for a landowner in Termessus (Pamphylia).[157] *Eirēnē* (Irene), whose specific date in the second or third century is uncertain, was an estate

---

and conclude that they were nothing more than peasants, though strict chastity was expected of them. This may have raised their status above ordinary peasants.

[152] Jeremias, *Jerusalem,* 108, 112–19. Sanders, *Judaism,* 179, in a rare moment, agrees with him: the priests worked at "fairly low jobs."

[153] Stern, "Aspects of Jewish Society," 580–96, portrays the priests as having prestige in the community apparently without regard to their economic station. Sanders, *Judaism,* 176–77, agrees with him.

[154] Magie, *Roman Rule,* 2.1518–19 n. 50. The Greek reads, γραμμα-τεύσασ[α], *grammateusas[a].*

[155] H. W. Pleket, ed., *Epigraphica: Texts on the Social History of the Greek World,* vol. 2 (Leiden: E. J. Brill, 1969), 27–28 (no. 12; for other female doctors, see nos. 1, 20, 26, 27). Cf. M. R. Lefkowitz and M. B. Fant, *Women's life in Greece and Rome* (London: Duckworth, 1982) 161 (no. 170). Many retainers were either slaves or freedpersons. As freedwomen, their status would have been mixed in the eyes of aristocrats (Corley, *Private Women,* 48–52). But we should not be too hasty in assuming that all these retainers were freedwomen when the texts and references do not say this explicity. None of the inscriptions cited in Pleket shows the doctors as freedwomen, and the same is true for the short inscription that names Antiochis. Per contra, other inscriptions are quick to point this status out evidently in order to segregate the social classes (cf. Lefkowitz and Fant, ibid., 162 [no. 174]).

[156] Ibid., 162 (no. 175). Cf. Pleket, ibid., no. 20.

[157] Broughton, "Roman Asia Minor," 675.

manager (οἰκονόμισσα, *oikonomissa*) for two landowners, Longil-
lianus and Severus, whose property was near the tetrapolis on the
Cillianian plains (between Pisidia and Lycaonia).[158] As noted with
women among the governing classes, it would be wrong to conclude
that these few inscriptions and references correspond to the actual or
maximum number of female retainers; rather, these few inscriptions
and references represent the women whose records have not survived. It is not at all improbable that other intelligent, productive,
and capable women would have been appointed retainers of estates
and businesses.

Plutarch, who is usually conservative towards women, recommends that women should study the works of Plato and Xenophon,
geometry, astronomy, and a wide variety of other subjects.[159] He also
knew a certain wealthy woman named Clea who held "a high office
among the priestesses at Delphi" and who "kept company with
books" (βιβλίοις ἐντυχοῦσαν, *bibliois entychousan*).[160] That is, she
was a religious scholar. It is likely that Plutarch's assessment of Clea
and other female scholars whom he knew or knew of reflects other
such women. In these two passages Plutarch is not depicting the
women as retainers, for wealthy priestesses came from the ruling
class, yet one may be able to surmise that these female scholars
formally passed on their knowledge, as Sappho formally did in her
school several centuries earlier. After all, the context in which Clea is
mentioned is Plutarch's introduction to numerous stories of heroic
and extraordinary women whom he and his contemporaries regarded
as historical. And these stories were "often cited," that is, circulated
throughout the Greek world, a practice that Plutarch heartily recommends and agrees with because of the high and noble values these
stories instill within the male and female hearers.[161] This wide

---

[158] Ibid., 674. These texts are conveniently collected in Pleket, ibid.
Pleket has *Eirēnē* living in the second or third century (p. 39). Broughton is
not sure of her date.

[159] Plutarch, *Mor.* 145B–D, LCL 2.337–41. The statement that Plutarch is
usually conservative towards women needs clarification. Plutarch's works are
vast and, as such, are complex and multifaceted. For example, according to
145B–D, he prefers that women should be educated in the domestic sphere by
their husbands. But in frs. 127–33, LCL 15.243–49, he believes that women
and daughters should be educated with men and sons; and the contexts of the
fragments, though lost, appear to enjoin public education. Generally, however,
Plutarch is conservative and even restrictive.

[160] The first quotation comes from Babbitt's introduction to Plutarch's
essay (LCL 3.473) and the second from the essay itself: *Mor.* 243D, trans.
Babbitt, LCL 3.479. It should be pointed out that βιβλίοις ἐντυχοῦσαν can
mean simply "read books."

[161] Ibid. 243D, LCL 3.479.

circulation indicates that ordinary women taught them informally. Dio Chrysostom heard a tale about Heracles from an anonymous old woman from the Peloponnese, a tale that he was about to adapt for the purposes of his speech.[162] The wide circulation also suggests that wealthy priestesses (or other wealthy women, for that matter) such as Clea taught them formally. Indeed, until any evidence turns up that wealthy pristesses could not be scholars and formally pass on their knowledge, Clea can serve as an example that such priestesses had it in their grasp to do this if they so desired.

For Jewish society (and Jewish communities in Asia Minor are included) women were mostly excluded from being retainers or religious leaders. Nevertheless, according to some inscriptions, women were synagogue leaders, among other roles.[163] Other inscriptions reveal that women, though not holding religious positions, donated their resources for the construction and upkeep of synagogues.[164] But the problem with the inscriptions is their late date (mostly from the third to sixth centuries). While this evidence poses no problem for a history of Judaism, much of it cannot apply to this study. It does not represent a trend beginning as far back as the Hellenistic period. But it does follow the increase in Gentile women holding public offices from the first to the third centuries C.E. With this caveat offered, however, there is one inscription from Smyrna, dated to sometime in the second century of our era.

> Rufina, a Jewess, head of the synagogue [ἀρχισυνάγωγος, *archisynagōgos*], built this tomb for her freed slaves and the slaves [θρέμασιν, *thremasin*] raised in her house. . . . [165]

As seen with Gentile officeholders, Rufina did not hold the office of synagogue leader only honorifically, nor did she depend on her husband. In this inscription Rufina's husband is not mentioned in a legal matter about burial.[166] That she had managerial skills and financial acumen is revealed by her decision to acquire a tomb and her control over numerous slaves. Rufina was obviously a wealthy woman who had money to spare if she could build a tomb for her slaves. But her kindness did not stop at slaves. "The slaves raised in her house" indicates that she took in infants exposed by their parents because, in the context of the other slaves, it is likely that the θρέματα, *thrematta,*

---

[162] Dio Chrysostom, *Or.* 1.49, LCL 1.27.

[163] B. J. Brooten, *Women Leaders in the Ancient Synagogue* (BJS 36; Chico, Calif: Scholar's, 1982) passim.

[164] Ibid., 157–65.

[165] Ibid., 5, trans. Brooten.

[166] Trebilco, *Communities,* 105.

were adopted free children.[167] But whether finding them exposed, raising them slave or free, or adopting orphans, Rufina provides a glimpse into the kindness of an aristocrat of the Roman era. Most did not share her purely humanitarian aid for the destitute.[168]

Talmudic literature knows of a female sage, Beruriah, living in the first to second centuries of our era, who garnered enormous respect from male sages.[169] Wife of the sage R. Meir and daughter of R. Hananyah ben Teradyon, she was a brilliant scholar, whose opinions are cited throughout the Talmud. This example shows that women could be engaged in Torah studies directly; they were not entirely passive in such matters. Unfortunately, the story of Beruriah and others like her, while inspiring, can only entice us to wonder how many more such women there were. It is true that ancient literature composed and maintained by men always tends to downplay women's roles, if not suppress out of hand any knowledge of these women's existence; but it is equally true that even after we take this literary suppression into account, male sages would probably still outnumber the women by far. Men dominated in this elite group of scholar-religionists.

As to secular female retainers, in the Book of Judith, Judith's unnamed servant woman (ἡ ἄβρα, *hē habra;* lit., "the graceful one") is depicted as the one "who was in charge of [τὴν ἐφεστῶσαν, *tēn ephestōsan*] all she [Judith] possessed" (8:10; cf. Gen. 15:2; 24:2; 39:4). In the name of her wealthy, powerful, and prestigious mistress, she walked alone in public and approached magistrates and elders— male political leaders—to demand that a conference be convened in order to discuss the crisis of the Assyrian invasion. She was a slave, and this reinforces the notion that slaves had mixed power and wealth and could be found up and down the model (fig. 1). One should not lightly dismiss Judith's servant as a literary character playing a powerful role in a topsy-turvy literary social world in which women were unrealistically prominent (like Aristophanes' play *Lysistrata,* of a few centuries earlier in confined Athens). When a comparison is made between this female Jewish retainer and female Asian retainers, the function of this Jewish servant becomes entirely plausible; in her case the literary world reflects the real world. As

---

[167] Ibid., 10.

[168] Hands, *Charities,* 175–209; for further discussion, see Arlandson " 'Fall and Rise,' " 90 n. 117.

[169] M. Kaufman, *The Woman in Jewish Law and Tradition* (Northvale, N.J.: Jason Aronson, 1993) 69. The summary in the text is based on his brief discussion, expurgated of the harsh polemics against Christianity. Ilan, *Jewish Women,* 197–200, argues that Beruriah existed as described by tannaitic scholars, but not by the amoraim.

noted with Asian retainers, it is highly probable that other intelligent and capable Jewish women working on the estates of the wealthy were appointed to manage the wealthy's affairs or a portion of their affairs.

Women in Jewish society begin the summary, since the results are straightforward. They were not priestesses, and data revealing that they were sages and other religious leaders are scarce. Despite Rufina, Beruriah, and Judith's servant, far fewer women than men occupied positions as retainers and religionists. Until more information turns up, it has to be conceded that women were behind the men in the roles of sages, religious leaders, and retainers, if only numerically.

Ample evidence suggests that women could also be counted among religious leaders in Asia Minor, as seen with Clea and the ἀρχιέρειαι. As with priests, priestesses were drawn from the very wealthy. Any woman wishing to advance in her religion had to be rich.[170]

To sum up the evidence in Asia Minor, women could be counted among religious leaders, as seen with Clea and the *archiereiai*. As with priests, priestesses were drawn from the very wealthy; any woman wishing to advance in her religion had to be rich. This means that only these women could ever hope to hold positions of leadership. At this economic level women enjoyed a high degree of equality with men. But the female *hierodouloi* were no more than peasants, so their status was open to question since frequently money and status were so tightly connected. It is not clear whether the people held them in higher esteem than they themselves. Women were retainers, but as with our conclusions of the governing orders, fewer women than men served in these positions. This conclusion, as well as the one for Jewish women, takes into account the numerical disparity between actual female retainers and the few surviving literary references and inscriptions which record their existence. Men filled in this class, and women were behind the men on a percentage basis.

Rural People. The urban aristocracies did not condescend to work the land. They hired estate managers to run their affairs, but not even the retainers actually farmed the land. They used farmers or peasants. D. Oakman makes the insightful distinction between two perspectives on the land, one from above, the other from below.[171] Viewed

---

[170] See Kraemer, *Her Share,* passim, for a discussion of wealthy priestesses in a variety of pagan religions.

[171] D. E. Oakman, *Jesus and the Economic Questions of His Day* (Lewiston, N.Y.: Edwin Mellen, 1986) 37–38.

from above or by the aristocrats, ownership of the land was economic. The more they owned, the more they earned. Viewed by the peasantry or from below, the land was "considered an inalienable heritage."[172] Any encroachment on the land was seen as an encroachment on the family heritage. The view from above has already been examined, so this descriptive survey now focuses on the view from below. In Palestine and the Greek East generally there were five different classes of peasants: small freeholders (upper and lower levels), tenant farmers, landless peasants, and day laborers.[173]

Small Freeholders. The landed peasants, or small freeholders (4–50 acres), were owners in their own right,[174] but they can be further divided into two groups:[175] the upper-level freeholders owned 15–50 acres and could support their families and live comfortably; the lower-level freeholders owned 4–15 acres and had to supplement their income. Besides supporting the priestly aristocracy through tithes, both levels of freeholders served the governing orders through their taxes, the benefits of which they never saw because the taxes were earmarked for building cities (Caesarea Maritima, Sebaste, etc.) and palaces (Masada and Herodium).[176] "The concept of taxation for the good of the nation as a whole is not an ancient one."[177]

Most lower-level peasants owned, on average, about 6 acres.[178] This would feed a family of six, the average family size, for only one-third of a year, and the family therefore had to supplement its income. And the peasants who owned only 1 or 2 acres[179] were day laborers more than freeholders.

Since so many freeholders owned so few acres, their political power was limited. At first glance their ownership of land may give the appearance of controlling the means of production. To some extent this is true, especially for the upper levels, but ownership did

[172] Ibid., 38.
[173] Fiensy, *Social,* 77–105. For a definition of "peasants," see Ste. Croix, *Class Struggle,* 210–11.
[174] Fiensy, *Social,* 92–105. Also see Ste. Croix, *Class Struggle,* 213–15; and P. Garnsey, "Non-slave Labour in the Roman World," in *Non-slave Labour in the Greco-Roman World* (ed. P. Garnsey; Cambridge: Cambridge Philological Society, 1980) 34–45.
[175] Fiensy, *Social,* 158, 164.
[176] Ibid., 92. But if the taxes went to the temple, as some of it surely did, then the peasants could benefit from the temple if they lived near Jerusalem or took a pilgrimage during a festival.
[177] Ibid.
[178] Ibid., 93–95.
[179] Ibid., 96.

not make the peasants' daily life secure. Although they were not subjugated to potentially oppressive landowners and some in the upper level lived comfortably, it has been observed that "the freer the ancient peasant, in the political sense, the more precarious his position"—a "deep paradox."[180] Their position was insecure because they were totally responsible for the harvest and for protecting their property from the incursions of officials, urban aristocrats, and bandits. One can surmise that, short of uniting together on a common front with a common cause, which happened rarely, they did not have much power, political or otherwise. Their status was low from the viewpoint of outsiders; the city dwellers generally despised the people of the land, and the peasants returned the favor.[181]

Yet this bleak picture must be counterbalanced. The growing debate in scholarship over the prosperity or poverty of first-century Palestine probably reflects historical reality: many peasants lived ordinary, untroubled lives—insofar as all peasants in all regions can—while many did not.[182] And the debate perhaps reflects class structure among the peasantry. After all, tenant farmers, landless peasants, and day laborers were below upper-level and lower-level freeholders. Scholars who see rural Palestine as oppressed economically are not arguing that small freeholders were losing land by the thousands each month, thereby being turned into tenants and landless peasants; nor are they arguing that peasants of various levels were unproductive (though perhaps some scholars are guilty of hy-

---

[180] Finley, *Ancient Economy,* 108.

[181] See MacMullen, *Roman Social Relations,* 28–32, 52–56, for enlightening discussions on rural-urban hatred. Fiensy, *Social,* 143–45, brings up the subject as well.

[182] For an optimistic view of the social and economic situation in Palestine, see T. E. Schmidt, *Hostility to Wealth in the Synoptic Gospels* (JSNTSup 17; Sheffield: JSOT, 1987) 17–30; and Sanders, *Judaism,* 157–67. In my opinion, Ste. Croix and Fiensy adduce more evidence than do Schmidt and Sanders. Sanders, p. 168–69, backtracks without explanation. Schmidt spends much time refuting F. Grant's outdated book, *The Economic Background of the Gospels* (1926), D. Mealand's *Poverty and Expectation in the Gospels,* G. Theissen's *Sociology of Early Palestinian Christianity,* and J. Gager's *Kingdom and Community* (Theissen's and Gager's books are widely acknowledged as fledgling attempts), and he does not offer enough of his own positive evidence for prosperity. Given that his book rises or falls on prosperity, he should have found at least as much positive evidence for prosperity as Ste. Croix does for, say, increasing landlessness and debt bondage in the Greek East. Oddly, Schmidt does not include Ste. Croix in his bibliography. My main points, however, in this section are the following: some peasants lived on the edge of poverty and potential ruin, but they still were productive, contributing members of society; and women played a vital role in making sure their families survived.

perbole). But surely some peasants among the lower-level freeholders (and even upper-level freeholders) were losing their land.

Tenant Farmers.   Tenant farmers had no or very little land of their own "and thus were compelled to enter into a contract with a landowner to farm his land, paying him a fixed amount of rent,"[183] in monies or in a percentage of the crops or in labor. Those who paid their rent by crop production usually paid one-third or a half, but the landlord could demand two-thirds, though one-half seems onerous and the demand of two-thirds impossible.[184] Those who paid in monies were subjected to the whims of the seasons and production. If the crops were plenteous, the rent was paid; but if they were poor, the rent was burdensome. Most of the tenants were so far in arrears that they might have been de facto bondsmen.[185] The farmers held their tenancies either for a fixed period of time (usually 4–5 years in the Greco-Roman world)[186] or at the will of the owners—that is, when the owner decided to eject the tenants, his will was law. Neither situation was very secure.

This economic insecurity and dependence on the whims of others could never have engendered power or high status. Like the freeholders, tenants never enjoyed honor from the city dwellers. The relationship between the landlords and peasants was mostly tense or hostile. Mark 12:1–8 pictures a landlord sending his retainers to collect the "fruit of the vineyard" (v. 2), but the farmers beat or killed them.[187] In fairness, however, it should be noted that relations were not always strained. The owners had an economic interest in protecting their land (and, subsequently, those who farmed it) from, for example, "the depredations of Roman officials and soldiers—always a terror to the peasantry in the Roman empire."[188]

Landless Peasants.   Landless peasants were increasing in Palestine and the Greek East, though precise numbers are impossible to

---

[183] Fiensy, *Social,* 75. Fiensy is basing his analysis squarely on that of Ste. Croix's in *Class Struggle,* 210–14.

[184] Fiensy, *Social,* 81–82.

[185] Ibid., 76. Oakman, *Questions,* 72–77, has a good discussion of indebtedness. The picture is very grim for the peasants. Ste. Croix, *Class Struggle,* 136–39, 162–70, 282, analyzes the situation of debt bondsmen throughout the Greek East.

[186] Ste. Croix, *Class Struggle,* 83.

[187] For peasant revolts, see ibid., 215–16; Fiensy, *Social,* 76; and J. D. Crossan, *The Historical Jesus: The Life of a Mediterranean Jewish Peasant* (San Francisco: Harper, 1991) 451.

[188] Ste. Croix, *Class Struggle,* 215.

obtain.[189] The Synoptic Gospels give evidence of this phenomenon (Mark 12:1–8; Matt 9:37–38; 10:10; 20:1–8; Luke 15:17). Loss of land resulted from expropriation by Rome and its emissaries, from limited resources in the face of hereditary laws (a large family living on a small plot could only provide the inheritance to the oldest son, so the others had to look elsewhere), and from takeovers by the urban aristocracy.[190] The latter were effected by foreclosures on farms when debts could not be repaid,[191] or by encroachment, which included moving boundary stones, threatening violence, or taking illegal court action.[192]

Cicero provides a tragic example of this violence in his prosecution in 59 B.C.E. of a Roman named Appuleius Decianus, a merchant, who had acquired land from the "wealthy but unwise" (Cicero's words) mother-in-law of Amyntas, a native of Apollonis (Mysia).[193] It seems Decianus attached her to himself with "flattery" (Cicero's word), while secretly sending one of his retainers to establish her estate as his own. Cicero objected to the legality of Decianus's actions because the mother-in-law did not have a male guardian, or *tutor,* a requirement according to "Greek law" (Cicero again).[194] Normally, Amyntas would have been the guardian, but Decianus had mistreated him by maiming his limbs with stones, clubs, and fetters, crushing his hands, breaking his fingers, and cutting his tendons, just as a Mafia gangster would do today. So Decianus registered his own

---

[189]Ibid., 162–70. Ste. Croix has a full discussion of debt bondage and its results in the Greek East from the Hellenistic to Roman periods. It is difficult to believe that Palestine would be exempt. Fiensy, *Social,* 77, analyzes Palestine and confirms Ste. Croix's results.

[190]Fiensy, *Social,* 77–78.

[191]Oakman, *Questions,* 72–77.

[192]Fiensy, *Social,* 79. Broughton, "Roman Asia Minor," 658–62, lists several illegal actions in Asia Minor. Dio Chrysostom, *Or.* 47.21–22, LCL 4.267–69, recounts how he had to sue to get his own estates back after his sister died. It is probable that he lost control of his property when he was exiled by Rome. In any case, two important facts emerge: his sister had absolute control over not only her own property in her own right but also over his; when she died, he had to fight to get control.

When my sister died I not only derived no profit from her estate but even lost everything of mine that she controlled [εἶχε, *eiche*] and had to make a loan for the purchase of my farm.

[193]T. R. S. Broughton, "Roman Landholding in Asia Minor," *TAPA* 65 (1934) 211. See Cicero, *Flacc.* 70–74, LCL 519–25.

[194]Cicero's use of the phrase "Greek law" is vague; for further discussion, see Arlandson, " 'Fall and Rise,' " 92 n. 143.

retainer, Polemocrates, as the *tutor*. Decianus also stole Amyntas's wife while she was pregnant. She gave birth to a daughter, and both were still living in Decianus's house when Cicero was prosecuting him. Cicero goes on to recount how Decianus violently and fraudulently confiscated the estates of other "weak-minded" women who did not have a guardian. Because the litigants in the case were wealthy landowners, the lesson can be drawn that if Amyntas had a difficult time recovering his property, then one can well imagine the utter lack of success a peasant farmer living anywhere in the empire had in a legal action against officialdom or friends of officials.

Aelius Aristides recounts a story of his own troubles. While he was away from his estate, his kin had bought him some property at Hadrianutherae (Mysia) in 142 C.E. Shortly afterwards, some neighbors wanted to appropriate it. Aristides describes the events:

> Certain Mysians, first saying and next doing many different things, tried to appropriate it. When they despaired . . . they gathered together as many servants and hired men as they could, and attacked, armed with every weapon. Then some of them from a distance tossed and cast stones and clods, and some joined in hand to hand combat, some took possession of the house and treated the contents, as if they belonged to them. Everything was full of confusion and wounds.[195]

A court case ensued, and Aristides won the property back because of his friends Julianus, the governor, and Rufinus, who was *consul ordinarius* of Pergamum.

There is also the case in which a woman seized property by force.[196] Babata was a Jewess who came from the village of Maoza on the southern shore of the Dead Sea in Nabatea and lived before and during the Bar Kokhba revolt against Rome (132–35 C.E.) During this revolt she and her entourage fled northward to a cave in the Wadi Nahal Hever in the province of Judea, just south of En-Gedi, on the western shore of the Dead Sea. She brought with her thirty-five legal documents varying in date from 93 to 132 C.E. These documents reveal that she was a wealthy rural landowner who exerted considerable control over her property. (She would occupy the middle strip, that for landowners, in the thinnest section of the model [fig. 1] but probably towards the bottom; she would not have been considered an aristocrat.) Six documents (nos. 20–25) pertain to establishing the

---

[195] Aristides, *Or.* 50.105–6, Behr 2.339. This account was written in 170/171 C.E. For other accounts of hostile takeovers, see MacMullen, *Roman Social Relations,* 6–14.

[196] N. Lewis, Y. Yadin, and J. Greenfield, eds., *The Documents from the Bar Kokhba Period in the Cave of Letters* (Jerusalem: Israel Exploration Society and Hebrew University of Jerusalem, 1989).

ownership of property that had belonged to a Jesus, the brother of her second husband, Judah. After the death of the brothers before 130, Babata took possession of three productive date orchards in lieu of unpaid debts. The guardians of the orphans of Jesus challenged this claim. Papyrus 23 summons Babata to court before Haterius Nepos, *legatus pro praetore* in Petra, "in the matter of a date orchard devolving to said orphans which you hold in your possession by force [βίᾳ, *bia*]. . . . "[197] It is not likely that Babata hired professional soldiers to fend off any encroachment onto the orchard but instead employed some day laborers, as the case of Aristides shows. The six documents do not reveal the outcome of the court trial, which dragged on for over a year, but "the fact that Babata kept these documents presumably implies that she emerged victorious in this litigation."[198]

As noted, if the wealthy attempted to take over the property of other wealthy landowners, then a fortiori they made the same attempts on the property of peasants of few acres; and perhaps these peasants attacked each other as well. But the frequency of both situations beyond the records that survive is impossible to ascertain. These three episodes notwithstanding, the main cause of landlessness was Rome's confiscation of property throughout the empire. This practice trickled down to its emissaries, then to the indigenous urban elite (officially permitted, unlike the two stories above) through investments and the entrepreneurial spirit (or, depending on the perspective of the victims, through loans at high interest with property as collateral), and finally to the victim-peasants.[199]

M. Goodman provides an analysis of how this shifting of landholdings and weakening in other structures may have affected the family.[200] As noted, the extended family broke up because a small plot of land could never sustain new families if it was divided equally through inheritance. This breakup occurred especially if the land was confiscated, even though the new landowners may have asked the disinherited farmers to stay and work. In any case, the inheritance and ownership completely disappeared. So family members, and with them their dependents, had to seek their livelihood

---

[197] Ibid., 103–4.

[198] Ibid., 102. The editor offers an alternative interpretation: "At the very least, these documents constitute evidence that she complied with the requisite legal formalities" (ibid.).

[199] Fiensy, *Social,* 79, and Broughton, "Roman Landholding," 207–39. We should remember MacMullen's summary, *Roman Social Relations,* 38, of over five centuries of Roman rule: "fewer have more."

[200] Goodman, *Ruling,* 68–70. Though I borrow from these pages, I will point out some disagreements.

elsewhere, such as in the city. "In place of the extended family the nuclear family became the primary social unit."[201]

But the nuclear family, too, was coming under attack. Burial customs reveal that while wealthy families could afford a loculus or common tomb, the poorer families may have buried their dead in individual graves separated from other family members. But against this picture, says Goodman, must be juxtaposed the idea that in times of stress the nuclear family adhered together. Josephus tells a story about a family of brigands who stuck together even in death.[202]

If the family was undergoing a slow disintegration, then the male head was also losing his control by the first century of our era. Some men asserted the importance of the individual over the family, as in the cases of the sectarians at Qumran and En el-Ghuweir. The individual interments in these two communities suggest that males denied their families. And even when men remained close to their relatives, they did not feel compelled to obey their father. The son in one high-priestly family led a faction opposing his father's in 66 C.E.

Finally, simultaneous with the father's loss of political power in the family came more freedom for adult females. "Divorce was evidently common—a fact confirmed rather than denied by moves made by some sectarians to ban divorce altogether, an innovation quite contrary to the plain meaning of the Torah."[203] And in some circles women could initiate divorce, though, Goodman concedes, this was probably not widespread. And a man could not often raise a heavy hand against a wife who infringed on the law or customs when everyone in the family was suffering equally from loss of land and from being forced to move around the country at harvest time and, at harvest's end, into the city when building programs were under way.[204] Thus, patriarchy was losing its grip, particularly over the extended family.

On the surface, some of Goodman's claims stand on their merits. Loss of land surely must have affected the family, and probably just in the way he described: families not having enough inheritance to provide the heirs with an incentive to stay on the land.[205] And the husband probably did lose some authority in the family, though it is

---

[201] Ibid., 69.

[202] Josephus, Ant. 14.429–30, LCL 7.671–73; J.W. 1.310–15, LCL 2.147–49; both are cited in Goodman, *Ruling*, 69.

[203] Goodman, *Ruling*, 70. Goodman is basing his information about divorce on Salome (Josephus, *Ant.* 15.259–60, LCL 8.123–25) and Herodias (*Ant.* 18.136, LCL 9.93).

[204] S. Freyne, *Galilee, Jesus, and the Gospels* (Dublin: Gill & Macmillan, 1988) 148–49.

[205] Cf. Fiensy, *Social*, 78.

hard to see how one can measure this phenomenon in precise terms. But at bottom, the major difficulty with Goodman's analysis is that he too often takes his evidence from the ruling elite or radical sectarians—neither group very numerous compared with the rest of the population—just when he is analyzing the economic deprivation in *all* levels of society. Consequently, it is not likely that a peasant woman experienced as much economic and social freedom from her husband as Goodman implies, if she ever had this goal in the first place. She did not initiate divorce unless she could go into a better οἶκος, *oikos,* and this was not probable, since she had no attractive dowry. Goodman may tacitly recognize this when the examples of divorce he offers come from the Jewish community in distant Elephantine and from two Herodian princesses. Rather, a woman living at the peasant level shared in the destiny of her husband and family. We should not look for upward social mobility here. If there were mobility, it would have been only one way—down.[206] For instance, if women came from poor families that owned 4 or fewer acres and married men with as many acres, then it would have been impossible for the women to escape from these conditions even if they had wanted to escape. They could never have accumulated enough resources.

Day Laborers.   Either day laborers never had land to begin with, or they were landless peasants who hired themselves out to work, especially during the harvest.[207] In Matt 20:1–16 laborers gathered at a known place in a village, waiting for work. When the landowner found them, he expressed surprise that they had been milling around during the grape harvest. On the same day, he hired many more at various intervals. This story perhaps indicates that unemployment was high even during a productive season. In any case, this passage perfectly reflects the life of the day laborer not only in Palestine but also in the Greek East.[208] They stood around in known places in towns and villages, waiting to be hired. Some of the more common jobs were weeding, harvesting, threshing, picking fruit, and ditch digging; transporting reeds, wood, crops, people, and so forth (there is a story of five men hired to carry a polished stone from Galilee to Jerusalem for use in the temple);[209] and guarding animals, fields, city gates, children, the sick, and the dead. Other laborers were barbers, bathhouse attendants, cooks, messengers, and manure gatherers.

---

[206] Finley, *Ancient Economy,* 99, says that "for movement one must look to the upper classes."

[207] Fiensy, *Social,* 85–90.

[208] Ste. Croix, *Class Struggle,* 186–88.

[209] Fiensy, *Social,* 86.

The daily life of the laborer was hard. In the cemetery of the Qumran community are skeletal remains, dated to before 68 C.E., of two males who were twenty-two and sixty-five years old.[210] The younger manifestly had worked with his hands from an early age and walked barefoot all his life. The older had probably carried burdens on his shoulders because the bone structure was deformed in a shape that indicates burden bearing.

It is not too difficult to assess the political power of day laborers: they had none. Landless peasants and day laborers were at the bottom of the peasantry because they either had already suffered from loss of land or had never had any to begin with. They had no voice in politics and were subject to the whims and incursions of the rich and powerful. But even though these peasants and the expendables overlap in class structure, most peasants should not be categorized as expendables. Most were productive—or tried to be—in society, unlike the expendables, who could not be productive.

To determine the daily subsistence of a laboring peasant without land in rural Palestine, where Jesus ministered, three parts of an equation are needed: the minimum amount of food for physical replenishment, the daily income, and the cost of obtaining the food. Scholars generally agree that the average wage for a laborer was one denarius per day.[211] But it would be misleading to stop at this datum and imply that his daily wage corresponds to modern, Western daily wages. It is better to ask about the buying power of the denarius.

For the minimum amount of food, the results of studies on peasants in underdeveloped countries reveal that a hardworking peasant needs about twenty-five hundred calories per day.[212] Those of heavier weight would need more, and others, such as children, would need fewer. Nevertheless, twenty-five hundred calories "offer a useful reference point."[213] This amount equals about one liter of grain.[214] So a peasant had to buy one liter of grain per day in order to replenish himself with enough food to perform his labor.

It is usually figured that a *se'ah* a common unit of measurement in Palestine, cost five-sixths to one denarius.[215] To be generous with our

---

[210] Ibid.

[211] Ibid., 86–87. For further discussion, see Arlandson, " 'Fall and Rise,' " 92 n. 150.

[212] Oakman, *Questions,* 58–61.

[213] Ibid., 58.

[214] Oakman says that twenty-five hundred calories work out to eleven American bushels per year (ibid., 60). Since 1.1 liters equals 11.5 bushels, we round off eleven bushels to one liter.

[215] D. Sperber, "Cost of Living in Roman Palestine," *JESHO* 8 (1965) 251. Sperber is referring to *m. B. Meṣiʿa* 5.1, Danby 355. Jeremias, *Jerusalem,* 122,

final calculations, we will use the lower amount. How many liters did a *se'ah* contain?[216] Evidence suggests that, depending on the region, a *se'ah* ranged from 8.64 to 18.6 liters; obviously, the smaller *se'ah* cost less than the larger.[217] The mean value of thirteen liters is settled on here.[218] As an independent confirmation that our twenty-five hundred calories or one liter is on target, the Mishnah states that a poor man's daily ration was one-twelfth of a *se'ah*, 1.1 liter.[219]

It would be almost meaningless to say that a single peasant spent one-thirteenth of five-sixths of a denarius to buy one liter of grain. In Palestinian society celibates or confirmed bachelors were very few.[220] Almost all peasants had families. Through talmudic references and excavations of villages (e.g., fifty people and six houses), scholars conclude that the average family had six to nine members.[221] Again, to be generous, our peasant is allowed to have a family of only six. He needed to purchase about six liters of grain for his family. And it was already agreed that a *se'ah* contained thirteen liters and cost five-sixths of one denarius. Therefore, a peasant had to spend about 38 percent of his daily wage just to buy his daily bread, not to mention other food items, such as oil or fruit in season; rent and taxes; and longer-term items, such as clothing, sandals, and household utensils, if he did not make them (even then the raw material would not be free).

There is a final important element. Up to now it is assumed that the day laborer or landless peasant had steady employment. This was tragically not the case. His work was seasonal, and because of Sabbaths and festivals, he probably worked only 200 days a year.[222] This amounts to a shortfall of 165 days, or 45 percent of the year, during

---

holds for one denarius, referring to Josephus, *Ant.* 9.85, LCL 6.47. It is unclear whether this price is limited to Jerusalem. Whatever the case, my calculations are only designed to give a rough estimate of the cost of living for a peasant.

[216] Jeremias, *Jerusalem,* 122. I am assuming, because Jeremias does not say, that the grain is wheat. See Arlandson, " 'Fall and Rise,' " 162 n. 102, for a discussion of the price of wheat in Cicero and of Jeremias's problematic reference to Cicero and other ancient authors.

[217] G. Hamel, *Poverty and Charity in Roman Palestine, First Three Centuries C.E.* (Los Angeles: University of California, 1990) 245.

[218] Ibid., 246; Jeremias, *Jerusalem,* 122. Jeremias appears much more confident than Hamel in asserting that a *se'ah* was thirteen liters and cost one denarius.

[219] Jeremias, *Jerusalem,* 122.

[220] G. F. Moore, *Judaism in the First Centuries of the Christian Era: The Age of the Tannaim* (3 vols.; Cambridge: Harvard, 1954) 2.119–20. He cites a few exceptions to the rule.

[221] Fiensy, *Social,* 87.

[222] Ibid., 89.

which he was unemployed and could not earn his one denarius. He was forced, therefore, to stretch the denarius that much further. And if he met up with injury, disease, landowners withholding wages, soldiers on expeditions requiring food, or poor crop yields, then life became even more difficult. Thus, at this level of society the economic contributions of the wife played an especially important role.

The Mishnah lists several typical contributions of a peasant woman: grinding flour, baking bread, washing clothes, cooking food, nursing children, and working in wool—in short, domestic chores.[223] Statements by Columella (fl. 1st c. C.E.), a Latin author on agricultural affairs who wrote about women's roles in agricultural production, match up with the Mishnah's comments. He maintains that women should and did work primarily in the house.[224]

It is possible that the view that women should be confined mostly to the house was held by Columella and other male writers of Greco-Roman agricultural literature because of their superstitious beliefs about women in general, beliefs common even among those of the highest circles.[225] Columella reports the claim of a Greek Egyptian named Bolus of Mendes that a menstruating woman could kill caterpillars by walking around the infested plant three times with loose hair and bare feet.[226] Columella himself believed that a menstruating woman could wither a rue plant just by touching it and could halt the growth of, or even kill, new cucumber and gourd shoots by looking at them.[227] Evidently, the successful farmer should keep women away from agriculture one week of the month.

---

[223] *m. Ketub.* 5.5, Danby 252. See S. Safrai, "Home and Family," in *The Jewish People in the First Century* (2 vols.; ed. S. Safrai and M. Stern; CRINT; Philadelphia: Fortress, 1976) 2.761; and Sanders, *Judaism,* 122, who regard the passage as genuinely reflecting what women did. It is interesting that the Mishnah suddenly jumps up into higher levels as the passage continues:

> If she brought him in one bondwoman she need not grind or bake or wash; if two, she need not cook or give her child suck; if three, she need not make ready his bed or work in wool; if four, she may sit [all the day] in a chair. (Danby, 252)

Some of the women mentioned in this excerpt may have been upper-level freeholders or even wealthy urbanites.

[224] Columella, *De re rustica* 12.praef.1–7, LCL 3.175–77. Following Ste. Croix, *Class Struggle,* 234–36, I do not hesitate to use Columella even though he lived in the West: he freely borrowed from Greek manuals on agriculture and says as much (*De re rustica* 7.5.15, LCL 2.271; and 12.praef.7, LCL 3.177–79).

[225] Ste. Croix, *Class Struggle,* 234–36.

[226] Columella, *De re rustica* 11.4.64, LCL 3.169.

[227] Ibid., 11.3.38, 50.

Yet, alongside these descriptions of women working in the house, two more passages are juxtaposed. The Mishnah reads,

> The School of Hillel say: We have heard no such tradition save of a woman that returned from the harvest. . . . The School of Shammai answered: It is all one whether she returned from the harvest or from the olive-picking or from the vintage. . . . [228]

And Columella reads,

> But in order that she may have recourse to wool-work on rainy days or when, owing to cold or frost, a woman cannot be busy with field-work under the open sky, there should be wool prepared and combed out already.[229]

Also, Plutarch in a passing comment notes that women worked as "gleaners."[230] It is clear from these passages that it is assumed, not questioned, that women left the domestic sphere to work in the fields. These writers are expressing crucial data in an offhanded manner, thereby increasing the chances of the reliability of the data. If the superstitions of intellectual Greek and Roman authors are left aside and if attention is paid to Columella's assertion that women worked inside but also outside the house, and to Plutarch's tidbit that women were gleaners, and if these are added to the Mishnah's view that Jewish women worked inside but also outside the house, then the three sources are indeed reflecting what happened in an agrarian society. It was typical for peasant women to feed, clothe, and care for their families from the domestic sphere; but they left these chores behind to work in the fields, especially during the harvest, in order to add more income to their families. The need to survive tends to break down customs that might hinder staying alive. Thus, as the wealth of women in the governing classes broke down some boundaries, so did the hardships of peasants.

In the Greco-Roman world two stories about female day laborers indicate that the privilege of childbirth was difficult for peasants. Strabo relates a story told to him by his friend Poseidonius in Liguria (on the southern coast of France, according to his geography).[231] Both men claim that Poseidonius' story illustrates the strength of other women in other regions, such as Thrace (northeast Greece, above northwest Asia Minor) and Scythia (north of Armenia, along the Caspian Sea). That is, they are implying that the following pathetic scene could have happened in other parts of the empire.

---

[228] m. Yebam. 15.2, Danby 241; par. m. Ed. 1.12, Danby 423.
[229] Columella, De re rustica 12.3.6, trans. Forster and Heffner, LCL 3.191.
[230] Plutarch, Mor. 784A, trans. Fowler, LCL 10.81.
[231] Strabo, 3.4.17–18, LCL 2.113.

First, a certain Charmoleon from Massilia hired some male and female ditch-diggers. One of the women was pregnant. When she was seized with the pangs of childbirth, she went away from her work, delivered the baby, and came right back to the job in order not to lose her pay. Charmoleon observed her doing her work painfully but did not find out the cause until later that day. Upon learning it, he sent her away with her wages. She took the baby to a spring, washed and swaddled it, then took it home. The fact that she was willing to suffer for a day's wage reveals how destitute she and her family were.

Second, in the later years of his life Varro (116–17 B.C.E.) re-counted a story of pregnant women from Illyricum (northwest of Greece, on the Adriatic Sea) who "often" stepped aside from their work when their time had come, delivered their babies, brought them back, and continued working.[232] One woman in particular brought hers back "so soon that you would say she had not borne it but had found it."[233]

These two anecdotes can be supported with a last one from modern-day Turkey (ancient Asia Minor). Pregnant peasants have been observed squatting in the fields, giving birth and resuming their work with remarkable strength and endurance. Only women having complications were sent with difficulty to the hospital.[234]

To sum up, six observations can be made: (1) Peasant women lived a precarious life politically and economically. Except for the upper-level freeholders and perhaps some lower-level freeholders, they lived at about poverty level and had no means to protect themselves. Their life was not one of ease and comfort. (2) Conse-quently, the extended family began to fracture. From this fact it may be conjectured that the nuclear family began weakening, and along with it, patriarchy. But until more information is literally unearthed, any conclusion about the weakening of the nuclear family and patri-archy is no more than guesswork. (3) Women shared in the destiny of their families. They could not have escaped economic and political insecurity by leaving their families behind. (4) Women worked mostly in the house, caring for their families; but they were also in the fields harvesting and doing other odd jobs in order to ensure their families' survival. Social and ideological boundaries that engender physical boundaries tend to become permeable when economic survival is at stake. (5) The privilege of birthing life into the world was very

---

[232] Varro, *De re rustica* 2.10.8–9, LCL 409–11.

[233] Ibid., 2.10.9, trans. Hooper, rev. Ash, LCL 411.

[234] This true story comes to me from a friend of mine who was stationed in Turkey during his stint in the army in the 1960s. He says he observed on more than one occasion women giving birth like this.

dangerous. Even with the successful results in the three anecdotes cited above, the stories still point to a high maternal death rate. (6) Despite their hardships, peasants were still the backbone of the macroeconomy of the Greco-Roman world. If individual families and even those in a given region hit hard by a bad year in production slid down the slippery slope into ruin, the majority were still productive, contributing members of society.

Slaves.   Although in the model they are placed below the day laborers and, indeed, had the lowest status in the empire, slaves occupied every corner of the Greco-Roman world, from field-worker peasants to retainers of huge estates, to domestics, and to artisans. But because most slaves in the East, numbering about 10 percent of the population,[235] worked in the city, usually as domestics of the wealthy, we will delay discussing them until the next chapter.[236]

---

[235] MacMullen, *Roman Social Relations,* 92.

[236] This a debated point. For a rural setting see Luke 17:7–10. Whether slaves were rural or urban, my remarks are so general that they remain unaffected by the debate and can be applied to either setting. For slavery in Jewish society, see Safrai, "Home and Family," 751. For the Greek East, see C. Whittaker, "Rural Labor in Three Roman Provinces," in *Non-slave Labour* (ed. Garnsey) 73–99; and Broughton, "Roman Asia Minor," 691. Levick, *Roman Colonies,* 98, finds no evidence of rural slaves in Pisidian Antioch. For an opposing view, see Ste. Croix, *Class Struggle,* 133–34, 144. He cites Jones and Finley, however, as disagreeing with his opinion (p. 144).

> One was like a workman, masculine,
> with unkempt hair, hands full of
> callous places, clothing tucked up, and
> a heavy layer of marble-dust upon
> her. . . . The other, however, was very
> fair of face, dignified in her
> appearance, and nice in her dress.[1]

3

WOMEN AND CLASS
IN THE ROMAN EMPIRE, II

To complete this description of women's life in the Greco-Roman world according to classes, urban people, the unclean and degraded, and the expendables are now examined.

URBAN PEOPLE

When Paul and his team walked into any city in the Greek East, they might have found a scene like this:[2] an indecent song from men near

---

[1] Lucian, *Somn.* 6, trans. Harmon, LCL 3.219–21. Lucian is recounting a dream he had as he and his father were deciding on his future. He had the choice of becoming a statue cutter like the first woman or educated and cultured like the second woman. Of course, the women are fictional. In any case, a statue cutter, except for the rare ones with widespread fame, lived a menial life. The one who pursues education becomes refined. Lucian chose the second course and recommends that other young men do the same.

[2] I borrow heavily from MacMullen's fine chapter, "Urban," in *Roman Social Relations*, 57–87, for the information in this paragraph.

the docks wafts its way like soot into their ears; a fuller hangs his clothing outside his shop; if the winds are right, they might smell the urine of a tannery because the tanners did not move their pungent business out far enough from the city; down one street butchers flay animals in preparation for a feast at an aristocrat's house; children run by with their dusty feet, playing at stoning another kid, just as they saw the adults do for real another day as they swiftly meted out neighborhood justice;[3] a mixture of vituperation and cheers resound as the loser and winner of the dice game shout out the results; a woman screams from the brothel in the back alley while men laugh derisively; slightly inebriated members of a *collegium,* having just eaten a fellowship meal in their meeting hall, discuss erecting a statue for a patroness; noisy bartering and dickering go on between buyer and seller in the marketplace; with wares in hand, vendors accost Paul and his team; the slightest commotion gathers a crowd; many in the crowd are destitute and live in the streets; women, young and old—an extended family—in dilapidated tenements[4] glare down at the newcomers from a second- or third-story window, perhaps like the one out of which Eutychus fell (Acts 20:7–12). Neighborhoods are not clean and tidy,[5] and their inhabitants are not always friendly to strangers. There should be little wonder why Paul, arriving in Corinth, for example, was fearful and trembling and sought out his fellow Jews for a place of familiar refuge (Acts 18:9–10; cf. 1 Cor 2:2–3).

Landowners.   Some landowners were not part of the governing classes, or at least their participation in local governments is not made clear from the available information. But it is typical of any analysis of class structure that there should be some overlap, and certainly these landowners overlap not only with the governing classes but also with upper-level freeholders (15–50 acres). In any case, those who never ascended to high political office could still be wealthy and aristocratic compared with most persons. They would have exerted their influence on politics in any way they could. In the

---

[3] Ibid., 66.

[4] Dio Chrysostom, *Or.* 47.15, LCL 4.261, rhetorically calls urban houses cheap and humble wrecks (φαύλων καὶ ταπεινῶν ἐρειπίων, *phaulōn kai tapeinōn ereipiōn*).

[5] Broughton, "Roman Asia Minor," 801–2, summarizes a second-century C.E. copy of a law for the maintenance of the metropolis of Pergamum in which fines were exacted on violators "for failure to keep roads passable, for removing materials, obstructing right of way, leaving water channels uncovered, failure to cooperate in the removal of filth, assessment of damages where walls and houses adjoin, dirtying the public fountains, failure to take proper care of cisterns and privies, etc."

model in chapter 2 (fig. 1) they are located up and down the middle strip proceeding out of the section for peasants, between the merchants and traders and the retainers and religionists. They are considered urban because many (not all) lived in the city yet owned property outside the city.

In Asia Minor the records of men who would fit into the class of landowners are many, each record varying in the amount of detail. One fuller example is provided here.[6] In the first century B.C.E. at Mylasa and Olymus (Caria), a Greek named Diodotus sold half of one piece of property and another whole piece, both of unknown size, for ten thousand drachmas.[7] The half-piece of property was in the country and contained an olive press and olive-pressing implements, building sites, vines, orchards, attached pasture land, and all the trees in it. The suburban property (κατὰ τὴν πόλιν, *kata tēn polin*) had houses, upper rooms, colonnades, a vestibule, a treading place for grapes, implements, a poultry house, cow stables, a well, and guaranteed right of ingress and egress. One property was worth four thousand of the total ten thousand drachmas, presumably the country estate.

In Palestine, there is evidence that men owned estates of comparable size and very likely with features similar to those owned by Diodotus.[8] It is argued in chapter 4 that such persons as Mary and Martha (Luke 10:38–42), Barnabas (Acts 4:36–37), Ananias and Sapphira (Acts 5: 1–11), and Mary, mother of John Mark (Acts 12:5–17), were landowners of this kind.

There is scanty and scattered evidence of women property owners. In an inscription of the second or first century B.C.E., found at Mylasa and Olymus, Artemisia sold property for five thousand drachmas.[9] In another inscription from this same region, Herais, daughter of Apollonius, residing in Olymus, adjoined in a sale of land to local tribesmen.[10] In Perga (Plancia Magna's hometown in Pamphylia), Mousas bequeathed to his mother, Cilla, a farm (μονάγριον, *monagrion*), which was to support her throughout her lifetime. Upon her death, it was to revert to the god Apollo.[11]

At least on an ideological level, and perhaps on an idealistic one, Hebrew Scriptures praise an industrious wife who is a landowner.

---

[6] Ibid., passim.
[7] Ibid., 665.
[8] Fiensy, *Social,* 53–54 and passim. Some of the men in the examples that Fiensy cites were politicians; but I assume that some were not, since landowners outnumbered the official political positions.
[9] Broughton, "Roman Asia Minor," 560, 665.
[10] Ibid., 664.
[11] Ibid., 670.

She, like a merchant ship, brings in food from afar; evaluates and buys a field; out of her own earnings plants a vineyard; makes sure that her trading is profitable; weaves; gives to the needy; makes linen garments and sells them; supplies merchants with sashes; and watches over or manages (Heb. ṣapha) the affairs of her household. She does all of this apparently at her own discretion (Prov 31:10–31). A suggestive passage in the Mishnah may faintly echo the managerial skills of this woman in Proverbs: "a wife that manages the affairs [nasaᶜ ve-natan] of the house."[12] This idiomatic Hebrew phrase can mean "conclude a bargain," "debate," or "barter" in commerce. Though this passage reflects a woman managing things within the household, it is reasonable to assume that her management skills would require her to interact with the outside world as it crossed paths with her household. But because the Mishnah does not go into detail about her daily life, it is unclear whether this woman was a landowner and how much financial freedom she enjoyed to take care of her household. Without this information, it seems that in the final analysis the Mishnaic woman is more limited than the woman in Proverbs.

Besides the fictional Judith, who appears to have surpassed the local politicians financially, we should recall a real-life woman, Babata, who exercised as much power over her assets as does the Proverbs woman. Babata lived in Maoza, a small town on the southern shore of the Dead Sea, so she is not, strictly speaking, "urban."[13] She was illiterate (διὰ τὸ αὐτῆς μὴ εἰδέναι γράμματα, dia to autēs mē eidenai grammata),[14] and no data describe her as playing a role in local politics. According to aristocrats residing in such cites as Jerusalem and Antioch on the Orontes, she probably would have been considered what Strabo calls a semirustic (μεσ-άγροικος, mesagroikos), though her papyri do not say this.[15] In any case, her power is seen in four instances.

---

[12] m. Šebu. 7.8, Danby 420. See M. Jastrow, A Dictionary of the Targumim, Talmud Babli and Yerushalmi, and Midrashic Literature (2 vols.; 1903; reprint, New York: Judaica, 1950).

[13] The information about Babata's life is drawn from Lewis, Yadin, and Greenfield, Cave of Letters, passim. It should be pointed out that in these documents Babata has a legal guardian. In my opinion, the guardian is necessary because she is appearing before a Roman tribunal and transacting business and writing up contracts (through a scribe) within Roman jurisdiction. The tone and spirit of many of the documents, however, suggest (to me at least) that Babata was, de facto, in control of the decisions to conduct business and initiate lawsuits. See the discussion of Nicerata below.

[14] Ibid., 60.

[15] Strabo 13.1.25, LCL 6.329. Classifying Babata as a semirustic is only my guess.

First, she initiates a lawsuit over her deceased husband's son because the guardians (ἐπίτροποι, *epitropoi*) are failing to maintain the boy's monthly allowance in a manner that would conform to his family's social standing or "splendid style." She set up a trust fund of four hundred denarii, the interest of which the guardians were to use for the boy's support. Second, in compliance with a provincial census ordered by a Roman governor, she declares that she herself owns four groves of date palms, two of which extend down to the Dead Sea. Third, she lends her second husband, Judah, three hundred silver denarii. The contract specifies that she can demand repayment whenever she chooses, and if he does not promptly repay the sum, he can be forced to pay twofold plus damages. Evidently, those rabbinic rulings that hand over to the husband control over his wife's assets while he is married to her never reached the ears of Babata, fortunately for her. Finally, it has already been noted that she seizes by force three productive date orchards in lieu of unpaid debts (see ch. 2, "Landless Peasants," pp. 37–50).

In Greece and one of its islands, two women from the ruling class[16] shed more light on Babata's fearless financial lawsuit. The widow Epicteta lived in the late third to early second c. B.C.E. on Thera, an island in the Cyclades.[17] In her inscription that numbers 288 lines, immediately after naming her *kyrios,* she proclaims, "May I continue to administer my assets in health and strength!"[18] This is the standard, obligatory precaution in any testament, but the self-assured manner in which Epicteta herself distributes her money imbues those typical words with a slight hint of pride and independence. She, not the *kyrios,* controls and dictates the terms of the foundation she establishes as to how the money should be spent. She funds two communities, one of men and the other of women, that are to preserve the memory of her dear friends (whose names appear in the inscription) by the maintenance of a chapel and statues and periodic sacrifices.

Nicerata also lived in the late third to early second c. B.C.E., in the town Thespiae, near the town Orchomenos in Boeotia, Greece.[19] Her

---

[16] Since the women lived in towns, it would be wrong to conclude that they were aristocrats on a par with aristocrats in a large city like Rome or Alexandria. Nonetheless, they were members of the ruling class in their own towns.

[17] R. Dareste, et al., ed., *Recueil des inscriptions juridiques grecques: texte, traduction, commentaire,* 2 vols. (Rome: "L'Erma" di Bretschneider, 1965) 1.77–115.

[18] Ibid. 1.78, my translation, borrowing from the French translation.

[19] Ibid. 2.275–311.

inscription numbers 178 lines and shows that, like Babata, she is involved in legal skirmishes, though, unlike Babata, her adversary is Orchomenos itself. She lent the town the huge sum of 18,833 silver drachmas. Its male leaders had difficulty in repaying her, so she has to sue them (or the city) several times. Showing no mercy, she refuses to remit the debt and eventually receives the payment after a year's delay. She also has a *kyrios* (her husband, Dexippos), but this inscription (and Babata's papyri) depicts the *kyrios* as a silent "straw man" serving only to prevent anyone from contesting the outcome of a judicial award or to prevent anyone from challenging the decision to spend a woman's own money in this or that way. A financially savvy woman *should* have a *kyrios* if the law in her region prescribes one, so that she does not lose a challenge or a favorable lawsuit on appeal over this small legal technicality. To show that Nicerata controlled her resources, when Nicerata's father died, why did not the burden of collecting his loan fall on Nicerata's husband instead of on her? If Nicerata's husband Dexippos had controlled his wife's assets, then why did not he sue the city instead of her suing it? Why is she even mentioned in the suit if he allegedly controlled everything? In Babata's and Nicerata's case, however, it is very clear that the women, not the *kyrioi,* are the driving force behind the lawsuit and the flow of resources.[20]

Though Epicteta and Nicerata were part of the ruling class in their own towns and therefore could be found in chapter 2 (see Governing Classes and Urban Elite, pp. 24–37), they confirm nonetheless that other women controlled their assets in the same powerful fashion that Babata did, who was not an aristocrat, but an illiterate, upper-level peasant. In no way do these three women appear weak or befuddled by their monetary decisions; rather, they are confident and have carefully planned their financial strategy. In no way do they ever appear oppressed by men in their own class. On the contrary, Babata and Nicerata are not afraid to sue men quite aggressively when they believe that they stand on solid legal ground. Since the three women span several centuries, two different social levels, and wide distances in the Greek East, we should not have a shred of doubt that they represent other women. Stated differently, it is impossible (for me, at least) to believe that they are the only women in the entire Greek East ever to have managed their affairs in a similarly powerful fashion. Fortunately, Babata's papyri and Epicteta's and Nicerata's detailed inscriptions survived the deleteri-

---

[20] The same could be said for Epicteta. Yet, despite these two inscriptions and Babata's papyri, a systematic study of other inscriptions and documents that mention the *kyrios* is still needed before dogmatic and universal conclusions can be reached.

ous effects of time measured in centuries. It can only be left to the imagination how profoundly our view of women in the Greek East would have changed if the papyri and equally detailed inscriptions of a hundred other such women were miraculously discovered.[21] Babata, Epicteta, and Nicerata are some of the best examples of how important it is to divide women up into classes before generalizing about them in the Greco-Roman world.

To sum up, many landowners did not necessarily hold seats in high political offices, though they and the governing class overlap, as seen with Epicteta and Nicerata. The estate owned by Diodotus in Asia Minor illustrates the typical size and features of other estates throughout the Greek East, whether owned by men or women. It should be reiterated that, as with women in other classes, the available inscriptions and papyri do not correspond at all to the maximum number of women who owned property; rather, they represent women whose records have not survived or been found. Accordingly, Babata, Epicteta and Nicerata are the quintessential examples of many other women who wielded a lot of power and exercised absolute control over their properties and assets.

Merchants and Traders. This category includes bankers (of whom there are three kinds: sacred, private, and public);[22] shop owners or shopkeepers; shipowners, importers, and exporters; intra- and intercity marketers; investors, vendors, slave dealers, and brothel keepers—to name just a few. Merchants and traders were very few in number compared with, say, the peasants. Even fewer, such as τραπεζίται, *trapezitai* (bankers), Jewish and Greek ναύκληροι, *nauklēroi* (shipowners), and slave dealers,[23] made much profit; the others were "small independent producers" and lived a little above or at poverty level.[24] Hence, the wealth, status, and power of most merchants were on a par with those of the artisans. Indeed, those who ran the shops either employed male or female artisans and day laborers—some

---

[21] And the inscriptions that have been uncovered so far, ranging widely in the amount of details, show that indeed women absolutely controlled their assets (see Menodora and Plancia Magna in chapter 2, Governing Classes and Urban Elite, 29–30 [Menodora]; 35–36 [Plancia Magna]).

[22] Broughton, "Roman Asia Minor," 888.

[23] Strabo 14.5.2, trans. Jones, LCL 6.329, calls slave dealing an "evil business" but also observes that it is "most profitable."

[24] Ste. Croix, *Class Struggle,* 271. P. Garnsey, "Grain for Rome," in *Trade in the Ancient Economy* (ed. P. Garnsey, K. Hopkins, and C. R. Whittaker; Los Angeles: University of California, 1983) 124–25, reports that many shipowners were landowners. See S. Applebaum, "Economic Life in Palestine," CRINT, 2.689–90, for a discussion of Jewish shippers.

slaves, some free—or themselves worked in the smaller ones. So the claim that there was a numerous merchant aristocracy is misleading: they were too few.[25] And because of their small numbers, they did not constitute a middle class in the modern sense. The difference between the owner of a small shop and those who worked in them is slight; but it is the difference between those who controlled the means of production—however small—and those who could not control the means; that is, those who could exploit the labor of others, and those who had to offer their labor.[26] In the aggregate, this made the shop owners more prosperous than the workers, if only a little.

The merchants and traders were mostly confined to the assembly. Several references show that they could not ascend to a councilship because of the requirement that all decurions own property.[27] During Hadrian's reign (117–38 C.E.) Ephesian council members were not prepared to accept a ναύκληρος, *nauklēros,* into the council.[28] "Investing in trade was normal for an aristocrat; to be a trader, humiliating."[29] Moreover, most merchants still had to work, and this was considered slavish. Plutarch can speak for every landowning aristocrat like himself:

> Surely taking up menial [βαναύσου, *banausou*] work fit only for the market-place [ἀγοραίας, *agoraias*] after holding public offices is like

---

[25] Ste. Croix, *Class Struggle,* 41. S. R. Joshel, *Work, Identity, and Legal Status at Rome: A Study of the Occupational Inscriptions* (Norman: University of Oklahoma, 1992) 78–85, discusses wealthy tradesmen in Rome, but her general findings can apply anywhere in the empire.

[26] Ste. Croix, *Class Struggle,* 270. He suggests (p. 199) that a truly free man was one who employed people, whence came his freedom to move about, versus someone who might be legally free but whose wages were so low that he was *as* a slave. Thus the first controlled the means of production, but the second could not, and was indeed controlled by them. H. Kreissig, "Free Labor in the Hellenistic Age," in *Non-slave Labour* (ed. Garnsey) 32–33, apparently agrees with Ste. Croix. Both Kreissig and Ste. Croix are writing from a Marxist viewpoint.

[27] Ste. Croix, *Class Struggle,* 124–29. H. W. Pleket, "Urban Elites and Business in the Greek Part of the Roman Empire," in *Trade* (ed. Garnsey, Hopkins, and Whittaker) 131–44, confirms this requirement.

[28] Pleket, "Urban Elites," 134.

[29] Ibid., 136. Dio Chrysostom, *Or.* 31.37, LCL 3.41, says the following to Rhodians about traders: "Nay, tradesmen [καπήλους, *kapēlous*] who cheat in their measures, men whose livelihood depends upon base gain, you hate and punish" (trans. Cohoon). And to his hometown Dio, *Or.* 36.25, LCL 3.443, says this about certain merchants: "As a usual thing those who come here are nominally Greeks but actually more barbarous than ourselves, traders [ἔμποροι, *emporoi*] and market-men [ἀγοραῖοι, *agoraioi*], fellows who import cheap rags and vile wine and export in exchange products of no better quality" (trans. Crosby). He does not, however, always speak badly of traders (cf. 36.11).

stripping a freeborn and modest woman of her gown, putting a cook's apron on her and keeping her in a tavern; for just so the dignity and greatness of high ability in public life is destroyed when it is turned to household affairs [οἰκονομίας, *oikonomias*] and money-making [χρημα-τισμούς, *chrēmatismous*].[30]

Money-making in commerce is considered menial (βάναυσος, *banausos*), a word that denotes baseness and contempt (though re-tainers could carry out this line of work). Those rare few lucky enough to make a fortune and who aspired to a councilship had to buy land, a much stabler means of production or of earning capital, though they did not necessarily have to sell their business if they could get retainers to do the practical side of things. There appear to be three notable exceptions to the rule about landownership, however.

The first are *negotiatores,* transplanted Italian businessmen who commanded respect and occupied positions of power.[31] Even though they were businessmen, they could have both invested in business and owned land, thus elevating their status through land ownership. The second exception is the purple merchants. To become one, the initial capital outlay was high but well worth it because the product brought in considerable profit. So, effectively, the purple merchants could buy their way into the town councils.[32] Third, in Palestine the loss of status incurred by working as a merchant and the subsequent loss of access to political power were not present. Some members of the Sanhedrin were businessmen. Even so, Sirach warns against the temptations in commerce: "A merchant can hardly keep from wrong-doing, nor is a tradesman innocent of sin" (26:29). Generally, how-ever, business was not frowned upon by the masses and some religious leaders. But even after we factor these exceptions into the model (fig. 1), nearly all the access of the merchants and traders to political power was blocked off except through landholdings.

Sometimes traders traveled from one city to the next, hawking their products. In the epistle of James, written to churches mostly in the Greek East, the author creates, as it were, a typical conversation between traders: "Come, now, you who say, 'Today or tomorrow we shall go into such and such a town and spend a year there, doing

---

[30] Plutarch, *Mor.* 785D, trans. Fowler, LCL 10.89–91.

[31] J. Hatzfeld, *Les trafiquants italiens dans l'Orient hellénique* (Paris: E. de Boccard, 1919) 101–42, 161, 296–99, 305–7. Ste. Croix, *Class Struggle,* 125 n. 12, cites Hatzfeld but does not critique or refute his thesis. Magie, *Roman Rule,* 1.251–56, says that *negotiatores* were a boon to the local economy. Broughton, "Roman Asia Minor," 543, estimates that there were no fewer than eighty thousand of them.

[32] Pleket, "Urban Elites," 142.

business and making money'" (4:13). Dio Chrysostom depicts a trader in a similar fashion. In a speech praising the city of Alexandria, he mentions "a trader with many precious wares who would land in any city."[33] The motive behind moving from city to city was market fluctuation. When this or that market dried up, the trader went to another one. Dio again observes perceptively that during a national festival in a given city "many too bring in merchandise of all sorts, the tradespeople, that is; and some display their own arts and crafts."[34] Some of these merchants lived in tents, congregating near each other during the festivals in a given city.[35] Or they would take the initiative and sell their petty wares door-to-door.[36] Living in a mobile manner would not enhance family life or offer much political power or social prestige.

In Ptolemaic Egypt queens and prominent women owned ships.[37] "Average" women also made loans of commodities and worked in commerce: one was a linen seller, another a general dealer, and some owned and operated home breweries.[38] It would be wrong to transport Egypt's historical realities pell-mell to Asia Minor or Palestine, but some features remain the same regardless of the region. During the Principate, women of Rome and the East also owned ships.[39] From the Principate to the imperial period, Rome—through such promises as exemptions from liturgies or from financial contributions to the polis or state—tempted wealthy merchants to remain in the shipping business and not only to invest in land.[40] In order to keep the benefits for future generations, shippers passed the trade on to their daughters and sons.

In Pompeii women engaged in every sort of business.[41] One was a pawnbroker who made small loans to a wide clientele; some sold middle-sized or smaller property; some managed middle-sized estates (retainers).[42] Nothing prohibited women in the Greek East from conducting the same kinds of business. Indeed, because of the growing prosperity in the eastern provinces, it is certain that they did.

---

[33] Dio Chrysostom, *Or.* 32.97, trans. Cohoon, LCL 3.267. I adapted the translation slightly.

[34] Ibid., 27.5, trans. Cohoon, LCL 2.353.

[35] Broughton, "Roman Asia Minor," 870–77, treats of mobile merchants.

[36] Dio Chrysostom, *Or.* 54.3, LCL 4.375.

[37] D. J. Thompson, "Nile Grain Transport under the Ptolemies," in *Trade* (ed. Garnsey, Hopkins, and Whittaker) 68.

[38] This list comes from S. B. Pomeroy, *Women in Hellenistic Egypt* (New York: Schocken, 1984) 148–73.

[39] Garnsey, "Grain for Rome," 124–26.

[40] Jones, *Roman Economy,* 58; and Garnsey, "Grain for Rome," 123–25.

[41] MacMullen, "Woman," 209–10.

[42] Ibid.

In Palestine the business transactions of the woman mentioned in Proverbs 31 and of Babata crossed over into the class of merchants and traders. But besides them, some wives of rabbis took care of the family business while the husband and possibly the oldest son studied the Torah.[43] This last datum is very revealing because apparently some rabbis were willing to suspend the primarily ideologically based notion that they should limit the women to the domestic sphere. If at least a few experts in the Torah suspended this custom, then it is not unreasonable to deduce that some common businessmen, comparatively unlearned in the Torah, did the same in order to increase profits. Their decision would have been primarily based on economics. Thus, a passing reference in the Mishnah reads, "if a man set up his wife as a shopkeeper."[44] This passage clearly assumes that shops were family owned and operated and that women were involved in business.

The Mishnah and the Tosephta report of a woman who sold produce and kept her earnings as pocket money for herself. "Abba Saul says, 'They purchase them [wine, oil, or produce] from a woman for five *denars*, so that she may buy a cap for her head.' "[45] She undoubtedly represents many other women. Unfortunately, it is difficult to translate this small and discretionary earning power into a woman's daily life, other than her making small purchases. It is likely that she could never have made enough money to improve her condition drastically, or even a little. Women at this level only very rarely moved up in the world. But at least this involvement in business offered her a measure of social freedom: she freely interacted with the public, men or women, who wished to purchase her products.

Except in the case of the women of prominence seen in chapter 2 ("Governing Classes and the Urban Elite," pp. 24–45), not much research has been done on merchant women in Asia Minor.[46] Probably representing many other women, Atalanta and one unnamed woman from Aphrodisias, the hometown of Chariton in Caria, lent

---

[43] Witherington, *Women in Ministry,* 10. He is citing *b. Ketub.* 62b–63a and is following R. Loewe, *The Position of Women in Judaism* (London: SPCK, 1966) 49–50.

[44] *m. Ketub.* 9.4, Danby 258.

[45] *t. B. Qam.* 11.5, Neusner 4.70. Cf. Safrai, "Home and Family," 761. He is referring to *m. B. Qam.* 10.9, which will be cited later (see "Artisans," p. 81). Abba Saul comes from the "fourth generation" of rabbis (ca. 140–65 C.E.), but his observation is relevant because it is confirmed by business transacted in the Greek East generally.

[46] Hatzfeld, *Traficants,* 110, 124, 161, and passim, shows the wives of the *negotiatores* enjoying prominent roles or the same honor as their husbands in some inscriptions, but he does not develop this theme any further.

money to the polis, fully expecting repayment.[47] In fact, Atalanta was an aristocrat, not a mere moneylender, and we saw earlier that Nicerata lent money to a polis, but she too was in the ruling class.

Dio Chrysostom very plausibly links the prosperity of a city and region with a wide variety of employment for women. The city of Celaenae "stood as a bulwark in front of Phrygia, Lydia and Caria"[48] on the Maeander River. Dio praises its citizens in glowing terms for their city's abiding prosperity; but he highlights the time when the courts were in session every other year because they brought in a numberless throng of people. Not only vendors took advantage of this influx. Dio claims that no one in the city was out of work (rhetorical exaggeration), including households (οἰκίας, *oikias*) and women.[49] Though he was delivering a flattering encomium to a partial audience and was exaggerating when he claimed full employment for the citizens of Celaenae, his point is still valid that prosperity gave more opportunities of employment for women. This information supports the conclusion that women were active and not passive outside the house. They produced, marketed, and sold the wares of their family's business and worked in other jobs. After all, economic common sense would dictate that women should be involved in production, marketing, and selling. The cities in Asia Minor were enjoying prosperity in the aggregate, so employment for women must have been undergoing a proportionate increase. Precise numbers, however, can never be known because of a lack of information.

In another speech Dio draws a series of analogies about competition between craftsmen. One of them is a dyer who sells to women.

> Well then, is it not preferable for a dyer to ply his trade all by himself rather than in competition with other craftsmen, so that he may be able to sell his dyes, of whatever quality they may be, to women? For they will then be satisfied to buy dyes even slightly better than the kind they are themselves accustomed to use for dyeing on their farms [ἀγροῖς, *agrois*], dyes picked up at random, and they will not demand fast colours and royal purples.[50]

---

[47] Van Bremen, "Women," 229.

[48] Dio Chrysostom, *Or.* 35.14–16, trans. Crosby, LCL 3.405–7. Jones, *The Greek City,* 263, generalizes this passage to include provincial capitals with governors; I link this passage with prosperity in general.

[49] Dio Chrysostom, *Or.* 35.15, LCL 3.407. In this passage the translation of a few words is misleading.

[50] Dio Chrysostom, *Or.* 77.4, trans. Cohoon, LCL 5.263–65. It may be argued that these women were freed slaves, but Dio does not say this. Moreover, that argument assumes a priori that only freedwomen could conduct such business. The truth is that "average" women throughout the empire would not have considered this line of work or any work as demeaning. (The aristocrats are another story.)

This observation about women is again spoken in an offhanded manner, which increases the reliability of the observation. Going out in public, women purchased dyes, on their own and after experienced and skillful examination, for use on their farms. From Dio's comment, women were involved in various stages of fabric making, not to mention some sort of production: inspecting the raw products, buying them, bringing them home, making them into various garments, and, very likely, selling them. They should therefore be considered merchant-artisans, though, if they employed workers, they would have controlled the means of production. This shows the overlap between merchants and artisans.

But as noted, this overall prosperity in the Greek East can be misleading if one were to assume that most merchants and traders were wealthy. Their products were sold locally and on a very small scale. (After all, it is entirely possible for prosperity and poverty to coexist, as they do even today in the West.) Impoverished women in Athens can serve as a more typical example. From the classical to the Roman periods they were *petites commerçantes* who lived on the "margins" of the city.[51] They were sellers of fruits and vegetables, ribbons, flowers, and perfumes. Women in Asia Minor surely must have transacted the same kinds of trade. Throughout the Greek East women made and sold garlands for the winners of contests. Says Plutarch, "For these women, culling flower-clusters and sweet-scented leaves, intertwine and plait them."[52] But these women should not be considered wealthy, since the contests and winners were few. Thus, not every woman's involvement in commerce brought in wealth.[53]

The kinds of living quarters and the prosperity (or lack thereof) of shops also provide revealing data about the daily lives of female (and male) shop owners and even artisans working in shops. Ostia was a port city for Rome, and during the reign of Domitian (81–96 C.E.), the Romans began constructing new insulae, a project taking on momentum in the second century.[54] The living quarters were brick apartment houses or blocks two to four stories high. The floor plans are divided into categories or types, with each having subcategories. Our attention is directed to the commonest.

The commonest type is connected with shops and has four categories: "those with single rooms; those with mezzanines; those

---

[51] Vatin, *Recherches*, 265.

[52] Plutarch, *Mor.* 41F, trans. Babbitt, LCL 1.225.

[53] Schaps, *Economic Rights*, passim.

[54] J. E. Packer, *The Insulae of Imperial Ostia* (MAAR 31; Rome: American Academy, 1971) 77–78.

with backrooms, and those with backrooms and mezzanines."[55] A mezzanine is an upstairs apartment whose staircase is away from the downstairs shop and shared by other apartment dwellers; only a few of the mezzanines were "relatively large."[56] The numbers for these subcategories are as follows: Of the 806 separate shops, 464 were composed of a single room or the shop-apartment; 141 had mezzanines; 155, back rooms; and 46, both mezzanines and back rooms.[57] Thus, most shopkeepers both worked and lived in a single room. And it is assumed that at least a few employees, if shop owners at this level had any, may have lived in the shops while the keepers or owners may have lived in one-, two-, or three-room apartments in the upper stories, unconnected to the shops.

Allowing for differences in detail, such as window sizes and door styles, it may be stated that similar numbers for shop-apartments existed in cities throughout the empire because shopkeepers and artisans, regardless of the city or town, almost always lived at subsistence level.[58] In other words, while it is futile to equate this or that apartment size with specific levels of prosperity or poverty, it can generally be believed that large apartments corresponded to wealthier people and smaller sizes corresponded to poorer people, especially the shop-apartments. It is inconceivable that other cities would have outstripped the prosperity of Ostia so much that nearly every citizen would have lived in multiroom apartments and that the numbers for the East would be the inverse of those for Ostia. The income of shop owners did not vary that much throughout the empire.

With this information about the shop-apartments in Ostia, two cities in Asia Minor, Pergamum and Miletus, can be examined.[59] In these cities, one-room shops line the agora and streets. In Miletus shops that face towards the agora have a small back room, but those butting against the backs of these shops and facing onto a street outside the agora do not have a back room.[60] Perhaps this difference in size indicates some division in prosperity or briskness of business. It is impossible to determine how many of these shops served as the living quarters for the owners or keepers, but as noted, Pergamum

---

[55] Ibid., 6.

[56] Ibid., 7.

[57] Ibid., 66.

[58] For further discussion, see Arlandson, " 'Fall and Rise,' " 160–61 nn. 80–81. By shop owners is meant not those who owned the insulae but the shops. Perhaps "shop renters" is more accurate.

[59] The sketchy and tentative analysis that follows is based on E. Akurgal, *Ancient Civilizations and Ruins of Turkey* (6th ed.; trans. J. Whybrow and M. Emre; Istanbul: Haset Kitabevi, 1985) 69–111, 206–22.

[60] Ibid., 214–17.

and Miletus surely did not outdo Ostia in prosperity. It is highly likely that in Asia Minor the same proportions of shop-apartments and one-room apartments in the upper stories of the apartment blocks served as living quarters for shopkeepers or owners, as opposed to multiroom apartments or houses, though it would be wrong to assume that all of them lived in their shops or one-room dwellings.

In the setting of this commonest type of floor plan, and especially the shop-apartments, it is not difficult to surmise how a woman might have participated in business life. It would have been sheer economic folly to exclude her from helping in the business in some capacity. In the shop-apartment, for reasons of space alone, it would have been impossible for a man to bar his wife from the "male sphere." Even if it is granted that an urban woman, as did her rural counterpart, indeed performed more domestic chores, such as tending the children and preparing the meal, then when the husband departed for the forum or marketplace or did anything else that took him away from the business proper, the wife would have taken over his duties of making and hawking the product to passersby A wife must have been inextricably tied to the profits (or lack thereof) of the shop. She would have been expected to increase the margin between costs (labor, production, purchasing of raw material, etc.) and the profits in any way she could. Thus, the boundary between the male and female spheres becomes more porous than expected.

This kind of contribution by wives in shops is illustrated in the Tosephta:

> Rabban Simeon b. Gamaliel says, "They purchase olives from women. For sometimes a man is ashamed to sell [things] at the door of his store, so he gives [them] to his wife and she sells [them]."[61]

It is unclear whether this store is a shop-apartment, but it certainly could have been. In any case, it is certain that under almost no circumstance would a common produce seller ever be ashamed of selling his product, so it difficult to surmise why he withdraws (besides the reason that this lone rabbi gives). But regardless of the reason, it is still very clear that a wife is involved in business in a shop while the husband retreats into the background. There must be no doubt that this practice of sharing labor between husbands and wives in shops was done throughout the Greco-Roman world. Profits demanded that this should take place.[62]

---

[61] *t. B. Qam.* 11.7, Neusner 4.70. The translation has been adapted slightly.
[62] We must remember Prisca who worked alongside her husband Aquila (Acts 18:2–3; Rom 16:3–4; 1 Cor 16:19).

It was already observed that some traders were no more than traveling peddlers who sometimes lived in, and sold their products from, tents, congregating in a city that was enjoying a festival. Since the wives of these peddlers accompanied them, male and female spheres disappeared for the same reasons that they disappeared for those who lived and worked in shops.

To sum up: (1) Evidence exists that there were female merchants and traders in Palestine and Asia Minor, evidence that Hellenistic Egypt and the Latin West confirmed. But these women were fewer in number than male merchants. (2) From the existing evidence, it may be said that a few women merchants and traders were wealthy but most lived a little above or at poverty, or even below. (3) The wealth of male or female shippers or purple merchants did not make them constitute some sort of middle class in the modern sense. They could afford to buy land, and probably most did so because of its greater stability, thereby allowing the male merchants at least to gain access to political power. The accumulation of landed wealth made them eligible for the council. But most traders and merchants, limited in political power, were restricted to the assembly. (4) Merchants overlapped with the artisans only when both made and sold their wares to the local markets. (5) Many shopkeepers and owners lived and worked in shop-apartments. Women in this situation were involved in business, and the domestic and public spheres coalesced. (6) Finally, despite merchants' and traders' limited political power and limited financial resources, they were productive members of society and in the aggregate did not suffer from long bouts of unemployment because of a lack of skill, as did common laborers.

Artisans. Because of the scattered and chaotic nature of the data, it is impossible to determine how many artisans lived in Asia Minor and Palestine. But there is much information about the kinds of jobs they did. A partial list for Asia Minor is provided in order to foster an appreciation of the variety: craftsmen and artisans, mostly free, but some slaves,[63] worked as builders and carpenters, wool dyers and washers, bakers, sandal makers, linen workers, tentmakers, silk weavers, weavers of all kinds, smiths of gold, silver, bronze, copper, and iron, potters, shipbuilders, fishermen, porters, fullers, leather-workers, and bed sawyers.[64]

---

[63] Broughton, "Roman Asia Minor," 839–40.
[64] Ibid., 841–44.

The products were exclusively intended for the local market, apart from textiles, ships, and luxury items, so most of the work was carried on by individuals in small shops.[65] There were rare large production centers, extreme examples of which are found in Hellenistic Egypt. Zenon, the owner of a vast estate, organized a working force of 320 in the town of Mouchis, 314 at Oxyrynchus, and 150 at Tebtunis, totaling 784, most of whom worked out of the home.[66] This same Zenon had a workshop employing about 40 workers, a number that more accurately reflects large shops in the Greek East.[67] In Sardis archaeologists have uncovered the remains of a few factories:[68] an Italian still living in Italy expanded his business there and bought a ceramics factory, fully operational in the last decades of the first century B.C.E.; it seems to have been of medium size, that is, with two dozen or so workers. Also, thirty to forty small workshops were found that made textiles of all kinds and operated 1 c. B.C.E.–1 c. C.E.[69]

Syria and Palestine can match the list for Asia Minor as well: glassmakers, makers of papyri and parchments, silk weavers, finishers of imported silk, tailors, dressmakers, fullers, dyers, ointment mixers in Jerusalem, workers in bronze, ceramic makers, and whole villages of potters, jewelers, goldsmiths, silversmiths, tanners, shoemakers, bakers, and butchers.[70] Craftsmen in Jerusalem worked in their homes or small shops.[71] Members of the same craft sometimes inhabited the same street and even, as noted, whole villages.[72]

Lucian's brief but revealing description of craftsmen can be applied to craftsmen working in their shops throughout the Greek East. He notes that if the workers ever heard about certain greedy philosophers living in "unlimited plenty" (Lucian's satire), they would react thus:

> All the men in the workshops would spring to their feet and leave their trades deserted when they saw that by toiling and moiling from morning until night, doubled over their tasks, they merely eke out a bare existence from such wage-earning. . . . [73]

---

[65] Ibid., 839.

[66] Pomeroy, *Women,* 168.

[67] Ibid., 179.

[68] Archaeological Expedition of Sardis (1958–), "The Hellenistic Period," in *Sardis: From Prehistoric to Roman Times,* ed. G. Hanfmann, L. Robert, and W. Mierse (Cambridge: Harvard, 1983) 127.

[69] Ibid.

[70] F. M. Heichelheim, "Roman Syria," in *An Economic Survey* (ed. F. Tenney) 4.189–209.

[71] Jeremias, *Jerusalem,* 19–20.

[72] Heichelheim, "Roman Syria," 198.

[73] Lucian, *Fug.* 17, trans. Harmon, LCL 5.73. I adapt the translation slightly.

In his endless quest to satirize insincere philosophers, Lucian ends up praising working people over them. His satire provides a glimpse into the long hours, menial work, and meager wages of an artisan. It is almost as if Lucian, before writing this passage, had walked by a shop and observed people at work, "doubled over their task," "from morning until night."

Most artisans, like most merchants, lived just a little above or in poverty. Used cautiously, the example of the "linen-workers" of Tarsus (Paul's hometown) can be instructive. Dio Chrysostom reports that the term "linen-workers" was a generic term for those "outside of the constitution," who consisted of "no small number."[74] They could not afford the five hundred drachmas to become full citizens and exercise political rights, a monetary requirement apparently unique to Tarsus.[75] They could attend the assembly; but because they were not full citizens, one must assume that they could not vote or speak. A large number of workers there could not afford the payment. It is very likely that throughout Asia Minor, if the requirement had been ordained as law, most semiskilled laborers could never have afforded the cost, as was also the case in Tarsus.[76] "This [inability to pay] suggests an organization in small family workshops, with a few apprentices and laborers, slave or free, as in the villages and towns in Egypt. It is possible that the Tarsian 'linen-workers' were free paid employees of factory-owners."[77]

---

[74] Dio Chrysostom, *Or.* 34.21–23, trans. Crosby, LCL 3.357–59. For a discussion, see Broughton, "Roman Asia Minor," 822; Jones, *Roman Economy,* 359; Ste. Croix, *Class Struggle,* 532; and Magie, *Roman Rule,* 1.600. Jones says they were "not necessarily very poor" (ibid.). I am not sure what Jones means by "very," but Ste. Croix's analysis (ibid.) is correct when he reminds us that the "linen-workers" were regarded as foreigners (δοκοῦντες ἀλλότριοι, *dokountes allotrioi*) and suffered some form of ἀτιμία, *atimia,* which certain other craftsmen did not suffer. I believe this shows that the "linen-workers" were indeed "very poor" in material and in status. But in any case, scholars are united over the fact that most artisans could never rise above subsisting day to day. Also see Jones, *The Greek City,* 268–69, who calls the "urban proletariat" "miserably poor."

[75] Jones, ibid., 174.

[76] R. F. Hock, *The Social Context of Paul's Ministry* (Philadelphia: Fortress, 1980) 31–37, esp. 35, describes craftsmen in grim terms. I do not wish to imply that all artisans were as badly mistreated as the "linen-workers." Indeed, in that same passage Dio goes on to say that the dyer, cobbler, and carpenter did not suffer the same reproach. It should be remembered that the silversmiths in Acts 19:23–27 made a good income from their craft.

[77] Jones, *Roman Economy.* It is by no means clear that these "linen-workers" were slaveowners, but some probably were free paid employees working in shops. Also, the word "family" here is important because it would have been economic folly for any male artisan living in or a little above poverty to

The artisans' political power was extremely limited.[78] They could never hope to achieve ownership of land or an equivalent monetary amount to buy their way into power, as a few merchants did, unless by extraordinary skill and luck; they could never advance to a councilship, though some were part of the assembly. And since the assembly's decisions had to be approved by the Roman rulers, the political office holders and the council, even the power of the assembly was subject to the rich landowners.

Like the Tarsian "linen-workers," the common masses in other cities were excluded from leadership in the assembly. Aristides observes,

> For who of you does not know that first of all such education is not within the capacity of the masses [πολλῶν, *pollōn*], no more than legislation and making proposals in the assembly?[79]

The "masses" include artisans in workshops and other occupations: "Yet shall we ineptly select our guides and teachers of the most serious matters from every workshop and every occupation?"[80] The vague term "every occupation" encompasses small traders and merchants who overlap with artisans and shopworkers. It is very likely that the leaders in the assembly were landowners, wealthy merchants, and prosperous shop owners who had not yet ascended to a councilship.

Artisans in Palestine suffered the same political liability. In a particularly enlightening passage in Sir 38:24–34 (2d c. B.C.E.), the author, Ben Sira, possibly a priest or scribe, describes how farmers, artisans, master craftsmen, those who cut the signets of seals, smiths, and potters—all of whom work "by night as well as by day" (v. 27)—are not regarded very highly for political wisdom. He acknowledges that a city is established on such men, who rely on the works of their hands, and that "they maintain the fabric of the world" (v. 34). But he also delivers this blow:

> Yet they are not sought out for the council [βουλήν, *boulēn*] of the people, nor do they attain eminence in the public assembly [ἐκκλησίᾳ,

---

exclude his family—and his wife—from increasing profits. It has already been argued that, in most cases, barring women from working in the shops would have been impossible because of the spatial dimensions of most shops' floor plans: many families both worked and lived in the shops.

[78] Joshel, *Work,* 63–69, discusses the views of work and workers in Latin literature, which was written from the elite's perspectives.

[79] Aristides, *Or.* 29.17, Behr 2.143. This oration was delivered at Smyrna between 157 and 165 C.E.

[80] Ibid., 29.18; Behr 2.143.

ekklēsia]. They do not sit in the judge's seat, nor do they understand the decisions of the courts; they cannot expound discipline or judgment, and they are not found among the rulers. (vv. 32–33)

Without sorting out what "council" or "assembly" meant in the second century B.C.E. (see in ch. 2 "Governing Classes and Urban Elite," pp. 24–29), we can still clearly see the class tension. Although taking part in the assembly, which was more democratic, workers, even skilled ones, did not have the leisure time to study the law and traditions (v. 24). Thus, they were not sought out for positions of authority. It is not difficult to transfer Ben Sira's assessment of his times to the first century C.E. The very fact that the governing orders in Jerusalem and other cities were still mostly a plutocracy indicates that old attitudes would not die easily. If artisans gained even a small degree of political prestige and power, they must have been confined to petty governing bodies in small villages.

Limited in power, the artisans formed, then, what are called *collegia* in Latin, usually translated as "guilds," but better as "societies."[81] In Greek the terms are numerous.[82] In Palestine there were societies of weavers, cheese makers, wool combers, bakers, dyers, sword makers, among others.[83] On very rare occasions one of the *collegia* might go on strike, as in the case of the bakers in Ephesus[84] or the temple utensil makers in Jerusalem.[85] But in the aggregate, the political power of the *collegia* remained static. Their *collegia* led the artisans beyond a camaraderie based only on their work, prompting them even to live in the same neighborhood or vicinity.[86] If a traveler asked for an individual, the reply might come back, "Go to Butchers'

---

[81] MacMullen, *Enemies of the Roman Order: Treason, Unrest, and Alienation in the Empire* (Cambridge: Harvard, 1966) 173, suggests this translation.

[82] Ste. Croix, *Class Struggle,* 597 n. 9, has a list of them: συνέδριον, συντεχνία, συνέργιον, σύστημα, συμβίωσις, συνεργασία, ἐργασία, ὁμοτέχνον, στατίων, πλατεῖα, κοινόν, οἶκος, *(synedrion, syntechnia, synergion, systēma, symbiōsis, synergasia, ergasia, omotechnon, statiōn, plateia, koinon, oikos)* and even ἡ ἱερὰ φυλή *(hē hiera phylē).*

[83] Heichelheim, "Roman Syria," 208–11; and Applebaum, "Economic Life," 683. Applebaum also notes that Jewish organizations were a little more concerned with political power then were their Eastern Greek counterparts.

[84] Jones, *The Greek City,* 219. Apparently the city controlled the imports of grain and thus controlled the prices.

[85] Heichelheim, "Roman Syria," 193. He adds that sometimes craftsmen from Alexandria were brought in to replace them.

[86] MacMullen, *Roman Social Relations,* 71–72, gives another reason for their close proximity: it was merely business convenience. This may be related more to working in shops than to forming societies. Joshel, *Work,* 106–12, discusses shops as communities in Rome.

Street or to the linen-makers' neighborhood."[87] Thus, another purpose of the *collegia* was to provide a fictive family for the members.
"For the poor artisans, excluded from the cult as from public life, the
collegium replaced therefore the family. . . . It formed for them a
religious family."[88] *Collegia* relished the patronage of wealthy women.
A grande dame would donate money for festivals or improvements on
their buildings, and the *collegium* would acclaim her as "Mother."[89]

Sometimes this notion of a fictive family breaks down because
some craftsmen had to travel. A group of sculptors from Asia Minor
lived in Rome in the second century C.E.[90] Some masons from a
quarry in western Asia Minor arrived in the city of Leptis in North
Africa for municipal improvements recently undertaken.[91] These
men were probably too poor to marry, or took their families with
them, or left them behind. Fortunately, their craft won a place for
them in the foreign society.

As to female artisans, in Hellenistic Egypt women and men
worked side by side in the textile industry, though the men were paid
three times more than the women.[92] As is true today, women did not
receive equal pay for equal work. This probably reflects the financial
plight of women throughout the empire. In the West, during the
Principate and earlier, *collegia* often enjoyed meals together, and
there is a frequent use of familial terms among the male members and
their families who were invited to the meals: *pater, mater, frater,
soror.*[93] For our purposes employment of the words *mater* and *soror*
is enlightening because they reveal women's involvement in the
collegia.[94] "Roman epitaphs depict women as active workers" and

---

[87] Heichelheim, "Roman Syria," 193; and MacMullen, *Roman Social
Relations,* 69–79.

[88] J.-P. Waltzing, *Etudes historiques sur les corporations professionelles
chez les Romains* (4 vols.; 1895–1900; reprint, Rome: "L'Erma" di Bretschneider,
1968) 1.75: "Pour les pauvres artisans, exclus du culte comme de la vie
publique, le collège remplaçait donc la famille. . . . Il formait pour eux une
famille religieuse" (the translation in the text is mine). Joshel, *Work,* 118, says,
"Membership conveyed a kind of belonging; office [in a *collegium*] signaled
one's elevation above one's fellows. Perhaps belonging and standing, even at
this modest level, were especially significant at a time when citizenship no
longer determined privilege." The same could be said for the Greek East.

[89] Waltzing, *Corporations,* 1.305–6.

[90] A. Burford, *Craftsmen in Greek and Roman Society* (London: Thames
& Hudson, 1972) 67.

[91] Ibid.

[92] Pomeroy, *Women,* 169.

[93] Waltzing, *Corporations,* 1.329.

[94] Ibid., 1.277. It is, however, at this point that Waltzing hesitates. He
says that during the second century women were not allowed to become

involved in *collegia* in their own right.[95] The Theodosian Code (432 C.E.) records the existence of women's industrial *collegia*, called *gynaeciarii* and *linteones*, located in the West and East.[96] Their job was to make clothing of silk, gold, and purple for the emperor and linen uniforms for the military.[97] The word "purple," the color of the clothing that the *gynaeciarii* made, stands out because the Theodosian Code reflects women's *collegia* that had already been operating for a long time in the East. This may indicate that Lydia the purple seller and the women who were accompanying her when Paul happened to meet them by the river in Philippi (Acts 16:13–15) formed a *collegium* of sorts.

Inscriptions and other sources depict freedwomen throughout the empire working as cobblers, shoemakers, leatherworkers, waitresses, innkeepers, amanuenses, butchers, and fisherwomen.[98] "Average" women who were born free would not have suffered loss of status from working at these jobs. Indeed, it can be safely assumed that they did work at them.

A woman from Lydia is credited with inventing linen thread.[99] Other women in Asia Minor spun wool at home,[100] though it could be conjectured that some might have belonged to workshops outside the home. And when they spun wool at home, they first kept clothing for their own family and then made every effort to market the surplus. This is illustrated by one of Lucian's dialogues. A certain woman named Crobyle had a famous smith for a husband, but he had died two years earlier. She sold some of his tools and belongings, which sustained her and her daughter Corinna for several months. "Since then I've barely provided a starvation diet, now by weaving, now by spinning, now by spinning thread for warp and woof."[101]

Pausanius (ca. 120–80 C.E.), while visiting the city of Patrae in Achaia, observed the following.

> The women of Patrae outnumber the men by two to one. These women
> are amongst the most charming [Ἀφροδίτης, *Aphroditēs*] in the world.

---

members despite the enrollment lists that have women's names on them. More recent scholars, such as Joshel, have to take up where he left off. She concludes that women were active participants in *collegia*.

[95] Joshel, *Work*, 141; she discusses further, pp. 142–45.

[96] Waltzing, *Corporations*, 2.232–46.

[97] Ibid., 2.361. Waltzing asks the question when were women allowed to become members between the second century and the time of the Theodosian code, but he again hesitates and then abandons the answer for lack of information.

[98] Corley, *Private Women*, 52, summarizes scholarship.

[99] Broughton, "Roman Asia Minor," 615.

[100] Ibid., 821.

[101] Lucian, *D. Meretr.* 6.293, trans. Macleod, LCL 7.387–89.

Most of them gain a livelihood from the fine flax that grows in Elis, weaving from it nets for the head as well as dresses.[102]

This excerpt shows that women could make a living from weaving, unlike Crobyle in Lucian's story. Lucian was therefore exaggerating. (See the discussion of Tabitha in ch. 4, pp. 143–44.) It appears that these women formed a *collegium* or, short of that, at least cooperated, in the loose sense of the word. Though married women worked at weaving, Lucian and Pausanius agree that single women—though Pausanius's statistic is likely false— turned to weaving to earn a living.

In Pausanius's travels through Elis, Greece, he also observed, "There is also in the market-place a building for the women called the Sixteen, where they weave the robe for Hera."[103] Like the women in Patrae, these women may have formed a religious *collegium*. In any case, it is clear that they were not consigned to their houses or to the domestic sphere but moved through, and worked in, the marketplace or the public sphere.

In Palestine it was said that "from women they buy garments of wool in Judaea and garments of flax in Galilee."[104] It is not clear whether some of these Jewish women formed *collegia*, but eighty-two maidens were known as skilled weavers for the temple, perhaps a faint hint that they formed a *collegium*.[105] These eighty-two maidens resemble the sixteen women in Elis whose sacred duty was to weave the robe for Hera. Still another faint hint exists. Women were known to have woven products in the marketplace or, generally, in a public meeting place: "if . . . she spins in the *shuq*."[106] It is likely that women who were spinners and weavers in this public arena formed a group, though the text does not say this explicitly. But it has already been shown that certain crafts occupied entire streets and neighborhoods in Jerusalem as well as in cities throughout the empire, so

---

[102] Paus. 21.14, trans. Jones, LCL 3.297–99. Hock, *Social Context,* 81 n. 48, observes that "weaving was often, though not exclusively, a woman's trade" and cites ancient authors.

[103] Paus. 2.14.9, trans. Jones, LCL 2.153.

[104] *m. B. Qam.* 10.9, Danby 347. Paus. 1.5.5, LCL 2.403, considers the flax from Palestine to be of high quality, though of a different hue: "The fine flax of Elis is as fine as that of the Hebrews, but it is not so yellow" (trans. Jones). But see the next note.

[105] Jeremias, *Jerusalem,* 5. Jeremias reports that the material was imported from Babylonia ready-made (38 n. 18).

[106] *m. Ketub.* 7.6. Danby, unfortunately, has "street" (p. 255). Neusner translates *shuq* correctly as "marketplace" (p. 392). In this passage the rabbis disapproved of such women. But our concern is not with this opinion but with the underlying assumption. Clearly, women worked in public and in groups.

perhaps women followed the same practice. In both examples, however, it is unlikely that these women formed *collegia* that were
politically and economically active, just as male *collegia* were not
politically or economically active.

In the fictional account of the trials and triumph of Tobit and his
wife, Anna, the author, writing two to three centuries before our era
and maintaining verisimilitude about social practices, appeals to
real-world customs about "women's work." Like Job, Tobit had been
wealthy, but severe testing swept over his life, including blindness.
At this juncture in the story his wife steps in to earn some money at
weaving.

> At that time, also, my wife Anna earned money at women's work [ἐν
> τοῖς ἔργοις τοῖς γυναικείοις, *en tois ergois tois gynaikeiois*]. She used
> to send what she made to the owners [κυρίοις αὐτῶν, *kyriois autōn*] and
> they would pay wages to her. One day, the seventh of Dystrus, when
> she cut off a piece she had woven and sent it to the owners, they paid
> her full wages and also gave her a young goat for a meal. (2:11–12)

The phrase "women's work" may be too easy a translation. The
combination of the plural and the article in τοῖς ἔργοις, and the
substantive τοῖς γυναικείοις, which, without the article, is usually an
adjective, probably indicates an industry or a large regional business.
(A variant reading has just ἐν τοῖς γυναικείοις, which may also
indicate an industry, for the same reason.) An industry would explain
the presence of the owners and the pronoun αὐτῶν, the antecedent of
which is "works." It also seems as though Anna worked out of her
house or at least not under the direct supervision of the owners. All
of these data bear resemblance to the situation of Zenon in Egypt,
who owned a textile industry employing 784 persons, most of whom
worked from their homes but some of whom worked in shops. Thus,
women individually worked at home and received wages or sold
their products to local owners who were probably also marketers.

Interestingly, this excerpt reveals that Anna "sent" her goods to
the owners and did not go herself. Other evidence has shown that
Jewish women themselves went to the marketplace to work or to the
owners to sell their goods. This was also seen with Gentile women,
who purchased dyes, as observed by Dio Chrysostom. Tobit and Anna
were once wealthy, so if the author's narrative world conforms to the
real world, and much of it evidently does, then she may not have
been accustomed to running errands to the marketplace and naturally
relied on her servants to do such chores. The passage continues by
stating that Anna retained enough discretionary power to receive the
goat as a bonus to her wages. Though Tobit, out of his ignorance and
bitterness, questioned the propriety of the goat, Anna won the debate,

as seen in Tobit's repentance for his distrust of his wife's good judgment.

So far the references depict women weaving and selling their products, but this was standard "women's work," as seen even with Penelope, the wife of Odysseus. But two brief references in the Mishnah show that individual women were also involved at home in crafts of the most general kind. One reference has a woman doing the "works of her hand."[107] It is probable that this refers primarily to weaving, but, as noted, the Mishnah is quite able to specify this trade when the need arises. It would be unnecessarily restrictive, therefore, to limit this reference just to spinning and weaving. This claim receives support from another passage: "A man should not teach his son a craft [*ummanut*] that is practiced among women."[108] This Hebrew word is also very general and should not be limited just to spinning and weaving, either for the son or the women. What is at stake is a young man spending too much time with women in the workplace, because women (that is, women generally, not just "bad women" such as prostitutes) were a negative influence (so many rabbis thought).[109]

In summary, seven inferences can be drawn from this survey: (1) In Asia Minor and Palestine most artisans lived in or barely on either side of poverty. Very few could ever manage to accumulate enough money to buy land, the quickest route to economic stability, political power, and high status. (2) If they participated in government, it was in the assembly or in a petty governing body in their small town or village. (3) *Collegia* had little or no political power because the members apparently did not concern themselves with strikes or wage controls. (4) Women were active members of *collegia* in Rome, and this probably reflects the situation in the East, since the East was undergoing prosperity and therefore social freedom for women. (5) Female artisans worked in small shops or in the home. While working in small shops, or large ones for that matter, the traditional boundaries between men and women became more permeable, thus offering a little more freedom to women. (6) It is likely that the difference in wages between men and women in Egypt reflects a disparity throughout the empire. This shows that women, as today, were behind the male artisans. (7) Because they had some trade or were skilled or semiskilled, the artisans were, despite their lack of wealth, contributing and productive members of society.

---

[107] *m. Ketub.* 5.4. The Hebrew reads, *maase yede ishto* (works of hand).

[108] *m. Qidd.* 4.14, Danby 414. Neusner translates, "A man should not teach his son a trade which he has to practice among women" (p. 498).

[109] Wegner, *Chattel?* 159–62, 166.

Day Laborers.[110]   In Acts 17:5 Luke writes that after Paul and Silas had reaped the fruit of evangelistic success in the city of Thessalonica, the Jews, out of jealousy, gathered together some πονηρούς, *ponērous* ("bad characters") frequenting the markets (ἀγοραῖοι). "Bad characters" in this passage means "loafers" or "corner-boys."[111] Dio Chrysostom describes them in the same way when he writes, "he [the king] does not covet the praise of the vulgar [βαναύσων, *banausōn*] and loungers about the market-place [ἀγοραίων, *agoraiōn*]."[112] This is a perfect picture of the μισθωτός, *misthōtos* (Lat. *mercennarius*)—or, in the NT, ἐργάτης, *ergatēs*—a day laborer who hired himself out for his unskilled (or, at best, semiskilled) labor power. The laborers gathered at a known location in the city waiting for a μισθωτής, *misthōtēs* (contractor) to hire them (cf. Matt 20:1–16).[113]

Overlapping with semiskilled workers, the laborers were not slaves, but they worked side by side with a few of them in seasonal construction, mines, and various menial tasks in public works, some as burden bearers and cleaners, others as ferrymen, dockworkers, and

---

[110] Ste. Croix, *Class Struggle,* 179–204, argues that free laborers did not play as significant a role in the macroeconomy as unfree laborers did. Finley, *Ancient Economy,* 65–70, also discusses labor. He uses the broad category of "dependent (or involuntary labor)" (p. 69). He defines this as consisting of those who were bound to work based on "some pre-condition, birth into a class of dependents or debt or capture or any other situation which, by law or custom, automatically removed some measure of his freedom of choice and action, usually for a long term or for life." Finley would have a "half-way" man (66) between slaves and "the perfectly free man" (67), the latter of whom never existed in real life. I believe that Ste. Croix has adduced plenty of evidence that free laborers existed; in my opinion Finley is waxing too philosophical about free will and determinism. Broughton, "Roman Asia Minor," 839–46, *pace* Ste. Croix, proffers much evidence that free laborers were in abundance in shops and industry in Roman Asia Minor, while slaves were not. "Slavery in industry was equally conspicuous by its absence" (p. 839). ("Equally" refers to slaves in agriculture.) The problem with Broughton's assessment is that he mixes skilled, semiskilled, and unskilled laborers together. Jones, *Roman Economy,* 358–59, independent of Broughton but in agreement with him, adduces evidence that more workers in the cloth industry were free than were slaves. My own opinion is that slaves and free men worked side by side. But in any case, in a survey of this kind the free laborers can represent other free urban poor, since they overlap.

[111] F. F. Bruce, *The Acts of the Apostles: The Greek Text with Introduction and Commentary* (3d, enl. ed.; Grand Rapids, Mich.: Eerdmans, 1990) 370.

[112] Dio Chrysostom, *Or.* 1.33, trans. Cohoon, LCL 1.19 (cf. *Or.* 66.25). The word ἀγοραῖος, *agoraios,* in the plural can mean "loungers about the market-place." It occurs in the plural genitive in Acts 17:5, but Luke makes it clear that only some of these loungers were ἄνδρας πονηρούς, *andras ponērous,* that is, not all of them were bad.

[113] Ste. Croix, *Class Struggle,* 186.

bargemen, since many cities were on a river. They often migrated to the country when harvest season arrived, so a gap has been placed between the urban and rural spheres in our model (fig. 1) in chapter 2. Like some artisans or semiskilled laborers, they were forced to migrate from one city to the next depending on their building programs, though construction was only seasonal at best, even in prosperous Asia Minor.[114] On occasion they also had to fend off competition. When a slave master hired out his slaves, the slaves took jobs away from the day laborers.[115]

The common laborer's daily life was very grim. In Lucian's story of an imaginary journey into Hades, a rich man is contrasted with a poor cobbler named Micyllus. Of his life on earth Micyllus says,

> But as for me, having nothing at stake in life, neither farm nor tenements nor gold nor gear nor reputation nor statues, of course I was in marching order . . . and sprang up at once . . . barefooted as I was and without even washing off the blacking. . . . And I infer that there is no dunning of debtors here and no paying taxes, and above all no freezing in winter or falling ill or being thrashed by men of greater consequence.[116]

A little later Micyllus exclaims,

> Alackaday, my rotten sandals! Unlucky man that I am, never again will I go hungry from morning to night or wander about in winter barefooted and half-naked, with my teeth chattering for cold![117] These two excerpts can be used for urban day laborers because in both literary contexts Lucian is painting an exceptionally bleak picture of a poor working man. It probably does not reflect the life of craftsmen but of laborers whose employment would have been intermittent, and in Micyllus's case more intermittent than usual. Micyllus claims that he did not even have one obol to pay his fare to Charon.[118]

---

[114] Ibid., 187. Ste. Croix has some good examples of workers in building programs (pp. 190–96).

[115] Ibid., 202–3, though Ste. Croix argues that this did not happen as often as one would suppose. Finley, *Ancient Economy*, 80, argues this point as well.

[116] Lucian, *Cat.* 15, trans. Harmon, LCL 2.33.

[117] Ibid., 20, trans. Harmon, LCL 2.41.

[118] That these two excerpts are exaggerated is seen in another of Lucian's dialogues, *Gall.* 22, LCL 2.217. The same Micyllus is described a little more positively. After he finishes his job, in the evening he receives his seven obols (very slightly over one drachma), buys some food, and then relaxes, having a good time. It should be remembered that a cobbler in Tarsus was not as debased as the "linen-workers" and was admitted freely into the assembly. So cobblers may have been stereotypical of the "working poor" in ancient times.

These two excerpts can be used for urban day laborers because in both literary contexts Lucian is painting an exceptionally bleak picture of a poor working man. It probably does not reflect the life of craftsmen but of laborers whose employment would have been intermittent, and in Micyllus's case more intermittent than usual. Micyllus claims that he did not even have one obol to pay his fare to Charon.[119]

In one of Dio Chrysostom's orations praising poverty he attempts to demonstrate how poverty in the life of a farmer, hunter, and shepherd was not a "hopeless impediment to a life and existence befitting free men who are willing to work with their hands."[120] Leaving the rural poor, he turns to the poor who lived in any city in the Greco-Roman world and contrasts them with men who lent money at excessive rates of interest and owned large tenement houses, ships, and many slaves.

> For the poor of this type suitable work may perhaps be hard to find in the cities, and will need to be supplemented by outside resources when they have to pay house-rent and buy everything they get, not merely clothes, household belongings, and food, but even wood to supply the daily need for fire, and even odd sticks, leaves, or other most trifling thing they need at any time, and when they are compelled to pay money for everything but water, since everything is kept under lock and key, and nothing is exposed to the public except, of course, the many expensive things for sale. It will perhaps seem hard for men to subsist under such conditions who have no other possession than their own bodies, especially as we do not advise them to take any kind of work that offers or all kinds indiscriminately from which it is possible to make some money.[121]

See Lucian, *Nec.* 17, LCL 4.103, and *Phaed.*, 1.14.1, LCL 343, in which cobblers are so depicted.

[119] That these two excerpts are exaggerated is seen in another of Lucian's dialogues, *Gall.* 22, LCL 2.217. The same Micyllus is described a little more positively. After he finishes his job, in the evening he receives his seven obols (very slightly over one drachma), buys some food, and then relaxes, having a good time. It should be remembered that a cobbler in Tarsus was not as debased as the "linen-workers" and was admitted freely into the assembly. So cobblers may have been stereotypical of the "working poor" in ancient times. See Lucian, *Nec.* 17, LCL 4.103, and *Phaed.*, 1.14.1, LCL 343, in which cobblers are so depicted.

[120] Dio Chrysostom, *Or.* 7.103, trans. Cohoon, LCL 1.43.

[121] Ibid., 7.105–7, trans. Cohoon, LCL 1.345–47. This speech may have been delivered in Rome, a city in which there were more free laborers than in other cities (cf. Ste. Croix, *Class Struggle,* 192). But it is noteworthy that Dio talks about cities (plural) as if to say that these conditions existed everywhere. Dio was well travelled and observed the poor in other cities.

When Dio states that some kinds of work are unsuitable, he is speaking as an elitist. He discourages jobs that are injurious to the body, sedentary, and inactive.[122] The poor, however, who were willing to work—the "respectable poor" (κομψοὺς πένητας, *kompsous penētas*)—would have gladly taken any odd job that might come their way.[123] He decides against banishing them into the country to live as rustics, a proposal that was realistically not out of the question because it would foster a life that would not be unsuitable for them.[124] Instead, he counsels them to take jobs that are not unbecoming, that is, those that do not injure health by inducing diseases or weaknesses. Jobs that are "becoming" are handcrafts of all kinds (those of artisans, in effect).[125] Seeing them work at these kinds of jobs, the rich, says Dio, would have to stop referring to them as the "poor class" (ἄπορος, *aporos*) and stop sneering at them.[126] Of course, Dio is merely theorizing about the availability of such employment for so many unemployed workers. In real life, jobs were not easy to find, as he himself notes in the first sentence of the excerpt.

In Plutarch's essay "The Education of Children" he offers advice on how to educate the children of the rich. He interrupts himself, however, because he imagines an objection.

> What is this? You, who have promised to give directions in regard to the education of free-born children, are now evidently disregarding the education of the poor children of the common people [τῆς μὲν τῶν πενήτων καὶ δημοτικῶν ἀγωγῆς, *tēs men tōn penētōn kai demotikōn agōgēs*], and you acknowledge that you are offering your suggestions for the rich only.[127]

Plutarch's reply is, first, that the poor should lay the blame not on him but on fortune and, second, that "they should avail themselves of that which is within their means."[128] This shows that the poor children of common people did not receive a proper education. But Plutarch quickly moves the discussion forward because it is being "burdened" with this matter of educating poor children.[129] In another essay Plutarch relates that poor men do not educate (τρέφουσι, *trephousi*) their children because they fear that this would

---

[122] Ibid., 7.110, LCL 1.347–49.
[123] Ibid., 7.107, LCL 1.345–47.
[124] Ibid., 7.107–8, LCL 1.345–47.
[125] Ibid., 7.107–24, LCL 1.345–59.
[126] Ibid., 7.113, LCL 1.349.
[127] Plutarch, *Mor.* 58E, trans. Babbitt, LCL 1.39–41.
[128] Ibid., trans. Babbitt.
[129] Ibid.

reveal their impoverished condition and that, as a result, the children will grow up "servile and boorish and destitute of all virtues."[130] Though Plutarch's conclusion about why the poor do not educate their children is only a deduction based on his observations, it may not be wholly inaccurate. His conclusion that poor people do not formally educate their children or perhaps do not even make an attempt to do this reflects not only his upper-class perspective but also historical reality. Throughout the Greek East children of poor commoners, such as urban day laborers, did not receive an adequate education, if at all, if only because they could not afford it.

To determine the weak purchasing power of a laborer's daily wage, about one denarius,[131] scholars usually rely on one commodity, wheat.[132] Grains, however, could fluctuate wildly, so the time and location need to be narrowed down. There are some revealing data from Pisidian Antioch, a city that will be used to exemplify other cities in Asia Minor.

From an inscription it is known that "in the reign of Domitian [81–96 C.E.] the governor of Galatia was asked to intervene"[133] at Pisidian Antioch because, during a famine, the landowners withheld the grain in order to inflate the prices. The governor demanded that they desist from profiteering and turn the grain over to the city. During his investigation the governor discovered that the normal price for a *modius* (one peck, or 8.75 liters) was about half a denarius or a little more.[134] Half a denarius will be used in our calculations.[135] (Under conditions of a famine it was one denarius.)

It has been calculated that a rural worker and, presumably, a hardworking urban laborer, needed about twenty-five hundred calories daily, which works out to about one liter of wheat.[136] Most city

---

[130] Ibid., 497E, trans. Hembold, LCL 6.357.

[131] Finley, *Ancient Economy,* 80; MacMullen, *Roman Social Relations,* 89; and Ste. Croix, *Class Struggle,* 129. MacMullen says a senator had a minimum monetary worth 250,000 times the wage of a laborer, and Ste. Croix says a senator needed HS 1 million. (HS is an abbreviation for sesterces, and 4 HS = 1 denarius).

[132] Jones, *Roman Economy,* 192; and Finley, *Ancient Economy,* 178, both agree with using grain as the test case.

[133] Jones, *Roman Economy,* 192–93.

[134] For further discussion of the difference between Palestine and Pisidian Antioch, see Arlandson, " 'Fall and Rise,' " 162 n. 102.

[135] D. Rathbone, "The Grain Trade and Grain Shortages in the Hellenistic East," in *Trade and Famine in Classical Antiquity* (ed. P. Garnsey and C. Whittaker; Cambridge: Cambridge Philological Society, 1983) 46–47, states that the price of wheat was usually two times that of barley but wheat has 35 percent greater nutritional value. For Palestine see Sperber, "Costs," 257–58, who agrees with Garnsey and Whittaker.

[136] Oakman, *Questions,* 58–61.

dwellers, however, had families, so for the sake of our scenario it is assumed that a family of city dwellers consisted of four members.[137] Therefore, he had to buy four liters of grain per day, and at half a denarius per *modius* of 8.75 liters, this cost works out to a little under 25 percent of his daily wage on his daily bread if the crops supplying the city yielded sufficiently—that is, if there were no famines or shortages, not infrequent in Asia Minor,[138] and no subsequent price increase; if the employers did not withhold wages; and if landowners in collusion with the ἀγορανόμος (controller of the market), another ruler, did not artificially inflate prices. The rest of the money had to be channeled to other foods, such as oil and pulses, and to other expenditures, such as clothing, sandals, household items, and rent.

Viewed superficially and somewhat anachronistically, 25 percent of a daily income spent on one item of food would not have been intolerable, although not pleasant. But unemployment must also be factored in. If a laborer worked 225 days—a generous amount, since his yearly wage would then equal that of a private in the Roman army—[139] because he found steady employment and did not succumb to sickness or get injured, then he was unemployed 38 percent of the year and would have to stretch the denarius that much further.

It is at this point that the woman played an important economic role. She would try by any means to contribute to the home education of her children, an inadequate one at best. And she would supplement the income by, say, weaving clothes for her household and selling the very small surplus. Women were excluded from construction and mines and from burden-bearing and barge work, but a few managed to find some wet-nursing and light odd jobs, such as cleaning. In the lengthy passage in Dio Chrysostom's seventh oration cited earlier (p. 94), a woman is said to have worked as a hired servant, a harvester of grapes, and a wet-nurse: "His [a working man's; ἐργάτης, *ergatēs*] mother was on occasion someone's hired servant or a harvester of grapes, or was a paid wet-nurse for a motherless child or a rich man's."[140] This shows that women migrated back and forth from country to city, depending on where they could make a little money. This mobility could never have fostered a stable family life. But their destiny, like that of the rural female day laborers, was tied together with their husband's. If the men could not find work, then the women suffered too.

---

[137] P. Brunt, *Social Conflicts in the Roman Republic* (London: Chatto & Windus, 1971) 35.

[138] Magie, *Roman Rule*, 1.581.

[139] For further discussion, see Arlandson, " 'Fall and Rise,' " 164 n. 107.

[140] Dio Chrysostom, *Or.* 7.114, trans. Cohoon, LCL 1.349–51.

To sum up, the most deprived group of working people was the day laborers. They enjoyed very little security in their family life. When a person's efforts and income were entirely devoted to just surviving, then he or she could never expect to see a better day. These people never escaped from merely subsisting day-to-day, wondering how long the job would last or when they would be forced to migrate into the country to harvest or into another city that had just embarked on a building program.[141] Social mobility for them was downward into the expendables. This picture reflects the laborers' wealth and political power: none. They were utterly dependent on the rulers and other property owners. Their status was no better; they lived humiliated lives. "It was as low as it could be, only a little above that of a slave, in fact."[142]

Slaves.   In the last chapter it was pointed out that slaves occupied every corner of the Greco-Roman world, even though they had the lowest status of any class. During the imperial period freedmen's sons advanced to the equestrian and even senatorial orders.[143] The most humble slave attached to a wealthy οἶκος had his basic needs met, whereas, say, a free day laborer or peasant, while theoretically having higher legal status, had to "work like a slave" just to survive from day to day. Even slaves working in the shops or fields next to the day laborers had a better daily life because the owners had an investment in them and took care of them, at least better than many laborers could care for themselves. Free but poor people had few dealings with aristocrats, so they never had access to wealth, as did, for example, slave estate managers. Nor had they the opportunity to advance into higher classes; their life was especially static. A few slaves found access to great power and wealth and took advantage of them and rapidly moved up. Josephus illustrates an extreme example of a sudden change in the rotating wheel of fortune (or misfortune).[144]

Pheroras was the younger brother of Herod the Great; to him Herod offered the honor of a wife from the royal family. But he degraded himself by marrying one of his slave girls, a δούλη, doulē, whom Josephus does not mention by name as if out of contempt for her and her kind. (Josephus calls Pheroras, however, Herod's lovesick brother.)[145] With her newfound power she, her mother, her sister, and

---

[141] Jones, *The Greek City,* 268–69, paints a grim picture.

[142] Ste. Croix, *Class Struggle,* 199–200.

[143] P. R. C. Weaver, "Social Mobility in the Early Roman Empire: The Evidence of Imperial Freedmen and Slaves," in *Studies in Ancient Society* (ed. M. I. Finley; Boston: Routledge & Kegan Paul, 1974) 121–23.

[144] Josephus, *J.W.* 1.484, LCL 2.229–31; cf., *Ant.* 16.194–96, LCL 8.287.

[145] Josephus, *J.W.* 1.484, LCL 2.229–31.

the mother of Antipater, Doris, one of Herod's wives, began to domi-
nate the other women, slave and free, in the οἶκος.[146] Most of the
other powerful women hated her and tried to charge her with sordid
misdeeds. Herod eventually banished Pheroras and his slave wife
from his realm. When Pheroras died later on, some eunuchs accused
the widow of poisoning him. Herod then believed, because of some
other evidence, that there was a plot against himself as well. To get to
the bottom of Pheroras's poisoning and of the plot against himself,
Herod tortured other slave girls from the group to which Pheroras's
wife had belonged.[147] Pheroras's wife attempted suicide by throwing
herself off a building but survived the fall. Herod called her in to
question her, and after she was restored, she confessed to the plot to
kill Herod but not to poisoning Pheroras. She went on to say that on
his deathbed Pheroras had renounced the plot and requested that the
poison be poured out in his presence, which she did. Soon afterwards, he expired. Josephus quickly turns the narrative away from
Pheroras's widow towards one of Herod's enemies, so it is not known
to Josephus's readers how her life turned out. But since Herod
despised her, notwithstanding his promise of immunity if she told
the truth—and she did—she did not live happily ever after.[148] Though
Josephus can exaggerate, this story illustrates a humble slave girl
rising from obscurity without legal status to a woman wielding much
power and finally falling back into oblivion.

This soap-operatic story, however, does not represent the harsh
realities common female slaves encountered. These hardships were
manifested in three areas of their sexuality: they were used for
breeding; this caused some women to abort; and when they did not
abort, they were put at risk while giving birth. There is a lot of
evidence that during the Republic and Principate some female slaves
were encouraged to breed in order to make the male slaves more
stable and to allow the owners to increase their profits by selling the
children or by not having to pay the costs of importing slaves.[149]
Slave breeding was a dangerous enterprise for women, since infant
and maternal mortality rates were high. In one of Dio Chrysostom's
imaginary dialogues, he matter-of-factly reminds his audience that it

---

[146] Ibid., 1.568, LCL 2.271.

[147] Free people could be tortured openly with probable cause, as were
the free women (ibid., 1.405, LCL 2.231) right along with the slaves. In secret,
however, free people could be tortured at any time. See Cicero's prosecution
of Verres, *Ver.* 5.63.163–65, LCL 2.647–51.

[148] Josephus, *Ant.* 17.71–78, LCL 8.405–9.

[149] Ste. Croix, *Class Struggle,* 229–39. Finley, *Ancient Economy,* 86,
agrees with Ste. Croix.

was commonplace for slaveowners to sleep with their female slaves.[150] If conception occurred from these liaisons, women were likely to abort so that they did not have to bear the burden of rearing children.[151] Religious convictions and doctors in Asia Minor condemned abortion, but women, not just slave women, did it anyway.[152] Callirhoe, the heroine of Chariton's novel, inwardly debated over whether to let the child in her womb live and grow up as a menial slave or to destroy it by abortion, thereby sparing it the wretched life of a slave.[153] She opted to keep it after having a dream in which her husband, Chaereas, appeared and exhorted her to keep it. These three unpleasant realia of slave women's life demonstrate not only that they lived miserably but also that just because a few slaves had access to wealth and power, it did not mean that all had this access. Exceptions only substantiate the rule.

Dio offers a revealing glimpse into the practice of brothel keepers and into the feelings of the women and children who were forced to become prostitutes:

> They must not take hapless women or children, captured in war or else purchased with money, and expose them for shameful ends in dirty booths which are flaunted before the eyes in every part of the city, at the doors of the houses of magistrates and in market-places, near government buildings and temples, in the midst of all that is holiest. Neither barbarian women, I say, nor Greeks . . . shall they put in such shameful constraint, doing a much more evil and unclean business than breeders of horses and of asses carry on, not mating beasts with beasts where both are willing and feel no shame, but mating human beings that do feel shame [αἰσχυνομένοις, aischynomenois] and revulsion [ἄκουσιν, akousin], with lecherous and dissolute men in an ineffectual and fruitless physical union that breeds destruction rather than life.[154]

In this passage slave women and slave children, according to Dio, feel a sense of shame and revulsion or unwillingness at engaging in this practice. There should be no trace of doubt about the accuracy of Dio's observation. It would have been far better for these women and children if they had been sold into the homes of the wealthy rather than picked up by brothel keepers.

But even in the homes of the wealthy, slaves were not completely free from abuse. In one of his innumerable comparisons ("just

---

[150] Dio Chrysostom, *Or.* 15.4–7, LCL 2.147–49.
[151] Ibid., 15.8.
[152] Vatin, *Recherches,* 235.
[153] Chariton 2.9, *CAGN* 46–47.
[154] Dio Chrysostom, *Or.* 7.133–34, LCL 1.363.

as . . . so," "this is like that") Plutarch observes that Epicurus and a certain Metrodorus, taking the position that escape from evil is "the reality and upper limit of the good," are like "slaves or prisoners released from their confinement, overjoyed to be anointed and bathed after cruel usage and the flogging."[155] Plutarch takes this treatment of slaves—who surely include females—for granted and assumes his readers would do the same. This does not even take into account the sexual abuse of slave children. In another essay Plutarch, through the ancient laws of Solon, encourages slaveowners not "to make love to slave-boys" because it is not "gentlemanly" or "urbane."[156] The concern is not for the children but for the reputation of slaveowners.

In Jewish society Gentile female slaves fared no better. Judging by the treatment of slaves in Palestine, many Jewish masters, from the time of Ezra to the Mishnaic period, took advantage of slave women sexually, since they were regarded as chattel or real estate.[157] The Jewish slave girl de jure could be treated better because, if sexual union occurred, either she was to become the slave wife of the master or of his son or she was to go free. But one always has to distinguish between de jure and de facto treatment. During the Second Temple period not many objected to the institution of slavery. Only the author of *Jubilees* (11:2), the Essenes, and the Therapeutae, according to Philo,[158] objected to the institution, whereas Sirach (41:22) and a few traditions in the Mishnah objected only to sexual liaisons.[159] However strongly traditions may have proscribed such liaisons between masters and Gentile slave women or taken the proscriptions

---

[155] Plutarch, *Mor.* 1091E, trans. Einarson and De Lacey, LCL 14.319. (Cf. Dio Chrysostom, *Or.* 66.13.) Ste. Croix, *Class Struggle,* 48, says that abundant references in Greek literature take the flogging of slaves for granted. Without offering evidence, Finley, *Ancient Economy,* 67, asserts, "There have been individual slaves who had the bad luck to be treated by their owners as nothing but a possession, but I know of no society in which the slave population as a whole were looked upon in that simple way." Though Finley does not offer evidence (unlike Ste. Croix), Finley's observation can serve as a balance.

[156] Plutarch *Mor.* 751B, trans. Helmbold, LCL 9.319.

[157] L. Epstein, *Sex Laws and Customs in Judaism* (American Academy of Jewish Research, 1948; reprint, New York: Ktav, 1967) 173–78. According to my brief survey of the scholarship, Epstein is one of the few who writes about this unpleasant aspect of slavery. Stern, "Aspects of Jewish Society," 628, says that slaves were in the categories of chattel and real estate. Safrai, "Home and Family," 749, briefly notes that slaves were used sexually.

[158] Philo, *Prob.* 79, on the Essenes; *Contempl.* 70, on the Therapeutae; both are cited in Stern, "Aspects of Jewish Society," 626.

[159] Cited in Epstein, *Sex Laws,* 174–77. He is referring to *m. Yebam.* 2.8, Danby 220; and *m. Tem.* 6.2, Danby 560–61.

for granted, "slave owners did not take them seriously. . . . Promiscuity was too much ingrained within the institution of slavery to be easily eradicated."[160] Many foundlings probably came from such unions.[161]

In *3 Baruch,* the Greek version of the apocryphal *Apocalypse of Baruch* (1st to 3d c. C.E., in the Greek East), the author imagines that Baruch, the scribe of Jeremiah, is transported to the second heaven by the angel Phamael. There he sees a vision of the men who "plotted" to build the tower of Babel, and he also sees the male and female forced laborers (cf. Gen 11):

> Among them one woman was making bricks in the time of her delivery; they did not permit her to be released, but while making bricks she gave birth. And she carried her child in her cloak and continued making bricks.[162]

The story in Gen 11 does not have this scene, so it is an embellishment that could be based on the author's own observation of at least some female slaves in his days who were working at various difficult jobs. This tragic story is mentioned because it resembles the three stories of female peasants who gave birth yet continued working (see ch. 2, "Day Laborers," pp. 64–65).

To sum up, slaves occupied nearly every level in Greco-Roman society. A few had access to much wealth and power, but the vast majority lived a degraded life. Men and women, not to mention children, were often misused sexually and economically. Slave women's children belonged to their master, who would not hesitate to sell them out from under their mothers. Realizing this, some women chose abortion. The few who became wealthy and purchased their freedom should not distract us from reality. Most slave women did not live happy lives.

The Unclean and Degraded.   Overlapping greatly with the expendables, the unclean or degraded are considered such because of occupation, heredity, or disease.[163] In Jewish society the religious leaders were concerned with the problem of purity. Occupations that certain religious leaders found unacceptable or unclean include ass drivers, camel drivers, male weavers, sailors, herdsmen, tanners, bath atten-

---

[160] Epstein, *Sex Laws,* 175. Not all slaves were mistreated. See Safrai, "Home and Family," 750–51. But it is not clear whether Safrai intends Jewish slaves here. He seems to do so but then mentions Gentile slaves a little later.

[161] Jeremias, *Jerusalem,* 343.

[162] *3 Bar.* 3.5, trans. Gaylord, *OTP* 1.665.

[163] Lenski, *Power,* 280–81, and Fiensy, *Social,* 164.

dants, gamblers, tax collectors, and prostitutes.[164] Moreover, if a man engaged in dung collecting, copper smelting, or tanning, some traditions said that his wife could divorce him even if she knew before the marriage that he worked in one of them. She only had to claim, "I thought that I could endure it, but now I cannot endure it."[165] This statement indicates that not only the religious leaders regarded some trades as degrading but some commoners did, too.[166]

The governing elite in all regions despised anyone, free or especially slave, who had to work at all. Farming manuals, written by Cato, Varro, or Virgil, for example, might wistfully extol the virtues of land and agriculture, but for the governing *ordines* to have to work the farms was demeaning. The common masses did not have this attitude because of economic realities. The eastern Greeks did not have the same concern for purity as did the Jewish leaders, but they nonetheless considered at least a few occupations as less than desirable, such as those of prostitutes, slave dealers, brothel keepers,[167] herdsmen, tanners, and fullers.

At first glance one might consider prostitutes, sacred or secular, as having at best a neutral status or at worse an ambiguous one in

---

[164] Jeremias, *Jerusalem,* 272, 303–12. He is referring to *m. Qidd.* 4.1, Danby 327; *m. Hor.* 3.8, Danby 466; *t. Meg.* 2.7, Neusner 2.285.

[165] Jeremias, *Jerusalem,* 308. Jeremias is referring to *m. Ketub.* 7.10, Danby 255.

[166] Sanders, *Judaism,* 460–64, has a slightly different perspective. He takes Jeremias to task for stating that the herdsmen were considered degraded. Maybe Sanders is correct, but in Palestine surely some other jobs were considered impure or less than desirable. The pagan Greco-Roman world held this view about some trades.

[167] Dio Chrysostom, *Or.* 4.96–98, LCL 1.213–15, describes a false king as being like a procurer, who trafficked in slavery and prostitution.

> So let him be a man insignificant in appearance, servile, unsleeping, never smiling, ever quarreling and fighting with someone, very much like a pander [πορνοβοσκός, *pornoboskos*] who in garb as well as in character is shameless and niggardly, dressed in a coloured mantle, the finery of one of his harlots. A foul and loathsome spirit is this, for he brings every possible insult and shame upon his own friends and comrades, or, rather, his slaves and underlings, whether he find them in the garb of private citizens or that of royalty. Or is it not plain to see that many who are called kings are only traders [κάπηλοι, *kapēloi*], tax-gatherers [τελῶναι, *telōnai*], and keepers of brothels [πορνοβοσκοί, *pornoboskoi*]? (trans. Cohoon)

Dio, an elite, would consider traders (κάπηλοι, local petty dealers) as less than desirable members of the community. Lucian, *Nec.* 11, LCL 4.91, lumps together adulterers, procurers [πορνοβοσκοί], and tax collectors [τελῶναι].

Asia Minor.[168] (Their status in Palestine is clear.)[169] But when their daily life is analyzed a little more closely, it was not glamorous; nor did people of that era think it was.[170] The long passage from Dio Chrysostom's speech cited earlier (p. 100) revealed that slaves who were turned into prostitutes felt shame and revulsion and were unwilling to ply their trade. Thus, their "career" choice was not their own. Many of them came from sorry ranks: they were exposed as infants or sold into slavery. The majority of the exposed infants were females because the expense of providing a girl's dowry was prohibitive for a poor family. In Longus's novel *Daphnis and Chloe* (ca. 2d c. C.E., the Greek East), two city dwellers exposed their two children, one male, the other female.[171] The male child was exposed because the father already had a large enough family, the female because the father was poor. The latter had lost his fortune to liturgies for the state. On the infrequent chance that these infants were found, they were destined to work as prostitutes or slaves or both. Any children conceived in prostitutes' line of work belonged to their master as property. He could take the newborns and sell them into slavery, or the girls might be kept for work in the brothel. They could never become legitimate wives, which was very important for women in order to be productive (and reproductive) in ancient society. Perhaps the only highlight of their daily life was the money they earned. An indication of their wealth is seen in a tariff inscription from Coptos in Roman Egypt in 90 C.E. stating that the passport fee for prostitutes was 108 drachmas while for other women it was only 20 drachmas. The reason for the disparity indicates not so much a direct tax on immorality as the economic power of prostitutes. But this last statement should not mislead us into thinking that people were neutral about the profession. It is possible to take advantage of prostitutes' services and tax their income while despising their trade.

Strabo offers a clue on the status of prostitutes and brothel keepers. The following anecdotes are legends, so our attention will be turned towards Strabo's attitude as revealing a prostitute's status.

The first is a story he had heard from the locals in Carura, a village in Asia Minor on the Maeander River just west of Antiocheia and

---

[168] I omit any discussion of the ἑταίρα, *etaira*, who far exceeds the few prostitutes mentioned in Luke–Acts. For a discussion of this powerful and wealthy woman, see Pomeroy, *Goddesses*, 89–92.

[169] See Epstein, *Sex Laws*, 152–78, for a discussion of a prostitute's status in Palestine. She was not highly regarded.

[170] The sketch that follows depends heavily on Pomeroy, *Goddesses*, 140–41. Pomeroy is surveying the Hellenistic period, but there is little doubt that her survey can be applied to the Greco-Roman world.

[171] Longus, 4.22–36, trans. Gill, *CAGN* 342–47.

northeast of Laodicea.[172] This region was subject to frequent earthquakes. One day, a brothel keeper and his troupe of women took lodging in one of the inns. On that very night, Strabo was matter-of-factly told, an earthquake opened up the ground below the inn, and the brothel keeper and his women disappeared. There is no hint of remorse from either the locals or Strabo over the fate of the brothel keeper and his bevy. Ancients liked telling such stories, and no doubt they had selected a particularly ugly profession for the object of a natural disaster.

Strabo illustrates that even sacred prostitutes, specifically those dedicated to the Armenian goddess Anaïtis, could never become legitimate wives.[173] That people dedicated these male and female slaves to a deity was not remarkable, he says. What he found shocking was that men of means dedicated their virgin daughters "first to be prostituted in the temple of the goddess for a long time and after this to be given in marriage."[174] He further cites a startling story from Herodotus, who said that every woman from Lydia engaged in prostitution.

Thus, if his shock at these stories reflect the attitudes not only of Strabo but also of the people, and it likely does, then it indicates that prostitution and legitimate marriage never mixed. One can be sure that a prostitute never earned high status from respectable people, even though respectable men might use her services. Aristides reflects Strabo's and most people's views when he observes, "the same conduct does not seem proper to a free woman and to a whore."[175]

The Jews were concerned with heredity. Those of questionable birth did not fit into certain communities. The blemishes ranged from slight (proselytes, freed Gentile slaves, illegitimate descendants of priests) to grave (bastards, temple slaves, the fatherless, foundlings, eunuchs, Gentile slaves, Samaritans).[176] The Greco-Roman world was also concerned with heredity. The rights, privileges, and possessions of the father were passed on to legitimate sons and daughters, ἐπίκληροι, *epiklēroi*.[177] Bastards were excluded.

The Greeks and Romans were ethnocentric as well, along with the rest of the ancient world. It is not necessary to pile on countless examples but only to state the obvious. The Romans thought themselves superior to all others; so, besides economic reasons, they easily justified conquering foreigners and despised them when the

---

[172] Strabo 12.8.17, LCL 5.513.

[173] Ibid., 11.14.14–16, LCL 5.335–41.

[174] Ibid., 11.14.16, LCL 5.341.

[175] Aristides, *Or.* 34.56, Behr 2.183.

[176] Jeremias, *Jerusalem,* 317–58.

[177] For a discussion of them, see Pomeroy, *Goddesses,* 60–62; and Ste. Croix, *Class Struggle,* 101–2.

foreigners overran their cities.[178] Many Greeks disdained barbarians, whose very name suggests that because they could not speak Greek but spoke gibberish ("bar, bar, bar"), they were inferior.[179] By Greek standards, the English word for foreigner would be "blabblabians."

People who were lame, blind, deaf, or leprous, four very common conditions in the Gospels, could never earn a living and participate in the ebb and flow of normal societal life. These conditions did not discriminate: they attacked men and women. If they were not born with these conditions or did not become such through injury, unclean contact, or natural causes, then another avenue of downward social mobility remained opened to people: prolonged sickness. Sickness and disease make the class of the unclean and degraded overlap with that of the expendables because people afflicted thus were never contributing and productive members of society.

Since the poor could not afford an adequate and well-rounded diet, they were subject to all sorts of diseases. That an inadequate diet caused diseases did not go unrecognized by doctors of the Mediterranean world. Galen of Pergamum (129–99 C.E.), for example, described this relationship. He used the most extreme evidence to support his claim, that of deficient diets caused by famines.

> The continuous famines throughout many of the provinces which have followed each other some years demonstrated clearly—except to utter blockheads—that unhealthy food tends to generate disease. The city-dwellers, as it was their practice to gather and store immediately after harvest corn sufficient for all the next year, lifted all the wheat together with barley and beans and lentils, and left the remainder for the rustics— that is pulses of various kinds (and a good deal even of these they took to the city). The country people during the winter finished the pulses, and so during the spring had to fall back on unhealthy foods; they ate twigs and shoots of trees and bushes, bulbs and roots of indigestible plants, they even filled themselves with wild herbs . . . or cooked fresh grass. You could see some of them at the end of the summer attacked by various ulcers springing up on the skin; these ulcers took different forms.[180]

Lurking behind the vague "city-dwellers" are the governing classes and aristocrats. They made sure that their needs were met first, even at the expense of the rural poor.

---

[178] MacMullen, *Roman Social Relations*, 58.

[179] Strabo 14.2.27, LCL 6.301. Ste. Croix, *Class Struggle*, 17, 247–49, 416–17, 509–18, discusses the notion of barbarians and their treatment by the dominant cultures.

[180] This passage is cited in Hamel, *Poverty*, 52. Hamel got it from M. P. Charlesworth, *The Roman Empire* (New York: Oxford, 1968) 48, and used Charlesworth's translation, as do I.

For Palestine, Josephus records remarkably similar effects of famine and droughts on the human body and soul.

> For in the first place, there were continual drouths, and as a result the earth was unproductive even of such fruits as it usually brought forth by itself. In the second place, because of the change of diet brought about by the lack of cereals bodily illnesses and eventually the plague prevailed, and misfortunes continually assailed them. For their lack of medical care and nourishment increased the intensity of the pestilential disease, which had begun violently enough, and the death of those who perished in this manner deprived the survivors of their courage also, because they were unable by any diligence to cope with their difficulties. And since, too, the fruits of that year were destroyed and those which had been stored up had been consumed, there was no hope of relief left, for their bad situation gradually became worse than they had expected.[181]

Though Galen's and Josephus' descriptions pertain to famines, droughts, and food shortages, their descriptions can be extended beyond them to inadequate food consumption insofar as Galen lists the foods that the very poorest would have been forced to eat with or without famines, especially during the winter.

The sick who could receive no or inadequate attention from their family flocked together at locations such as temples or shrines. In the cities of Pergamum, Ephesus, and Smyrna they spent many days and nights in the open air at the temples, for example, of Asclepius, Isis, and Sarapis, waiting for a divine visitation from the god or goddess, or treatment by a doctor, or gifts from devotees visiting the temples.182 At Epidaurus in Greece a Roman senator

---

[181] Josephus, *Ant.* 15.300–302, trans. Marcus and Wikgren, LCL 8.145. This famine occurred in 25/24 B.C.E., the thirteenth year of Herod the Great's reign.

[182] H. C. Kee, *Miracle in the Early Christian World* (New Haven: Yale, 1983) 78–104. Aristides, *Or.* 28.132, Behr 2.134, states the following about his own life:

> Even when we were stricken, we did not come to ignoble supplication of the doctors. But although, to speak by the grace of the gods, we possessed the friendship of the finest doctors, we took refuge in the temple of Asclepius, in the belief that if it was fated for us to be saved, it was better to be saved through this agency, and that if it was not possible, it was time to die.

Aristides was wealthy, so he could enjoy a friendship with "the finest doctors." The poor could never have had this friendship. For the interesting, not to mention superstitious, life of the sick among the temples, see Aristides, *Or.* 47–52, Behr 2.278–355.

named Antoninus provided a dwelling near the bath of Asclepius because "the women had no shelter in which to be delivered and the sick breathed their last in the open. . . . Here at last was a place where it was hallowed for a human being to die and a woman to be delivered."[183] If women had no shelter in which to give birth, this may indicate the homeless condition of day laborers and other urban poor, or it may indicate that women in all levels of society preferred a sanctuary in which to give birth, or both. The author of the Gospel of John depicts "a great number" of the crippled and sick gathered by the pool of Bethesda in Jerusalem waiting for an angel to stir the water so that the person who managed to jump in first would be healed (5:1–7). Forming these groups or subsocieties only reinforced their knowledge that they were not part of the larger and normal society.

According to Christian writers, another condition made people unclean: demonization. For the Greeks and other eastern peoples a woman possessed by a δαίμων, *daimōn,* or a divinity was not necessarily viewed with abhorrence. Certainly the women at Delphi and other places who spoke prophecies were not considered unclean or degraded. But for the Christians, such as Luke, any woman who came under the influence of a δαίμων needed help and rescue in the worst way. Thus, sometimes Luke assesses these people as being oppressed with an ἀκάθαρτος δαιμόνιον (usually: ἀκάθαρτος πνεῦμα), *akathartos daimonion,* or unclean spirit.

To sum up, economic necessity forced some Jews to work in degraded occupations—at least they were degraded according to the religious leaders. But there is also an indication that even commoners thought some jobs were degrading. Prostitution in Jewish society was seen as unclean, even though it existed in Palestine and must have received its business from Jews and Gentiles who lived there. Even pagans in Asia Minor thought it was unclean if it crossed over their boundaries into "normal" society. Prostitutes could never hope to fit into the larger society and lead a decent and respectable life. Finally, the sick formed a subsociety because of their uncleanness. Rejected, many gathered at religious places hoping for a divine visitation from the gods, help from the doctors, or monetary gifts from the people.

The Expendables.   Numbering 5 to 10 percent in an agrarian setting and 15 percent in an urban,[184] the expendables lived below the majority of society, in the bottom margins, and consisted of those "for

---

[183] Paus. 27.6, trans. Jones, LCL 1.395. I adapted the translation.
[184] Lenski, *Power,* 283.

whom the other members of society had little or no need."[185] They were separated off by three kinds of boundaries: economic, legal, and both. Not every corner in the Roman world was experiencing prosperity. Prosperity and poverty can coexist, and impoverished conditions throughout the Greco-Roman world spawned beggars,[186] widows and orphans without οἶκοι, *oikoi,* underemployed laborers (so Lenski),[187] and pirates and criminals (by definition outside the law); the law made some philosophers, magicians, astrologers, prophets, and diviners enemies of Rome (so MacMullen)[188] and, by extension, of its puppet governments in the Greek East and Jerusalem. But the only group that concerns us here is the widows.

We have mentioned that in one of Lucian's dialogue a certain Crobyle had a husband who died.[189] She spent some time weaving but was not able to make enough money to provide for herself and her daughter Corinna. As a result of their poverty, Corinna was forced to become a prostitute. Of course, not every female weaver was so poor that she or her daughter had to become a prostitute to survive. Lucian was possibly describing the process of a wife-turned-widow sliding down to the expendables, and her daughter to the unclean and degraded. It seems that his audience would have also accepted this slide (though perhaps not the direction the daughter's slide took) as a simple fact of life.

Widows had an ambiguous status, depending on their household. Concerning property rights, in Ephesus and on certain islands in the eastern Aegean off the coast of Asia Minor down to the second century B.C.E., the laws and customs for women, including widows, resemble the liberal ones at Gortyn on the island of Crete.[190]

---

[185] Ibid., 281.

[186] Aristides, *Or.* 28.139, Behr 2.136, notes, "But if you are a beggar and without means for daily nourishment and with your ambition fixed on two or three obols . . . " Seven obols equalled one drachma. In Jewish culture, at least Sirach did not like beggars and their lifestyle:

> My child, do not lead the life of a beggar; it is better to die than to beg. When one looks to the table of another, one's way of life cannot be considered a life. One loses self-respect with another person's food, but one who is intelligent and well instructed guards against that. In the mouth of the shameless begging is sweet, but it kindles a fire inside him. (Sir 40.28–30)

[187] Lenski, *Power,* 283.

[188] MacMullen, *Enemies,* passim. He calls enemies whom I would call expendables.

[189] Lucian, *D. Meretr.* 6.293, LCL 7.387–89.

[190] Vatin, *Recherches,* 189–90. The authority on women's property right laws in Greece and at Gortyn is Schaps, *Economic Rights,* 58–60, 84–88; so I rely on his findings and blend them with Vatin's.

Throughout Greece the father or nearest male relative (i.e., brother or paternal uncle) or even the husband or son might give a dowry to a woman.[191] In this he was acting as a κύριος who then maintained control. But at Gortyn a law was passed eliminating the "essential economic power"[192] of the κύριος over a woman's property or the inheritance she stood to receive at her father's death, if she had not already received them as her dowry. A woman could own property and was entitled to it at the end of the marriage, either by divorce or the death of her husband.[193] And when she died after her husband's death, their children inherited it. If upon her husband's death they had no children, the woman left his household. Just before his death she could even leave with a gift from him or with an increase by him of the sum of her dowry. "The purpose of the gift must have been to make the widow more attractive to a prospective husband, and to ensure that the marriage actually took place."[194] It seems, then, that in the Greek East widows retained quite a bit of control over property and possessions.

But one should be careful about what abolishing the "essential economic power" of the κύριος means. For the eastern Aegean and certain cities on the coast and inland, the power of the κύριος was not entirely eliminated when legal decisions or illegal activities were challenged.[195] The court case in which Cicero was prosecuting Decianus for stealing property from a woman who was without a legal *tutor,* or κύριος, indicates some vestige of power for the guardian (see ch. 2, "Landless Peasants," pp. 56–57). But in many cases a κύριος was only a formal "shadow" with no substantive power in making decisions, if he was involved at all (see ch. 2, "Governing Classes and Urban Elite," pp. 36–37 and ch. 3, "Landowners," pp. 70–73). In any case, as at Gortyn, a widow was amply provided for, and she retained some measure of power over her dowry and inheritance from her father when her husband died.[196]

---

[191] Schaps, *Economic Rights,* 58.

[192] Ibid., 58–59.

[193] Ibid., 86–87.

[194] Ibid., 87.

[195] Vatin, *Recherches,* 243.

[196] As evidence that laws did not become more restrictive, I include an inscription cited in Hands, *Charities,* 191, about a woman in the late second century C.E. from Termessus in the province of Pisidia. I also include this excerpt because Atalanta, a widow, exerted a considerable amount of monetary power, apparently without a κύριος. The translation is Hands's.

In the month of Soterios, the thirteenth day in the regular assembly, it was resolved by the people, on the proposal of the presiding committee;

A widow in Jewish culture had at least five choices. Leaving her husband's grave, she could (1) go into her husband's house or (2) return to her father's house.[197] In her husband's house she could support herself from his property.[198] Since the dowry was intended for the husband and his family, it had to be included in the property.[199] (3) Another means of support was the levirate marriage, in which one of the brothers of the deceased carried on his dead brother's name by taking the widow into his house and begetting children for him. The Torah, however, made provision for a brother to exempt himself (Deut 25:9). He was summoned to court and underwent a ceremony called *haliṣah*.[200] Its original purpose was for his degradation because he refused to "build up his brother's house." But in tannaitic tradition this degradation had long since disappeared and was seen as an alternative to the levirate marriage. (4) After a waiting period that lasted as long as one could detect pregnancy, a widow could remarry. Formal law and accepted custom strongly encouraged this.[201] (5) Alongside this tradition, however, should be placed another: some groups considered a widow's abstention from marriage a pious and holy act.[202] Evidently, Luke depicts Anna in this positive light (Luke 2:36–38).

---

since Atalanta, daughter of Preterabis . . . , a *widow* [my emphasis], adorned both with nobility and with a sense of what is right, and who reveals to the full the quality of a woman emulating by her exertions the accomplishments of her forefathers in the ambitious services *(philotimeisthai)* towards the city, both in expenditure of no mean kind and in advancing moneys and in public subscriptions and gifts and priesthoods, has promised in time of great corn shortage to provide an ample supply for the commons, and in fulfillment of her generous promise (φιλοτιμία, *philotimia*) she provides corn unstintingly from the month Idalianos of the present year. . . . [bronze and golden crowns are voted in her honour, a statue in a prominent place, close to the Attalus arcade].

[197] Safrai, "Home and Family," 787. He is referring to *m. Ketub.* 9.6, Danby 258; and 12.3, Danby 262.

[198] *m. Ketub.* 4.12, Danby 251. Wegner, *Chattel?* 97–113, discusses the levirate widow; on pp. 138–42, she discusses the autonomous widow.

[199] L. Epstein, *The Jewish Marriage Contract: A Study in the Status of the Woman in Jewish Law* (New York: Arno, 1973) 178–79, discusses three kinds of contracts, employed during the tannaitic days, that depended on the region: Jerusalem, Judaea, and Galilee. Economic conditions tended to favor the Judaean contract, since it favored the husband's family. If not, a widow could live for an indefinite period of time consuming the entire estate.

[200] Safrai, "Home and Family," 789.

[201] Ibid., 787.

[202] Ibid., 788–89.

Words such as "property," "estate," "rights," and "power" call to mind the aristocrats, or at least the upper-level freeholders of land. When their widows had property and possessions, they received care. But what happened to the widow who could not take refuge in any of these Greek or Jewish provisions? Most people in Palestine and the rest of the Greco-Roman world were not wealthy. Statistically, it was more likely that a woman recently widowed already lived among the lower classes. Thus, the carefully constructed laws dealing with property and estates would not apply to her, or only minimally. What is more, a skilled literary artist such as Luke could deliberately omit some information so that he might elicit the maximum sympathy from his audience for the (stereotypically) destitute widow. A primary example is the widow in Luke 21:1–4, who is there called the "poor-generous" widow. A few verses earlier Jesus denounces the scribes for devouring widows' houses. Then he observes the poor-generous widow giving money to the temple out of her poverty and praises her. Fitzmyer correctly states that Luke never says that she was elderly or sickly or had no family.[203] By this he implies that she probably was not faring badly. But he misses the key point: Luke omits these facts so that he can make his own case about the poor versus the rich under the gaze of Jesus and his kingdom. So, if historical realities do not hold widows down, then an author's literary realities will.

In summary, the expendables are those whom society rejects. If widows (and beggars and orphans) without an οἶκος, did not receive help, then they faded away into obscurity. Laws were passed in Asian and Jewish societies to protect widows, or at least give them some power, but these laws pertained to women of means. The laws were empty if women's hands were empty. Their plight was then potentially life-threatening.

MEN AND WOMEN IN LUKE–ACTS

A text that spans the Mediterranean world as Luke–Acts does—from Judea, Samaria, and Galilee to Asia Minor, Greece, Rome, and even Ethiopia—should include persons who fit within our adapted model of an advanced agrarian society. This outline[204] is a brief textual

---

[203] Fitzmyer, *Luke,* 2.1322.

[204] One of the disadvantages of an outline is that it reinforces the misleading notion of layers in society. For example, the rural day laborers are now placed above urban day laborers. But I see no alternative. This outline serves a purpose if the reader understands its limitation. For further discus-

application or filling out of our model and anticipates a more detailed analysis of women in chapters 4 and 5. It makes up the second
of the four groups and is a nearly complete picture of the men and
women in Luke–Acts.

I. GOVERNING CLASSES
   A.   Emperors: Augustus (Luke 2:1), Tiberius (Luke 3:1), Claudius (Acts
        11:28; 18:2), Nero ("Caesar," Acts 25:11, 21; 26:32; 27:24)
   B.   Senators (Luke 2:1; Acts 13:7; 18:12; 19:38)
   C.   Equestrians (Luke 3:1–2; 20:20; Acts 23:24–25, 33)
   D.   Provincial authorities (urban)
        1.   Legates: Quirinius (Luke 2:1)
        2.   Proconsuls: Sergius Paulus over Paphos (Acts 13:7); Gallio
            over Achaia (Acts 18:12); those over Asia, residing in Ephesus
            (Acts 19:38)
        3.   Kings (Luke 1:5; Acts 12:1–23), kings in general (Luke 10:24;
            14:31; 21:12; 22:25, 35), Candace (Acts 8:27)
        4.   Tetrarchs (Luke 3:1, 19; 9:7; Acts 13:1)
        5.   Prefects/Procurators: Pontius Pilate (Luke 13:1, Acts 4:27),
            Felix (Acts 23:24), Festus (Acts 24:27–26:32) (see above,
            Equestrians).
        6.   Priestly aristocracy: high priests (Luke 3:2; Acts 4:6; 5:17, 21,
            27; 7:1; 9:1; 23:2, 4, 5), Sanhedrin (15 times in Luke–Acts),
            captain of the temple (Acts 4:1; 5:24), chief priests (23 times
            in Luke–Acts), elders (11 times in Luke–Acts), ἄρχων, *ar-
            chōn* (Luke 23:13, 35; 24:20; Acts 3:17; 4:5, 8, 26; 13:27; 14:5)
        7.   Lay aristocracy: πρῶτοι, *prōtoi* (Luke 19:47) (see below,
            Urban Landowners)
        8.   The "first man" (Acts 28:7)
        9   Δῆμος (Acts 12:22), ἐκκλησία (Acts 19:32–41)
   E. Political offices (urban)
        1.   Duoviri (Acts 16:22)
        2.   Asiarchs (Acts 19:31)
        3.   Politarchs (Acts 17:6f.)
        4.   Leading men and women? (Acts 13:50; 17:4; 17:12)
        5.   Magistrates (Luke 12:58; Acts 14:5; 16:19)

II. RETAINERS AND RELIGIONISTS
   A.   Retainers
        1.   Town clerk (Acts 19:35)
        2.   Judges (Luke 11:29; 12:58; 18:2, 6; Acts 13:20; 17:34?; 18:15;
            23:25; 24:10; 25:6, 10, 17)
        3.   Assistants to magistrates (Acts 16:35, 38)
        4.   Ethiopian eunuch (Acts 8:27)

---

sion of the finer points of classifying this or that person into this or that class,
see Arlandson, " 'Fall and Rise,' " 169–72 nn. 170–91.

5. Tax farmers (Luke 3:12; 5:27, 29, 30; 7:29, 34; 15:1; 18:10, 11, 13; 19:2)
6. Military personnel: chiliarchs (ca. 18 times from Acts 21:31 to 25:23), centurions (Luke 7:2, 6; 23:47; 14 times in Acts), soldiers (17 times in Luke–Acts), guards (Luke 22:4, 52; Acts 5:23; 12:6, 19; 16:23, 25, 27, 36), of debtor's prison (Luke 12:58)
7. Estate managers (Luke 8:3; 12:42; 16:1–8)

B. Religionists (overlaps with Retainers)
1. Scribes: γραμματεύς (19 times in Luke–Acts); νομικός, nomikos (6 times in Luke)
2. Pharisees (ca. 36 times in Luke–Acts)
3. Priests
    a. Palestine (Luke 1:5; 5:14; 6:4; 10:31; 17:14; Acts 4:1; 5:24; 6:7)
    b. Lystra: priest of Zeus (Acts 14:13)
4. Levites (Luke 10:32; Acts 4:36)
5. Leaders of synagogues (Luke 8:41, 49; 13:14; Acts 13:15; 18:8, 17), synagogue attendant (Luke 4:20)

III. RURAL
A. Peasants and day laborers
1. Sower (Luke 8:5)
2. Plowman (Luke 8:61)
3. Laborers into the harvest (Luke 10:2, 7)
4. Gardener (Luke 13:6: ἀμπελουργός, ampelourgos)
5. Garden (Luke 13:19)
6. Hired men (μίσθιοι, misthioi) (Luke 15:17)
7. Unprofitable slave farmers (Luke 17:7–10)
8. Wicked tenant farmers (Luke 20:9–19)
9. Crowds (ca. 46 times in Luke)

IV. URBAN
A. Landowners
1. "Powerful" man (Luke 11:21)
2. Foolish landowner (Luke 12:16–21)
3. Master and faithful manager (Luke 12:41–46)
4. Vineyard owner (Luke 13:6–9)
5. Man buys a field (Luke 14:18)
6. Loving father's estate (Luke 15:12–32)
7. Landlord and dishonest manager (Luke 16:1–8)
8. Landlord and unprofitable slaves (Luke 17:7–10)
9. Landowner and wicked tenants (Luke 20:9–19)
10. Ananias and Sapphira (Acts 5:1–11)
11. Barnabas (Acts 4:36–37)
12. Mary (Acts 12:12)

B.   Merchants
1.   Purchase of property (Luke 14:18)
2.   Financial investments (Luke 19:12–27)
3.   Money changers (Luke 19:45–46)
4.   Lydia (Acts 16:14–15, 40)
5.   Shipowners (Acts 25:41)
6.   Cargo ships (Acts 20:13, 38; 21:2, 3, 6; 27:2–44; 28:11)
C.   Artisans
1.   Fishermen (Luke 5:5)
2.   Tabitha (Acts 9:36–42)
3.   Temple builders (Acts 17:24)
4.   Idol makers (Acts 17:29)
5.   Tentmakers (Acts 18:3)
6.   Prisca and Aquila (Acts 18:2–3)
7.   Paul in a σχολή, *scholē* (Acts 19:2–3, 9)
8.   Silversmiths (Acts 19:24)
D.   Day laborers
1.   Crowds in Jerusalem (ca. 29 times in Luke; ca. 6 times in Acts)
2.   Crowds in urban centers in Acts (ca. 17 times); i.e., unemployed rabble (Acts 17:5)

V. SLAVES
A.   δοῦλος, *doulos* (13 times in Luke; none in Acts without theological connotations)
B.   παῖς, *pais,* and παιδίσκη, *paidiskē* (8 in Luke; 2 in Acts without theological connotations)

VI. UNCLEAN AND DEGRADED
A.   Occupations
1.   Swineherds (Luke 8:34)
2.   Shepherds (Luke 2:8, 15, 18, 20)
3.   Simon the tanner (Acts 9:43)
B.   Afflictions and infirmities
1.   Sick
a.   General (ca. 21 times in Luke–Acts)
b.   Specific: fevered (Luke 4:38–39; Acts 28:8), paralytics (Luke 5:18, 24; Acts 8:7), dropsy (Luke 14:2), hemorrhaging woman (Luke 8:43–48), woman bent double (Luke 13:10–17), blind (Luke 4:18; 6:39; 7:21–22; 14:13, 21; 18:35), maimed (Luke 7:22; 14:13, 21; Acts 3:2, 11; 14:8), lepers (Luke 4:27; 5:12, 13; 7:22; 17:12), centurion's servant (Luke 7:1–10), death (Luke 8:41–42; 49–56), Tabitha (Acts 9:36–42)
2.   Demonized (ca. 30 times in Luke–Acts)
C.   Prostitutes
1.   "Sinful" woman (Luke 7:36–50)
2.   In parable of Prodigal Son (Luke 15:30)

D. Ethnic
    1. Good Samaritan (Luke 10:33)
    2. Leprous Samaritan (Luke 17:16)
    3. Samaritans (Acts 8:4–25)

VII. EXPENDABLES
   A. Widows
   B. Poor (πτωχοί, ptōchoi)
       1. Rural (general: Luke 4:18, 6:20; 7:22; 18:22)
       2. Urban (Luke 14:13, 21; 16:19–31; 19:8; 21:2, 3)
   C. Criminals and outlaws
       1. Barabbas (Luke 23:18)
       2. Crucified (κακοῦργοι, kakourgoi) (Luke 23:32)
       3. Theudas (Acts 5:36)
       4. Judas (Acts 5:37)
       5. Bandit from Egypt (Acts 21:38)
       6. Sicarii (Acts 21:38)
       7. Robbers (Luke 10:30, 36; 19:46; 22:52)

The characters in Luke–Acts easily fit into the classes described in the previous two chapters. Besides confirming Lenski's nomenclature of the classes and our own additions and adaptations, this outline reveals how important social hierarchy is to Luke. He attaches to people labels that can be overlooked today in a post–Enlightenment culture that stresses *égalité*. Or Luke describes the characters by their actions, as in the case of the business deals of landowners. But for Luke's first-century audience these epithets, titles, adjectives, and actions evoked and carried lively meaning necessary to understand his stories to their fullest.

CONCLUSION

Very generally, the graph (fig. 1) in chapter 2 depicts three overlapping levels in Greco-Roman society: (1) The thinnest sections belong mostly to the aristocracy, though on rare occasions in the aggregate a retainer or a prosperous merchant could force himself or herself into this class if he or she bought land, the major and most stable source of wealth. (2) The widest or most populous portion represents persons who lived a little above, at, or below the poverty line and who could never hope to improve their lot in life unless by extraordinary skill or luck. Therefore, it would be wrong to consider them a middle class in the modern sense. But despite their static condition or inability to move up, they were what has been called "productive and contributing" members of society because they did not suffer to the same degree as those in the classes below them. (3) The very bottom portion represents the unclean and degraded and the expendables. Overlapping greatly, they were the refuse and rejects of Greco-Roman culture. It must be emphasized, however, that these levels are not rigid layers in the geological sense. The graph attempts to show that there was a continuum of wealth, status, and power.

Despite these three levels, society was undergoing a social bifurcation between the haves and the have-nots, that is, between (a) the aristocrats in the thinnest sections of the graph and (b) people in the widest portion. (By definition those in the very bottom were always deprived.) It will be seen, however, that a literary artist, such as Luke, could play with or manipulate the bifurcation: some who would normally be placed in the widest portion were depicted as prosperous or slightly above the widest portion of the graph. Luke's manipulation of a person's social location confirms viewing people along a continuum of wealth, status, and power.

In chapter 1 it was noted that NT scholars too often see women in the Greco-Roman world as homogenous and thereby make their studies imprecise. Some assert (or at least imply) that women were uniformly oppressed or at least uniformly badly off. The source of these indiscriminate conclusions is found in the failure to separate persons according to classes. People of the ancient world did not view themselves as homogenous. Wealthy landowners would not admit most merchants into their council, rich urbanites disdained country bumpkins, peasants hated and distrusted city dwellers, and Tarsian assemblymen despised the "linen-workers," to name only a few examples.

An alternative assessment is offered: not all oppression was created equal. When oppression did rear its ugly head, as in the situations of the rural and urban day laborers or the sick and destitute, both women and men suffered. One could speculate that in the first century a widow without an adequate οἶκος, such as the poor-generous widow in Luke 21:1–4, or even a male beggar, such as the pitiful Lazarus in Luke 16:19–31, whose open wounds dogs licked, would give any-thing to enjoy for a day the oppression experienced by a wealthy female officeholder when she realized that men in her own privileged class were ahead of her in political power. Upper-level women lived far better lives than lower-level men and women (with, e.g., better food, cloth-ing, and shelter). Anachronistically speaking, one has little sympathy for a female plantation owner in the pre–Civil War Old South who might complain to her male slave about oppressive patriarchy.

Inasmuch as geography connotes politics, Palestine was more conservative than other regions in the Greek East in religious matters. Jewish women did not hold leadership positions. Still, Jewish women

among the peasantry and urban lower classes enjoyed freedom analogous to their eastern counterparts. But in all societies, upper-class
women lived better than lower-class women and men on a daily
basis. Whenever necessary, in the next two chapters attention will be
paid to geopolitical differences.

The inscriptions and literary references concerning productive
and contributing women in society represent many other women
whose records have not survived or been found, or who did not
bother to record their own existences. And in most cases, whenever
these women were mentioned in literary works, their lives were not
described as fully as they could have been. Even with this literary
suppression, the focus of this descriptive survey has zeroed in on the
meager scraps elite male authors left us, that is, on offhanded or
incidental passages about women. Paradoxically, these few and impoverished passages worked against male authors: when the men
consciously waxed eloquent about women, they tended to view them
as subservient and domestic, but in passing references the men more
accurately described women in Greco-Roman society.

Thus, according to both the surviving inscriptions and the
meager, offhanded literary references, women were engaged and
involved in every area of life. Boundaries between male and female
spheres were permeable. Percentagewise, women did not progress as
far as men, and boundaries were certainly not obliterated; but women
in their own classes were not necessarily locked indoors or barred
from the public square. Although women in the governing classes in
Asia Minor were not completely equal with men, they enjoyed much
freedom, power, and esteem; those who were shopkeepers and artisans contributed to the profit margins of the shops and small factories; and those who were peasants worked inside and outside the
house. (Likewise, it would be wrong to believe that women today in
the United States are equal with men, that wife beating no longer
occurs, that as many women as men occupy positions of power, that
women receive equal pay for equal work, and so forth.) To be sure,
some laws gave women rights, such as control over the dowry upon
the death of, or divorce from, their husbands and, for Jewish women,
the ability to appear in court without a male guardian; but most laws
in Gentile and Jewish societies favored men over women. It was still
a man's world (as, admittedly, it is today), but women were making
inroads within their own classes.

Thus, the next chapter claims that, much like their unconverted
counterparts, competent and forward-looking Christian women, such
as Lydia (Acts 16:13–15) and Dorcas (Acts 9:36–42), were not faring
badly before their conversion and would have still succeeded in their
respective enterprises without Christianity. They were not suffering

socially in the first place—surely not any more than other non-Christian women in their class. To answer how and why they converted would exceed the central thesis of this study, but the conclusion in chapter 4 offers a brief suggestion. In any case, where, according to Luke, did Christianity make—or ought to have made—the greatest social impact or change if every woman was not suffering equally before her conversion?

To understand how Christianity affected women most profoundly, one must turn to the truly oppressed: the unclean and degraded, the expendables, and the slaves. It is on this point that this study diverges from many others, simply because it makes class distinctions. In fact, the claim that Luke wants to elevate women among these oppressed classes at the expense of rich and powerful men would be strengthened if it can be shown that many women converts and disciples are not depicted in Luke–Acts as oppressed but that when the genuinely oppressed women came into their ranks, the upper classes, according to Luke's stories, had to esteem and value them. These women above all had to receive honor in the Christian communities.[205]

---

[205] This survey (and it is *only* a survey) barely scratches the surface of a vast subject. From it I am convinced that we must systematically re-evaluate all the sources—literary or papyrological or inscriptional—according to classes, a rural or urban context, geography, time frame, and so on. For example, scholarship needs to re-examine women's place in Josephus, not just according to his prescriptive statements, but in light of any inconsistent and contradictory claims; even more important, his writing must be compared with writings contemporary with him, such as the one by Strabo. How does Strabo treat Hellenistic queens and "regular" women? How does Josephus treat them, and which author is more liberal or conservative? Can we reach conclusions about women's life in the Greek East from such a comparison? To cite another example of more work that must be done, scholars should compile a resource book of all the women's inscriptions (see Epicteta and Nicerata, pp. 71–73), papyri (see Babata, pp. 57–58; 70–71) and other references in the Hellenistic and Greco-Roman periods in the Greek East; this time frame would make the book relevant to NT scholarship. The compilation should contain the original language with a facing translation, a quick introduction of the date and region, and perhaps brief notes serving as a commentary. Accomplishing this task would involve searching through all the inscriptions gathered in many volumes of many series, such as *Bulletin de correspondence hellénique* and *Supplementum Epigraphicum Graecum*. This would make the resource book rather bulky and exceed the existing books (e.g., Lefkowitz and Fant, *Women's Life*); indeed, it might reach two or more thick volumes. But its value would be priceless and therefore worth the team effort. To sum up, if these two sketchy chapters were to gain even partial acceptance, then I hope they will spur on more detailed analyses and studies of women's daily life in the Greek East and during the period bearing on the NT.

"I told you," Dionysius said,
looking away at Leonas,
"that she is not a slave.
I predict that she is εὐγενής. "[1]

4

WOMEN AND CLASS IN LUKE–ACTS

WOMEN AND THE KINGDOM OF GOD

Before examining women's class location in Luke–Acts, we should complete the intermediary step of clarifying women's location relative to the kingdom of God, one of the major themes in Luke–Acts, if not the major theme. This step is important because it shows the kinds of women who can or cannot receive the kingdom or be favored by it.

The advancement of the kingdom is manifested in the words and works of Jesus in the Gospel and the words and works of the church in Acts. Every time the kingdom is preached, or deliverance or healing occurs in either book, there is a response of some kind; the kingdom by its nature evokes a reaction. It is possible to classify women in two categories based on their interactions with the kingdom: (1) those who receive it or are favored by it, and (2) those who are resistant to it or are not favored by it.[2]

---

[1] Chariton 2.5.6 (my translation) (see *CAGN* 43). Dionysius, the first man of Miletus, is reprimanding his slave Leonas for thinking that Callirhoe was a slave. From her beauty and demeanor, Dionysius believes that anyone could have detected her noble origins.

[2] My interpretation of the kingdom of God in Luke–Acts is a sociological one in its simplest form. When Jesus and the apostles teach on the kingdom and do its works, they are instilling its values, norms, ethics, and even

It is also possible to classify female characters on a completely different basis, namely, whether they are portrayed (1) as historical persons or (2) as characters in the sayings of Jesus or in the speeches of the apostles. The women in the second classification appear to reflect the prosopography of the Greco-Roman world and pose no problem of historical credibility beyond that posed by the sayings of Jesus and the speeches of the apostles as such. The format of two columns is designed not to make comparisons between the Gospel and Acts but is for convenience; the women are listed in their order of appearance in Luke–Acts.

Women Receptive to or Favored by the Kingdom of God

Luke	Acts
Elizabeth 1:5–7, 24–25, 39–80	Mary 1:14
Mary 1:27–36; 2:41–51; 8:19–21	Praying disciples 1:14
Anna 2:36–38	At Pentecost 2:4
Simon's mother-in-law 4:38–39	Jerusalem disciples 5:14
Grieving widow 7:11–17	Hellenistic widows 6:1–7
"Sinful" woman 7:36–50	Hebrew widows 6:1–7
Healed and delivered disciples 8:2	Persecuted 8:3
Mary Magdalene 8:2; 24:10	Samaritans 8:12
Joanna 8:3	Persecuted 9:2
Susanna 8:3	Tabitha 9:36–42
Financial contributors 8:3	Widows 9:39–41
Jairus's daughter 8:41–42; 49–56	Mary 12:12
Hemorrhaging woman 8:43–48	Rhoda 12:13–15
Mary 10:38–42	Timothy's mother 16:1
Martha 10:38–42	Lydia 16:14–15, 40
Daughter of Abraham 13:10–17	Pythoness slave 16:16–24
Poor-generous widow 21:1–4	Prominent Thessalonians 17:4
At crucifixion 23:27–31	Prominent Bereans 17:12
At crucifixion 23:49	Damaris 17:34
At burial 23:55	Tyrian disciples 21:5
At resurrection 24:1–8	Prisca 18:2–3, 18, 26

customs into the members of the Jesus movement and later into the adherents of the sect called the Way. Jesus and his emissaries are resocializing persons living in the Greco-Roman world with a new vision of life on earth as this life meets up with the heavenly kingdom. Resocialization is paramount for any group or faction. Done through a variety of ways (codification of rules, parables, myths, hero legends, modeling in-group behavior and curtailing out-group behavior, and even miracles and the outpouring of the Holy Spirit), it produces boundaries and differentiates "us" from "them." For further analysis of a social interpretation of the kingdom of God, see G. Lohfink, *Jesus and Community,* trans. J. P. Galvin (Philadelphia Fortress, 1984). For a survey of other interpretations of the kingdom and a bibliography, see D. C. Duling, "The Kingdom of God," *ABD,* 4.49–69.

Mary, mother of James 24:10

Reporters of resurrection 24:9–11

Philip's daughters 21:9

Paul's sister 23:16

Women in Sayings

Widow of Zarephath 4:25–26

Doers of the word 8:21

Queen of South 11:31

Beaten slaves 12:45

Οἶκος divided[3] 12:52–53

Baker 13:21

Οἶκος divided 14:26

Woman and lost coin 15:8–10

Divorcees[4] 16:18

One grinding grain 17:35

Persistent widow 18:1–8

Honor your mother 18:20

Οἶκος divided 18:29

Widow in levirate marriages 20:28–40

Widows 20:47

Οἶκος divided 21:16

Persecuted 21:23

Reporters of resurrection 24:22–23

  (cf. 24:9–11)

Women in Speeches

Prophetic disciples 2:17–18

Persecuted disciples 22:4 (cf. 8:2; 9:3)

---

[3] The four οἶκοι have divisions in them, so some members opposed the gospel of the kingdom. They should also be placed on the outside of the kingdom. Schüssler Fiorenza, *In Memory,* 145–46, reports that in Luke 14:26 and 18:29b wives are said to be on the list of persons left behind by Jesus' followers, whereas Mark and Matthew omit them. She draws this conclusion: "Thus, Luke presents the only textual basis for assuming that the Jesus movement was a charismatic movement of wandering men. . . . By not including the wife among those left behind, the Q and pre-Markan traditions do not restrict entrance into the radical discipleship of Jesus to men." This conclusion is misleading because it overlooks Luke 8:2–3. In these two verses Luke shows, demonstrates—in a way Matthew and Mark do not—that women are radical followers. Therefore, far from restricting women, Luke improves (in the sense of expanding) the earlier tradition by making women in 8:2–3 live out radical discipleship. Now, men *and* women can leave their homes. Tannehill, *Narrative Unity,* 1.138, also makes this connection between 8:2–3 and the οἶκοι pericopes.

[4] Divorcees are numbered among those whom the kingdom favors because when Jesus makes the pronouncement that divorce and remarriage constitute adultery, he is protecting the women who potentially would have been abandoned without an οἶκος. There is the well-known debate between Hillel and Shammai. Hillel was more liberal in his interpretation of the law and allowed for divorce, whereas Shammai was stricter. That Jesus followed Shammai on this matter is not surprising when we consider the social protection of the woman. Also, if a peasant or day laborer had to take back his divorced daughter, then life became that much harder on the other members of the family, not to mention the shame placed on the woman and the family.

Women Resistant to or Not Favored by the Kingdom of God

Luke	Acts
Herodias 3:19	Sapphira[5] 5:1–11
Woman from crowd[6] 11:27–28	Candace[7] 8:27
Servant accusing Peter[8] 22:55–62	Prominent Antiochenes of Pisidia 13:50
	Philippians[9] 16:13
	Drusilla 24:24
Women in Sayings	Bernice 25:23
Newlywed 14:20	
Prostitutes 15:30	
Women in Noah's days 17:27	
Lot's wife 17:32	
One grinding grain 17:35	

WOMEN AND STRATIFICATION IN LUKE–ACTS

Making up the third of the four groups as we move towards our target group—those women whom Luke exalts at the expense of rich and

---

[5] Sapphira is the only woman who was apparently once favored by the kingdom—she is, after all, part of the Christian community—and yet falls out of favor. That Luke intends this to be an exception is seen in his summary at the end of the tragic episode: "And a great fear came upon the whole church and upon everyone who heard this" (Acts 5:11). I am not speaking so much theologically as I am socially. She was a member of the sect called the Way and, as such, took part in its community life. There is no need to engage in the theological debate over whether or when a person may become disenfranchised from the gospel or "lose" salvation. I have placed her outside the kingdom since her life ends tragically. It should not be overlooked, however, that she who falls is wealthy, not poor. She is an example of negative equality with her husband, Ananias, because Peter did not allow her to hide behind Ananias's legal authority to control the property. For her wealth, see the data on Barnabas (Mary, mother of John Mark [pp. 138–40]). She, too, owned at least a medium-sized estate.

[6] She shouts that Jesus' mother is blessed, but Jesus contradicts her. Those who hear the word of God and obey it are blessed. There is no evidence that she remained outside the kingdom, but likewise, no evidence exists that she entered it or was favored by it. With Jesus' rebuke serving as the only clue, she is placed outside the kingdom.

[7] Regardless of later tradition, it is not clear in Acts what happened to Candace, "a hereditary title of the Ethiopian queen mothers" (Bruce, *Acts*, 226), after her (or their) eunuch returned with the gospel. Thus, she is placed outside the kingdom.

[8] It should be pointed out in her defense that she speaks the truth, whereas Peter lies. Peter was fulfilling the prophecy that he would deny Jesus (Luke 22:34), but Jesus never said that the prophecy had to be fulfilled through her.

[9] Luke never says that the Philippian women joined Lydia in her conversion and hosting of the apostles. Therefore, they are tentatively considered as ignoring the kingdom, even though they may have converted later.

powerful men—this section is a nearly complete picture of the women in Luke–Acts divided according to the stratification model. The women in the outline below are historical figures and are not found in sayings or speeches, unless noted. The women in italics either resist the kingdom or are not favored by it.

I. GOVERNING CLASSES
A. Ruling families
1. *Herodias* (Luke 3:19)
2. Queen of the South (in story) (Luke 11:31)
3. *Candace* (Acts 8:27)
4. *Drusilla* (Acts 24:24)
5. *Bernice* (Acts 25:23)
B. Prominent women
1. *Pisidian-Antiochenes* (Acts 13:50)
2. Thessalonians (Acts 17:4)
3. Bereans (Acts 17:12)

II. RETAINERS AND RELIGIONISTS
A. Retainers
1. Joanna (Luke 8:3)
2. Susanna? (Luke 8:3)
3. Jairus's daughter (Luke 8:41–42, 49–56)
B. Religionists
1. Elizabeth (Luke 1:5–7, 24–25)
2. Timothy's mother? (Acts 16:1)
3. Damaris? (Acts 17:34)
4. Philip's daughters (Acts 21:9)

III. RURAL
A. Peasants
1. Followers of Jesus (Luke 8:3)
2. *Woman from crowd* (Luke 11:27–28)
3. Baker (in story) (Luke 13:21)
4. Woman and lost coin (in story) (Luke 15:8–10)
5. Two *(One)* grinding flour (in story) (Luke 17:35)
6. Mary, mother of James (Luke 24:10)

IV. URBAN
A. Landowners
1. Mary and Martha?[10] (Luke 10:38–42)
2. *Sapphira* (Acts 5:1–11)
3. Mary, mother of John Mark (Acts 12:12)

---

[10] Because they lived in a village, Mary and Martha should not be considered urban. The emphasis here is placed on their being landowners, a subject we will discuss momentarily.

B.   Merchants
     1.   Lydia (Acts 16:14–15, 40)
     2.   *Philippian women with Lydia?* (Acts 16:13)
C.   Artisans
     1.   Mary, mother of Jesus (Luke 1:27–36; 2:41–51; 8:19–21)
     2.   Peter's mother-in-law (Luke 4:38–39)
     3.   Tabitha (Acts 9:36–42)
     4.   Prisca (Acts 18:2–3, 18, 26)
D.   Crowds
     1.   Jerusalem disciples (Acts 5:14)
     2.   Tyrian disciples (Acts 21:5)

V. SLAVES
A.   Beaten slaves (in story) (Luke 12:45)
B.   *Servant accusing Peter* (Luke 22:55–62)
C.   Rhoda (Acts 12:13–15)
D.   Pythoness (Acts 16:16–24)

VI. UNCLEAN AND DEGRADED
A.   Sick
     1.   Peter's mother-in-law (Luke 4:38–39)
     2.   Healed crowds (Luke 8:2)
     3.   Hemorrhaging woman (Luke 8:43–48)
     4.   Daughter of Jairus (Luke 8:41–42, 49–56)
     5.   Woman bent double (Luke 13:10–17)
B.   Demonized
     1.   Mary Magdalene (Luke 8:2; 24:10)
     2.   Delivered "many" (Luke 8:2)
     3.   Joanna (Luke 8:3)
     4.   Susanna (Luke 8:3)
     5.   Woman bent double (Luke 13:10–17)
     6.   Pythoness (Acts 16:16–24)
C.   Prostitutes
     1.   "Sinful" woman (Luke 7:36–50)
     2.   *In parable of Prodigal Son* (Luke 15:30)
D.   Ethnic
     1.   Samaritan converts (Acts 8:12)
     2.   Zarephathian widow (in story) (Luke 4:25–26)

VII. EXPENDABLES
A.   Widows
     1.   Anna (Luke 2:36–38)
     2.   Zarephathian (in story) (Luke 4:25–26)
     3.   Bereft of only son (Luke 7:11–17)
     4.   Persistent widow (in story) (Luke 18:1–8)
     5.   Widows with houses "devoured" (in story) (Luke 20:47)
     6.   Poor-generous (Luke 21:1–4)

7.   Hellenistic and Hebrew (Acts 6:1–7)
8.   Mourners (Acts 9:39–41)
B.   Persecuted
1.   Οἶκος divided (Luke 12:52–53; 14:26; 21:16)
2.   By army (Luke 21:23)
3.   By Saul (Acts 8:3; 9:2–3; 22:4)

Luke's narrative contains a minimum of sixty-seven women, and of them only the slaves, the unclean and degraded, and the expendables are potentially involved in a social transaction in which they are elevated at the expense of wealthy, powerful, and privileged men. Luke employs this type of transaction as part of the theme of falling and rising, which is foregrounded in the words of Simeon in Luke 2:34:

> So Simeon blessed them and said to Mary his mother, "See, this child is set for the falling and rising of many in Israel." (my translation)

Since only women coming from the lowest levels in society can fulfill this theme of rising while wealthy and powerful men fall, it stands to reason that women who are wealthy and powerful or women who, short of that, are at least productive members in society are excluded from the vertical movement. Whenever these women are paired with men and whenever the possibility emerges that they may not be excluded, then their rise and the men's fall will become shortened or ambiguous, as the rest of this chapter will show. Luke does this to preserve his theme that only women from the lowest levels of society may rise at the expense of high-level men. This confirms the findings in the previous two chapters that men and women in the slave, unclean and degraded, and expendable classes lived far worse lives than women above them. This claim that Luke excludes women living in higher social levels—though apparently obvious—represents a departure from the common view (or at least the common implication), noted in chapter 1, that all women were oppressed equally and uniformly and therefore could be candidates for rising as men fell. Luke did not see women so indiscriminately.

This exclusionary strategy, which is the focus of this chapter, can be formally stated in a hypothesis: Women who come from high levels in society or who are at least contributing and productive members of society will not undergo a striking upward movement contrasted with high-level men's downward movement. If there is a possibility of this, then the women's rise and the men's fall will become shortened or ambiguous.

Socially and literarily, Luke treats of four categories of women favored by the kingdom of God:

1. Women who are not paired with men will keep their social standing or will be elevated, if only spiritually, when they confront the blessings of the kingdom, and if only a little. They will certainly not suffer demotion. This shows that the kingdom of God does them no social damage.

2. Women who are paired with men favored or not favored by the kingdom *from approximately the same class* will keep their social position or will receive some measure of elevation over the men, if only spiritually, when they confront the blessings of the kingdom, and if only a little. The men may or may not be demoted. This shows that women in the kingdom of God are at least equal with men.

3. Women (or men) *from a higher class* will not receive further elevation at the expense of women (or men) from a lower class. If there is a possibility of this, either the women's (or men's) social standing will become ambiguous or the lower classes will triumph ultimately over the upper classes, if only spiritually in the kingdom of God. This preserves the theme of the humble rising and the proud falling, and not vice-versa.

4. Women who are paired with men *from a higher class* will receive some measure of elevation over the men, if only spiritually, when they confront the blessings of the kingdom, and if only a little. Ideally, the men should undergo a demotion. This shows that the kingdom of God will raise the women's position in the new, spiritual society even if at the expense of men.

The concepts used in these four categories will become clear when they are applied, but some are defined now: (a) *Pairing a woman with a man* means that both appear textually in close proximity and share similar features or functions, such as Anna and Simeon (Luke 2:25–35, 36–38).[11] Luke plays one off the other. (b) *A woman keeping her social standing* as she encounters the kingdom of God signifies that if, for example, Lydia the purple seller converts, no evidence exists that she ceases from being a prosperous merchant. (c) *Elevation* is the same as the rising movement in Luke 2:34. It indicates that a woman receives a blessing from the kingdom of God and its emissaries, as when Elizabeth loses the social stigma of barrenness. This, however, is only a partial fulfillment of

---

[11] D'Angelo, "Women in Luke–Acts," 443–45, discusses the meaning of male/female pairs in Luke–Acts. J. Kopas, "Jesus and Women: Luke's Gospel," *TT* 43 (1986) 192–202, says that pairs do not compare or contrast women and men but express equality. She is overlooking class structure.

the falling and rising theme because men may or may not be present in the story, or they may or may not be explicitly demoted if they are present. (d) *A woman being elevated over a man* occurs when there is evidence that the woman was equal or inferior to the man with whom she is paired in their standing in society but at the end of the story she occupies a more powerful position or receives more benefit from the kingdom or more praise from an emissary of the kingdom. An example is Prisca (Acts 18:2–3, 18, 26). Apollos is an eloquent and educated orator, but Prisca the tentmaker will end up teaching him. When, however, mitigating circumstances arise in Prisca's case and when Apollos is not explicitly said to be demoted, then this, too, is a less than adequate fulfillment of Luke 2:34; in Apollos's case, his falling movement is not clear. (e) If *the man comes from a higher class and is demoted while the woman rises* (category 4), this is the ultimate fulfillment of Luke 2:34: "the fall and rise of many." But, to repeat the hypothesis, no women in the analysis in this chapter will fit into this category. But if there is a possibility that they may, it will turn out that their rise and the men's fall become shortened or ambiguous.

To sum up, it should be clarified that the working of the kingdom of God in people is always manifested visibly, that is, socially. Society always witnesses the effects of the kingdom of God, according to Luke. Whenever Jesus or the apostles heals the sick, crowds can see the healing. Whenever Jesus confronts a religious leader with the truth, the crowds can see that the religious leader loses the battle and that Jesus gains social prestige; Luke shows this by having the people rejoice. When Saul of Tarsus converts, this sends shock waves not only into the Christian communities but also into those Jewish communities (usually the upper echelon) that resist the upstart sect called the Way. Thus, the rising and falling movements in Luke's story are both social and spiritual, as the rest of this book will demonstrate; the two coalesce. In Luke–Acts, as the social undergirds the literary and the literary assumes the social, so the social undergirds the spiritual and the spiritual assumes the social.

However, it would be wrong to take this visible social benefit too far. Women who are impoverished, healed of their diseases, or widowed do not become wealthy, nor do they advance into the ruling class, to cite extreme shifts in social standing. Rather, in the kingdom of God they receive—or ought to receive—honor and prestige from the followers of Jesus or the members of the fledgling church; humiliated women who are eligible to receive benefit from the power of the kingdom are therefore eligible to receive daily sustenance—material benefit—so that they can survive; they should become wealthy in the kindness and love shown to them by the employed and productive members in the community; they should receive honor that manifests itself in practical things. On the other side, as noted, women who are rich or at least productive members of society must not suffer social demotion, visible or otherwise. In both cases the kingdom offers blessings, not hindrances, according to Luke's writings.

Governing Classes. *Queen of the South* (Luke 11:31). Addressing a crowd, Jesus says that the queen of the South will rise up in judgment against the men (including women) of this generation because she traveled from the ends of the earth to hear Solomon, whereas the men will not listen to someone, Jesus, who is greater than Solomon. The queen of the South reaches the heights of wealth, power, and prestige, yet Jesus esteems her more highly than common people; she will judge them. This apparently contradicts the first part of category 3.

But Jesus is not emphasizing her money and political power but her ethnicity vis-à-vis the chosen people. Her low status through birth and origin (according to Jews), if it does not cancel out her wealth and power, makes them be ambiguous or drop away into the background.[12] She is a pagan without the benefit of Torah, but the people of Israel worship the true God under its direction. Furthermore, Jesus, although addressing the crowd, denounces the men (and women) of an entire generation. This includes the upper reaches of Jewish society and government as well. The queen can be paired with Jewish equivalents. Thus, the second half of category 3 applies to the queen's story.

Prominent Women (Acts 13:50; 17:4, 12). It is not clear where precisely they are situated socially. Are some of them political office holders in their own right? Are some wives of Roman decurions or Greek βουλευταί? From the same adjectives used to describe all of the groups (πρώτη, *prōtē*, and εὐσχήμων, *euschēmon*), Luke wants to signal his audience that the women come from the same class. In Chariton's novel *Chaereas and Callirhoe* Dionysius is called the "first man" (πρῶτος, *prōtos*) of Miletus, and Hermocrates is the "first man" (πρῶτος) of Syracuse, and even of Ionia and Sicily.[13] In Acts 28:7

---

[12] To forestall criticism that Luke is suppressing women, we should observe that he does the same with Naaman, the leprous Syrian commander (Luke 4:27). By stating openly that Naaman was a Syrian and a leper, Jesus calls into question the commander's ethnicity and cleanness not only as contrasted with the lepers in Israel in Naaman's time but also with the healthy Jews of Jesus' audience.

[13] Dionysius: Chariton 2.4, 5, *CAGN* 41, 43; Hermocrates: Chariton 1.1, 2.11, *CAGN* 22, 49.

Publius is also the "first man" (πρῶτος) of the island of Malta, whose father Paul heals of a fever and dysentery. All three men are extremely wealthy and powerful and enjoy the highest esteem. Because the women (and men) in Acts 13:50; 17:4, 12 are mentioned in a group, it is unclear whether they live in the same high levels as the three men who are cited alone, which denotes that the men are unique in their societies. In any case, the presence of the two adjectives πρώτη and εὐσχήμων was probably sufficient to clarify for Luke's audience that the women are wealthy landowners, since the primary source of wealth was land,[14] and that they enjoy a high measure of political power and social prestige.

The Berean women (17:12) are paired with men from their same level, but the women do not suffer demotion upon conversion at the expense of men, or vice-versa (category 2). The Thessalonian women (17:4) are not paired with men and do not undergo demotion when they convert (category 1). Both groups of women reveal that according to Luke, high levels of wealth, status, and power do not necessarily disqualify people from the kingdom. It is a question of the heart. Both rich and poor may enter or be favored by the kingdom.

On the destiny of the prominent women Luke is silent.[15] Do they enter the church assuming leadership roles? It is not unreasonable to assume that Mary (Acts 12:12) and Lydia (Acts 16:14–15, 40) are analogous models. If the poor are to receive honor in the Christian community, however, then it is better for Luke to remain silent about these women's place in the community. In fairness, he is also silent about the place of even the prominent men who convert.

The power of these women is demonstrated by the Pisidian-Antiochene women (Acts 13:50–51), who, along with men, can muster enough clout to oppose the gospel and drive the socially deprived apostles out of their region (cf. 2 Cor 4:7–12; 6:4–10). On a political level, these unconverted women temporarily prove more powerful than converted men, who are, to the women, nothing more than another wandering band of troublesome philosopher-preachers. The

---

[14] This contradicts W. A. Meeks, *The First Urban Christians: The Social World of the Apostle Paul* (New Haven: Yale, 1983) 73, that there were no landed aristocrats among the Christians.

[15] Schüssler Fiorenza, *In Memory*, 161, believes that Luke slights women's lives and ministry in Acts, a silence that she calls the "Lukan silence." Her complaint is valid up to a point. Luke is the master of ellipsis. We should not look for an historian in the Greek or Roman mold. Equal or worse omissions include the lives of the ten apostles besides Peter and John. What ever happened to Bartholomew or Thomas or Andrew? And why is Luke so terse with Peter's destiny when he has no more use for him? Peter "departed and went to another place" (Acts 12:17). Other examples of ellipsis abound.

women's wealth, power, and status are left intact. This supports the conclusion in the previous chapter that not all women were oppressed socially and that powerful women could oppress men from any level.[16] That women oppressed men illustrates best why it is imperative to divide persons up into classes. These women appear side by side with men in the public arena, making the political decision to persecute Paul and his team. Apparently, the men do not hold more power than the women, and they do not serve as the women's guardians. On the contrary, the women are mentioned first as being approached by the Jews who instigated the persecution. In this situation the leading women do not act alone, though they could if they are typical of other women in the Greek East. This confirms the findings about the governing classes in chapter 2, that wealthy women in the Greek East generally were powerful enough to participate in such decisions. If the presence of the men makes this conclusion unsettling or unconvincing, however, their presence still confirms the findings about women in the governing classes that, though powerful, they were a step behind the men within their own class.

In either case, the deprived ultimately triumph over the privileged. First, Jesus predicted that Paul would suffer persecution (Acts 9:16; cf. Luke 12:11–12; 21:23), so the women unwittingly fulfill Jesus' plan for Paul's life. Second, before leaving, the apostles accomplish their goal of establishing a Christian community (13:52). Third, they return to the city and region without incident (14:21–23). The representatives of the kingdom of God emerge in triumph, a triumph that fits into category 3.

Retainers and Religionists.   Joanna and Susanna (Luke 8:3; 24:10). Joanna was the wife of Chuza, Herod's estate manager (ἐπίτροπος, *epitropos*), and therefore had access to much money and power.[17] Susanna was probably on the same socioeconomic level as that of Joanna because retainers rarely associated closely in public with their superiors; likewise retainers did not associate publicly with underlings unless the retainer came from among the slaves, which was often the case. After all, even in long-established Christian communities,

---

[16] See Nicerata (pp. 71–73), who sued the male leaders of a city.

[17] D. Sim, "The Women Followers of Jesus: The Implications of Luke 8:1–3," *HeyJ* 30 (1989) 52–53, argues that Joanna comes from a wealthy home but is as good as poor, since women could not control financial resources. Again, his evidence is based on a generalization of women throughout the empire. Women's lives were not homogeneous and uniform. The survey in chs. 2 and 3 leads to the conclusion that wealthy women had a strong voice in financial matters. Even poor women could pocket money they earned (see ch. 3, "Merchants and Traders," p. 77).

preferential treatment threatened to discriminate between the rich and the poor (Jas 2:1–4). But the presence of Mary Magdalene and the "many" who serve argues in favor of a breakdown in class hierarchy.[18] Jesus' teachings on honoring the less fortunate was apparently taking hold. The "many" likely came from the crowds and were not wealthy. Some commentators rightly understand that women who left their home to follow an itinerant preacher were courageous.[19] This is true only if their courage is seen in their leaving home to follow an itinerant preacher and not to work. Otherwise, leaving the domestic sphere per se was normal and required no special courage. Women in a variety of classes could appear in the public domain and make decisions on their own.

Two passages indicate that Jesus can exalt these two women disciples over even the twelve. First, the word διηκόνουν, diēkonoun, encompasses a wider definition than giving. Serving is at the heart of Jesus' message. When the male disciples spark a dispute over who will be the greatest, Jesus has to remind them that the one who serves is the greatest (Luke 22:24–27). "I am among you as the one who serves [ὁ διακονῶν, ho diakonōn]" (22:27). These women, in contrast, do not have to be reminded; they simply act.[20] Second, the women reappear in the Easter narrative as believers in the resurrection, whereas the twelve doubt and call their report worthless (23:55–24:11).[21] A

---

[18] So I. H. Marshall, *The Gospel of St. Luke: A Commentary on the Greek Text* (Exeter: Paternoster, 1978) 316, and Witherington, *Women in Ministry,* 118. But A. Plummer, *A Critical and Exegetical Commentary on the Gospel according to S. Luke* (5th ed.; ICC; Edinburgh: T. & T. Clark, 1922) 216 (and Fitzmyer, *Luke,* 1.698, follows him), assumes that the many women were "persons of substance." Plummer's argument is not likely, given the economic condition of the day. Some persons of substance fit with the tone of the passage, but not many. If they were women of substance, however, then Joanna (and Susanna) can serve as their representative in the argument that follows. For opposing arguments, see Witherington, *Women in Ministry,* 118. If they are peasants, then Mary Magdalene in the next chapter will serve as their representative.

[19] Marshall, *Luke,* 317; Whitney, "Women in Luke," 201; and B. J. Malina and R. L. Rohrbaugh, *Social-Science Commentary on the Synoptic Gospels* (Minneapolis: Fortress, 1992) 334.

[20] Corley, *Private Women,* 115–17, argues that Luke does not reverse the role of the twelve with that of the women because the twelve have a special position. This is true, but Luke is not afraid of humbling the twelve when they do not walk according to the kingdom as Jesus reveals it.

[21] Corley, ibid., 114–15, points out that Peter is the first to see the resurrected Jesus (24:34); so the women are subordinated again. But it is the women who have to prod him into action (24:11–12). E. Schüssler Fiorenza, "Word, Spirit, and Power: Women in Early Christian Communities," in *Women of Spirit* (ed. R. R. Ruether and E. C. McLaughlin; New York: Simon &

problem occurs when it is realized that Joanna and perhaps Susanna are wealthy and socially powerful retainers, but the twelve are fishermen and peasants. These passages combine to make the two women from a higher class receive more esteem in the kingdom than the apparently deprived and poor twelve, a prospect that contradicts the first half of category 3.

But against this contradiction it may be argued, first, that Joanna and Susanna had been unclean and degraded by their demonic oppression and illnesses. It was the kingdom of God and its emissaries that liberated them to serve as disciples. Second, they may be slaves, as was often the case with estate managers. Their status in society may be mixed. But this is far from clear. Yet, there is a more significant possibility. Third, for reasons that refer back to Israel's twelve leaders of twelve tribes (Luke 22:30),[22] the twelve enjoy higher status with Jesus and more authority or power from him than all other male or female disciples. They are the "Christian" equivalent of prestigious and powerful men, whereas the women are a secondary corps behind them (as are all other male disciples). Of all disciples, the twelve should be the first to serve and the first to believe in the resurrection. Therefore, with these three factors, the exaltation of prominent women over lowly men is ambiguous or canceled out. Instead, it turns out that Luke exalts two women whose beginning was ambiguous over the now prestigious twelve.[23] All these ambiguities combine, however, to flatten out or shorten the vertical movement seen in Luke 2:34.

The falling and rising theme is far from clear because in the end Joanna and Susanna are never divested of, or condemned for, their wealth and power to contribute to the Jesus movement. Luke does not

---

Schuster, 1979) 52, sees Luke as downplaying the women's roles by this rebuke in v. 11. She fails to take into account the irony of the situation. The eleven are wrong, the women are right. Ergo, the eleven's unbelief is λῆρος, *lēros* (nonsense).

[22] Corley, *Private Women,* 116–17, discusses the importance of the twelve in Luke's writings.

[23] E. Schüssler Fiorenza, "Luke 13:10–17: Interpretation for Liberation and Transformation," *TD* 36 (1989) 310, believes that when Luke mentions the illness and demonic oppression of the women, he is suppressing their chance for social status. It is my argument that if he can widen the social gap between them and the twelve, then when the women triumph over them, as seen below in the next chapter (Mary Magdalene), their exaltation seems that much higher. It should be remembered that Luke could in no way dispense with the twelve even if he had so desired. Short of that, how better could he fulfill his theme in Luke 2:34 than by exalting a secondary corps of disciples—who are women—over the twelve prestigious men in the context of two important issues for Jesus: servanthood and the resurrection?

take away the wealth of the women, and the twelve are raised up, in terms of status with Jesus, more highly than the women (and other men). Luke artfully preserves the women's monetary position while maintaining his theme that the humble may rise and the privileged may fall if the latter do not take care. One has to look to other persons for the theme in Luke 2:34 to be acted out.

Jairus's Daughter (Luke 8:41–42, 49–56). Jairus's only girl, twelve years old and dying, belongs within the household of her father, who is a synagogue ruler (ἀρχισυνάγωγος). Therefore, she is not an expendable (though she is unclean) because she receives the care that a man of Jairus's status can give. Synagogue rulers enjoyed high prestige in the Jewish community and were well-off. They often had to maintain most of the upkeep on the building, which could involve considerable expense.[24] Since wealth almost always came through land, he is probably a landowner. This powerful man falls at the feet of Jesus (v. 41). As the ruler lowers himself, he becomes a beneficiary of the kingdom. When Jesus raises his daughter from the dead, he reveals that the kingdom of God favors the rich and power-ful who show humility (v. 41). Tragedy is usually an effective agent to bring about the requisite humility.

A woman hemorrhaging for twelve years (cf. the daughter's age), coming from the unclean and degraded, is paired with Jairus and his daughter because her story is interwoven in the middle of theirs. (Perhaps it is more accurate to say she is paired with the daughter.) Jesus heals the woman, and she ceases from her uncleanness and from being an expendable.[25] Paired with her, Jairus and his daughter are therefore placed in category 3, but this does not present a problem because they are not elevated over the woman as the result of his daughter's restoration. The ruler falls and rises on his own, not at the woman's expense. In effect, the synagogue ruler catches up with the woman and her kind because the rich are eligible to receive the blessing of healing if they become humble. In the kingdom of God, the woman is made equal to Jairus (and his daughter) because both

---

[24] G. Theissen, *The Social Setting of Pauline Christianity: Essays on Corinth* (trans. and ed. J. H. Schütz; Philadelphia: Fortress, 1982) 73–74. That a ruler had to maintain the building makes his responsibilities resemble those of a gymnasiarch, discussed in ch. 2, "Governing Classes and Urban Elite," pp. 34–35.

[25] Though not part of this study in ch. 4, the woman with the hemorrhage would approximately belong in category 4 because according to the standards of the heavenly society, if not the earthly society, she comes from a lower class yet is made equal to the ruler, as seen in her healing. Unlike women in category 4, however, she is not exalted at the expense of the man who also receives healing or a benefit of the kingdom.

are raised up, but neither at the expense of the other. The falling and rising theme is not fulfilled in their situation.

Elizabeth (Luke 1:5–7, 24–25, 39–80). She is descended from Aaronic lineage (1:5), so she enjoys status through birth. As the wife of a priest, her status is heightened. Both are described as "righteous in the sight of God, walking without fault in all the commandments and requirements of the Lord" (1:6). But all is not well with this esteemed couple; two problems erode this otherwise positive description. First, a priest such as Zacharias, living in a town nestled in the hill country of Judea (1:39), typically was poor.[26] He is not part of the powerful priestly families of Jerusalem. Second, Elizabeth is barren, a particularly shameful condition for a woman.

But when God breaks in through Gabriel, the poverty is assuaged because God shows that he does not favor the rich over the poor. And with this intervention, the shame of barrenness is removed (1:25). As the mother of John the Baptist, so popular with the people, Elizabeth was probably ascribed high honor. Thus, as stated for category 1, she keeps her social position with the added blessing of fertility and an honorable son.

Mother of Timothy (Acts 16:1). According to 2 Timothy 1:5, her name was Eunice, and Timothy's believing grandmother's name, incidentally, was Lois. As was true for Elizabeth and her son, Timothy's mother enjoys the privilege of having a spiritual and celebrated son. The people of Lystra and Iconium attest to his character (Acts 16:2). His mixed heritage does not detract from his popularity. But it was Eunice and Lois who instructed their son and grandson in the Scriptures, a nurturing process that gave him the opportunity to become popular and recognized as a leader (2 Tim 3:15). Because of her apparent knowledge of the Scriptures, she is placed among the religionists, though this placement is only tentative because of lack of information. The occupation of her Greek unbelieving (?)[27] father is unknown, however. F. F. Bruce, following Ramsay, makes the enticing observation that in Phrygia (and the same was true for Lycaonia) "the Jews married into the dominant families."[28] This implies that Eunice (and Timothy) is well-off, but this is only a guess. It may be assumed that she is paired with her husband and is exalted more highly than he, according to Luke's ecclesiology, because she is a believer. She fits into category 2. She is not a candidate

---

[26] Jeremias, *Jerusalem*, 108.

[27] Luke implies that he is an unbeliever, though he does not state it explicitly. It is likely that Luke would have mentioned his faith in the same breath as his wife Eunice.

[28] Bruce, *Acts of the Apostles*, 351.

for Luke 2:34 because they are in the same class and her husband is not explicitly said to fall.

Damaris (Acts 17:34). Her social location is unknowable, but Bruce is on target when he writes that "they [Dionysius and Damaris] were presumably of sufficient note for Luke to single them out by name."[29] It is not unreasonable to assume that she is at least a religionist or retainer, though she could be an aristocratic landowner. It should be remembered that religionists outside Palestine were drawn from among the wealthy. There is no evidence that she loses her status after conversion, that she lags behind the few male converts, or that she is honored above them. She is paired with Dionysius, but since neither suffers demotion or exaltation at the expense of the other, she conforms to category 2.

Four Daughters of Philip (Acts 21:9). Philip's daughters carve out a good reputation for themselves by their spiritual gifts and their famous father. Because of the daughters' connection with their father and because of their own spirituality, they are tentatively placed among the religionists. Certainly Luke depicts Philip's daughters as devout. They are not paired with anyone, so they are part of category 1.

Landowners. *Mary and Martha* (Luke 10:38–42). It is impossible to untangle the different pericopes on Mary and Martha (John 11:1–12:11; Matt 21:17?; 26:6–13?; Mark 11:11?; 14:3–9?; Luke 7:36–50 [not likely]; 10:38–42). If the anointing pericopes (Mark 14:3–9; Matt 16:6–13) and the traditions in John, Mark 11:11, Matthew 21:17, and Luke 10:38–42 contain at least a kernel of history, and they do,[30] then three indicators speak of their wealth and social location: the size of Lazarus's tomb, the size of their house, and the price of the perfume.

Evidently, Lazarus's tomb was large. Peasants and day laborers could never have afforded it. The size of their house is an ambiguous indicator because peasant houses, grouped together into insulae, had courtyards, and it is possible that Jesus and a few disciples could have been invited into the main room, while the other disciples stayed in the courtyard.[31] Matthew 26:7, 9 says that the ointment was

---

[29] Ibid., 388.

[30] It is widely believed to be methodologically unacceptable to use the Gospel of John for excavating historical tidbits. As this analysis is sociological in purpose, however, I use any clue available for locating a person socially. Besides, I see no reason to doubt John's verisimilitude. He is not utterly devoid of historical facts, any more than are explicitly fictitious stories written by Lucian or Chariton.

[31] Fiensy, *Social,* 123–32.

costly and could have been sold for a large sum; and Mark 14:5 and John 12:5 record that the ointment was worth 300 denarii. This amount is well over the yearly wage of a common, laboring peasant (ca. 200 denarii in a good year). Mary and Martha might resemble the rural and wealthy landowner Babata (minus Babata's aggressive litigations).[32] It should be recalled that Babata could not read or write, lived in a small town called Maoza on the southern shore of the Dead Sea, and therefore would not have been considered an aristocratic urbanite. Ultimately, however, no decisive evidence of Mary's and Martha's social location is available, though they appear well-off. Wherever they are to be located, they do not lose their position when they meet Jesus. The two sisters are not contrasted with men in the immediate pericope and do not lose their position in the larger society or in the spiritual society; thus they fit into category 1.

Yet, since there is some debate over whether Jesus is elevating or lowering the status of early Christian women represented in Martha and Mary, a brief discussion is in order. Schüssler Fiorenza, for example, sees the pericope as restricting women, whereas Witherington sees it as liberating them.[33]

Schüssler Fiorenza's reasoning is based on her historical reconstruction of the house-church, following her "hermeneutics of remembrance." This reconstruction juxtaposes NT patriarchy to historical realities. In the setting of the house-church, the spiritual and practical ministries of women coalesced. So when Jesus praises the silent Mary yet silences the active Martha, he is being used by later male ecclesial leaders to rob women of both halves of their power, the activity of hosting-leading *and* proclaiming.[34]

Witherington holds to the view that Jesus elevates Mary's role of being discipled by a rabbi—supposedly unheard of in Jewish culture—but artfully does not lower Martha's role of hospitality.[35] (Even if some women were in fact disciples of itinerant sages and teachers, one could still argue that women were *rarely* disciples, and that Jesus

---

[32] See ch. 2, "Landless Peasants," pp. 57–58; and ch. 3, "Landowners," pp. 70–71.

[33] E. Schüssler Fiorenza, "Theological Criteria and Historical Reconstruction: Mary and Martha: Luke 10:38–42," *Center for Hermeneutical Studies Protocol Series* 53 (1987) 1–12; and Witherington, *Women in Ministry,* 100–103.

[34] Schüssler Fiorenza, "Theological Criteria," 9.

[35] Witherington, *Women in Ministry,* 101. A. Reinhartz, "From Narrative to History: The Resurrection of Mary and Martha," in *"Women Like This": New Perspectives on Jewish Women in the Greco-Roman World* (ed. A.-J. Levine; Society of Biblical Literature; Atlanta: Scholar's, 1991) 164–66, notes that Witherington does not document his claim.

was aligning himself with those liberals who permitted women to follow them.) For men and women, continues Witherington, discipleship comes first, practical things second. "One's primary task is to be a proper disciple; only in that context can one be a proper hostess."[36] Hospitality is not eliminated or even denigrated, but sitting at the feet of Jesus is placed over it.

My view takes into account the two audiences of Luke's double work, one Jewish, the other Gentile. Jewish women hearing of Mary sitting at Jesus' feet may have been surprised, since it was indeed rare for women to do this. But Gentile women hearing of Mary would not have been surprised, since in their social experience women followed itinerant philosophers.[37] But one thing is certain: no woman would have been surprised at Martha's role. The first impulse of a hostess would have been to show hospitality as Martha does. Not surprisingly, then, Martha (and the culture) attacks Mary for sitting and neglecting the hospitality custom that was so deeply embedded in the first-century ethos. Defending Mary from Martha's (and the culture's) aggression and offering a valid alternative, Jesus protects and upholds her rare role—listening—as Jesus often commanded even of male disciples: "Mary has chosen what is better, and it shall not be taken away from her" (10:42). This statement clearly indicates Martha's aggression; if Martha had not threatened Mary's discipleship, then the competition between the two roles would never have arisen.

Witherington is therefore correct when he claims that Jesus elevates discipleship over practical things without degrading the latter. This passage is liberating and not oppressive because Jesus preserves both roles but makes discipleship take priority.[38]

Mary, Mother of John Mark (Acts 12:12). Mary was wealthy, as evidenced by her ownership of a house large enough to host church meetings: "It was a house of some size, with a gateway [πυλών, *pylōn*] on the street, from which the house proper was separated by the intervening courtyard."[39] Mary assumes a leadership role in a private

---

[36] Witherington, *Women in Ministry,* 101.

[37] I am not arguing that Jesus should be considered a wandering philosopher in the Greek sense. But his Gentile audience may have taken him as such. Corley, *Private Women,* 63–66, notes that these women were viewed stereotypically as prostitutes in their days, but this view emanates from elite male authors. It is doubtful whether "average" persons would have shared this view.

[38] Tannehill, *Narrative Unity,* 1.137, rightly points out that Mary and Martha fill out the picture of discipleship pronouncements—"those who hear and do the word of God" (8:21; 11:28)—that have women as the subject. Luke is protecting Mary's role.

[39] E. Haenchen, *The Acts of the Apostles: A Commentary* (trans. R. McL. Wilson; Philadelphia: Westminster, 1971) 385.

and public sphere, similar to women in shops. Her regular prayer meeting during "mounting opposition in Jerusalem to the Christian movement is evidence that Luke is portraying one woman's courageous contribution to the community of faith."[40] Traditionally, it was here that Jesus and the disciples ate the Last Supper and where the disciples were praying when Pentecost arrived.[41] Another tradition says that John Mark was Peter's interpreter in Rome.[42] If this is so, then this datum—a Jew (John Mark) residing in Jerusalem *and* learning Latin—means that Mary could afford a good education for her son, either by hiring a tutor or sending him to Rome for studies.

John Mark, Mary's son, was a cousin of Barnabas (Col 4:10). In Acts 4:36–37 it is revealed that Barnabas's real name was Joseph and that he was a Levite. Persons not lower than the apostles themselves gave him the nickname Barnabas, which, Luke clarifies for the Gentile members of his audience, means "son of encouragement." To receive this name meant that he was active and honored in the Christian community. He had some status in society through his Levitic lineage, and now he acquired more in the Christian community from the apostles. He was also a landowner, but he was so generous that he sold the tract and laid it at the feet of the apostles (v. 37). Undoubtedly he sold only his share of the inheritance. It is impossible to know precisely where and how big the parcel of land was, but if Barnabas's case was typical, then it was out of town and supported his living in Jerusalem. It was at least a medium-sized tract (50–315 acres)[43] because he was too active in the Christian community in Jerusalem to have owned anything smaller, which would have forced him to live outside the city and work the land from sunrise to sunset. Besides, he was a Levite, and Levites were not allowed "an inheritance" in the land (Num 18:8–13, 20–21; but cf. Neh 13:10). (Many in Palestine interpreted this as not being allowed to work the land, so they owned land instead, with retainers serving as intermediaries.)[44] If he owned property within the city, then it is impossible to find out how much it was worth. One may conjecture that it was profitable, since city-owned property was at a premium price, more so than property in a rural setting.

To sum up, Mary (with John Mark and Barnabas), an active and honored participant in the Christian community, belongs to a wealthy, land-owning family. Not contrasted with men, she maintains her

---

[40] Witherington, *Women in the Earliest Churches*, 147.
[41] Haenchen, *Acts*, 384 n. 11.
[42] Bruce, *Acts of the Apostles*, 285.
[43] Fiensy, *Social*, 23–24.
[44] Sanders, *Judaism*, 77.

position in society and the Christian community after conversion. She is therefore part of category 1.

Merchants. *Lydia* (Acts 16:14–15, 40). To any listener in the Mediterranean world of Luke's day, the Greek word πορφυρόπωλις, *porphyropōlis* (purple seller) as a description of a woman's profession would have evoked a semantic association with other words: wealth, luxury, regal clothing, highly specialized trade for an elite product.[45] Purple merchants had to be wealthy even to enter the business.[46] Purple clothing was a luxury item consumed by the rulers and the other rich in the major cities throughout the empire, especially Rome. Moving quite easily in the public sphere—though not entirely alone if the women with her at the river are her business associates—and marketing her product in competition against, presumably, men, Lydia was involved in this regal and lavish line of work. It should be recalled that Dio Chrysostom cites the case of women fabric makers who were involved in every aspect of their trade: they inspected the raw products, including purple dyes, bought them, had them transported to the workplace, made them into various garments, and sold them.[47] If the second half of Lydia's occupational epithet, "seller," did not restrict her only to merchandizing the finished product, then undoubtedly she operated in precisely the same way that these women did.

The first known convert in Europe, she is also a God-worshipper, most of whom came from among the wealthy.[48] The identity of the women accompanying Lydia is not known (Acts 16:13). They could be her slaves. It is my guess that they are God-fearers, or in the same occupation as Lydia's (since persons of the same trade associated with each other), or both. Her fate in the Christian community is seen when she hosts the apostles in her house (v. 40). She probably thereafter assumed a leadership role. Her house is the nerve center and retreat for the mission in this region. She is not contrasted with men,[49] and she keeps her position in society (category 1).

---

[45] R. Ryan, "Lydia, a Dealer in Purple Goods," *TBT* 22 (1984) 285–89, has an excellent discussion of Lydia, even though the article is written for the laity and has no references to scholarship. She covers all the main points of Lydia's life, however.

[46] See ch. 3, "Merchants."

[47] Dio Chrysostom, *Or.* 77.4, LCL 5.263–65. See ch. 3, "Merchants and Traders," p. 78.

[48] Theissen, *Social Setting,* 103. Bruce, *Acts of the Apostles,* 358, points out that "Lydia" probably means "Lydian woman" but concedes that "Lydia, however, is elsewhere attested as a personal name for women of high station as well as for slaves and freedwomen."

[49] Witherington, *Women in the Earliest Churches,* 147–48, pairs her with the jailer (16:23–39), but this is a stretch. If this is valid, however, then it is

Artisans.   Mary, Mother of Jesus (Luke 1:27–56; 2:5–52; 8:19–21).
Mary comes from Aaronic lineage (Luke 1:5, 36).[50] Her status through
bloodline is established. But this does not always translate into
wealth. Presenting Jesus in the temple for circumcision (Luke
2:21–24), Mary and Joseph offer a pair of doves or two young pigeons
for Mary's purification according to the law (Lev 12:8). According to
Leviticus, the preferred offering was a young lamb. If a woman could
not afford it, however, she could offer doves or pigeons. Evidently,
Mary and Joseph do not have enough money to buy the lamb and
have to settle for the more economical animals.

She was married to Joseph the τέχτων, *techtōn*. Usually this
word is taken to mean a carpenter, so Joseph was numbered among
the artisans.[51] This decision, for financial reasons, to sacrifice
pigeons would have been in keeping with what is known of other
artisans in the Greco-Roman world had they been required to make
a similar offering.[52] However, it is not Luke who reveals that Joseph
was an artisan, an omission for which there are two possible
reasons:

(1) The omission was not deliberate because the first and second
generation of believers already knew of Joseph's occupation. Mentioning it would have been redundant. But this is not very satisfac-
tory because when his fellow Nazarenes question Jesus' authority,
Mark 6:3 (and Matt 13:55) omits Joseph's name and refers to him as a
carpenter, whereas Luke 4:22 refers to Joseph without the occupation.[53] The omission therefore seems deliberate.

(2) A better answer lies in the emphasis placed on Jesus' priestly
and royal lineage. As noted, through Mary's family tie with Elizabeth,
a daughter of Aaron, Jesus has at least a spiritual heritage. It is almost
as if Mary should have been placed among the religionists in our

---

impossible to determine whether they belong on the same social level in terms
of their power, wealth, and status. In whichever category they belong, neither
one is exalted above the other; so the rising and falling theme is not fulfilled
with them.

[50] Fitzmyer, *Luke*, 1.344.

[51] C. C. McCown, "ὁ τέκτων," in *Studies in Early Christianity* (ed. S. J.
Case; New York: Century, 1928) 173–89, discusses what τέκτων means and
concludes that wood was the main, if not exclusive, product with which he
worked.

[52] Some decades later, Herod commenced an ambitious building program in Sepphoris, a few miles from Nazareth. It is probable that Joseph and
his family profited from the boon in the local economy. But at his birth, Jesus
came from a family of modest means.

[53] Apparently, Joseph's Davidic lineage did not impress his fellow Nazarenes. Though this option is not likely, they may not have known of it;
otherwise, they would not have sneered.

outline. Joseph comes from the royal house of David (1:27; 2:4), a fact having many prophetic ramifications for Jesus. Joseph, Mary, and Jesus have family connections with Zacharias, Elizabeth, and John the Baptist and share a common lineage. In support of this emphasis, the financial status of both families is downplayed; this further accentuates the spiritual status. In the discussion about Elizabeth and Zacharias it was noted that they come from a town in the hills of Judea (1:39) and are therefore not part of the ruling priestly families in Jerusalem. This obliquely indicates that they are not wealthy; but only an informed audience could draw this conclusion. Mary and Joseph can offer only two pigeons at Jesus' presentation in the temple, an offering that is another oblique indicator of their low financial standing; but only an informed audience could draw this conclusion also.[54] If Joseph's occupation had been stated, this would have immediately called to a first-century audience's mind financial matters and distracted them from Jesus' religious heritage. In sum, both families come from approximately the same religious and economic class, though the religious aspect is brought to the foreground in the first two chapters of the Gospel. Luke puts a religious aura about them that conforms to the supernatural atmosphere of the nativity scene.

It is difficult to assess fully the implications of the emphasis placed on Mary's religious heritage and the de-emphasis of other factors except for the obvious reason that Jesus must be seen to have come from this kind of family. But for our purposes the net result is clear. Mary is placed in category 2 because when she and Zacharias are paired together in the narrative, they start off on roughly an equal footing religiously and economically. Mary will not be exalted at the expense of a poor and irreligious commoner.

The well-known pairing occurs when Gabriel visits Mary and Zacharias with the promise of children. Mary questions the angel, and she receives no punishment (1:34–36); but Zacharias is punished for his question by being struck mute (1:19–20). This is a shameful condition for a man because he is made passive and cannot live effectively outside the house.[55] Therefore, Zacharias is humbled, while Mary is exalted. This is apparently a fulfillment of the falling

---

[54] Of course, a Jewish audience, if they had any children, would probably know about the two choices of animals, two pigeons (the more economical offering) and the lamb (the more expensive). But the allusion is still oblique for Luke's wider audience.

[55] Malina and Rohrbaugh, *Social-Science Commentary,* 284–85. While Elizabeth is rid of her shame, Zacharias takes on his own shame. But they come from the same class (category 2), so the fall and rise are shortened.

and rising theme, but the social hierarchy is missing because they come from roughly the same level in society. The upward and downward movement is not as striking as it could have been. (A woman from the slave, the unclean and degraded, or the expendable classes would have done nicely.) Nevertheless, since women in the first century had not progressed as far as men in roughly the same social levels, Mary's exaltation at Zacharias's expense should not be lightly dismissed.

Long after this episode, mitigating circumstances surface. Normally, one would expect Mary's son to garner high public status for her during his earthly ministry, but this is not necessarily the case. In Luke 8:19–21, when Jesus is informed that his mother and brothers are on the periphery of the crowds that are pressing him, he clarifies who his family is: "My mother and brothers are those who hear and do the word of God" (v. 21). And at a woman's outburst over the blessedness of being Jesus' mother (11:27), Jesus corrects her as well: "On the contrary [μενοῦν, *menoun*], blessed are those who hear and keep the word of God" (v. 28). Jesus is creating a fictive family, which expands the boundary of his real or biological family, and he is now at the head of it. The message is clear enough: a woman who joins the Jesus movement has a part in it and enjoys a position of honor if she obeys the word.

Peter's Mother-in-Law (Luke 4:38–39). This woman is placed among the artisans because of Peter's occupation. Both he and she, however, should be considered no higher than village peasants. Her story is simple. She is sick with a fever, Jesus rebukes it, and she is healed and rises to serve them, the very thing a woman of her social position would do. (A rich woman would have called in a servant.) In context, she is paired with a demonized man who is also freed from his affliction (vv. 33–37). It is unclear where he is situated socially. But he was unclean and degraded by his affliction for an unknown duration, whereas Peter's mother-in-law was sick with only a fever for a short while. She is productive in society; he is not. Still, they probably come from the same social level, the peasantry, and are raised up, but not at the expense of each other. This puts Peter's mother-in-law into category 2. Or she fits into category 3 because she comes from the peasants, and he from the unclean and degraded. But this ambiguity does not pose a problem because neither is promoted or demoted at the expense of the other; indeed, the man from the slightly lower class catches up to the woman in that his affliction is worse and yet both are restored without preferential treatment. The theme in Luke 2:34 is not pertinent here.

Tabitha (Acts 9:36–42). When the widows point out all the tunics and cloaks Tabitha made, it may be asked whether she had a small team helping her (the other widows in v. 39?), despite the explicit claim that she herself made them out of her deep charity. Otherwise, her industrious working habits produced a sizable surplus of goods. Though she did not pursue her own need above those of others according to Luke's characterization of her, it is obvious that her needs were met sufficiently so that she could afford to give many items away. One can guess that she also sold part of the surplus to those capable of buying it, thereby making a profit. If power is measured by an ability to move people and if status is ascribed by people's praise, then in the Christian community at Lydda, Tabitha enjoyed a surplus of both.

Tabitha has been paired with Aeneas, who was paralyzed for eight years (vv. 32–35).[56] Before the paralysis he may have been prominent, as indicated by the mention of his name. He and Tabitha may have come from roughly the same social level in terms of their prosperity. Otherwise, his social location is unknowable except that his affliction, making him unclean, also turned him into an expendable. Thus, Tabitha is part of category 3, since it is likely that her sickness and subsequent death did not last as long as his paralysis. But this is not a problem for our analysis of the theme in Luke 2:34, since neither is exalted at the expense of the other. Both a man and a woman are suffering yet are favored equally by the kingdom of God through its emissary, Peter. Again, the falling and rising theme is not relevant in their situation.

Prisca (Acts 18:2–3, 18, 36). According to Paul's epistles (Rom 16:5; 1 Cor 16:9), Prisca and her husband, Aquila, were another example of prosperous artisans, a rarity in the aggregate. Paul writes that she hosted a congregation in her house. Since a common artisan, even a semiskilled one, working in the shop could never have afforded a house large enough to hold a gathering of even moderate size, they were probably shop owners. It should be remembered that some mezzanine apartments had two or three "relatively large" rooms.[57] It is probable that Prisca lived in an apartment like these. According to the definition outlined in the previous chapter, that those who controlled the means of production should be regarded as merchants, Prisca and Aquila should therefore be considered merchants. Though not afraid of working with their hands, they must have overseen production and marketing. They were merchant-artisans.[58] Also, it is likely that as they offered Paul lodging (Acts

---

[56] D'Angelo, "Women in Luke–Acts," 446.

[57] Packer, *Insulae,* 7.

[58] This guess about their being merchant-artisans accounts with a little more precision for the discrepancy between their apparent wealth and average

18:3), they also offered him a job.[59] After all, Paul heard of them and went to them as if he were in need of employment (vv. 18:2–3).

Their ability to travel and immediately acquire houses out of their own means, not out of an offering from Christians, also speaks of economic independence.[60] Aquila came from Pontus in northern Asia Minor. They were in Rome when Claudius's edict forced them to leave. Paul met them in Corinth and sent greetings for them from Ephesus (1 Cor 16:19). Upon moving to Corinth and Ephesus, they had enough capital to buy or rent a large house and host a church almost immediately.

But most of the above description is not found in Acts. In Acts, Prisca comes onto the stage after being expelled from Rome (Acts 18:2). In other words, she and Aquila are persecuted and have to scramble to work at their trade in Corinth. For Luke's audience the word σκηνοποιοί, *skēnopoioi*[61] (tentmakers) would not have elicited images of wealth. There is no hint that they are prosperous artisans; that they host a church in their large house; that they are merchant-artisans or own their own shop; and that after traveling, they could procure a large house upon arrival in a city. Travel for artisans was not unusual because they did this to find employment—anyone in the first century would know this. Worse yet, she and her husband were unemployed by an edict from the most powerful man in the empire. They lost political protection and were vulnerable.

By omitting the data found in Paul's letters and mentioning some of his own, Luke has three possible strategies in mind: (1) He depicts the couple as average workers, living like the thousands of artisans around the Mediterranean who could not hope to improve their lot in life unless, perhaps, they entered the Christian community. It should be remembered that artisans did not hold any real political power outside the assembly. Upon entering the Christian community, they may have had easier access to power. (2) Prisca's power and prestige come from God's giftings. Accordingly, when she is paired with Apollos, she instructs the eloquent and educated

---

trade. See Meeks, *First Urban*, 59, who conjectures that they operated on a "fairly large scale."

[59] The Greek in Acts 18:3 says, ἔμενεν παρ αὐτοῖς καὶ ἠργάζετο, *emenen par' autois kai ērgazeto*. The καί seems to separate the preposition παρά, *para*, from ἠργάζετο, so that it does not mean "he lived and worked with them" but "he lived with them and worked." The word παρά with the dative of a person can be equivalent to the French *chez*.

[60] Theissen, *Social Setting*, 91–92. He should add, however, that artisans traveled to look for employment.

[61] Hock, *Social Context*, 20–21, discusses what σκηνοποιός, *skēnopoios*, meant in the Greco-Roman world.

(λόγιος, *logios*) speaker in the way of God more adequately. (3) Apollos' birthplace, Alexandria, might also elicit semantic association with education, learning, and sophistication. His education speaks of wealth. A man who has time to study usually does not work by the sweat of his brow.[62] Just as Josephus and the two traveling orators Dio Chrysostom and Aristides were supported by their properties,[63] so it would not be unreasonable to assume that Apollos is a landowner whose property supports him nicely. Therefore, the ironic picture that emerges is this: the social gap between Apollos and Prisca is now widened more than if Luke had revealed what Paul revealed in his epistles. A mere female tentmaker (or leatherworker) instructs the well-studied, powerful, wealthy, male rhetorician. This places her in category 4, which holds the most hope for the fulfillment of the theme in Luke 2:34.

Although Prisca is tentatively a member of category 4, it is difficult to maintain that Apollos suffers a social demotion; Prisca takes him aside out of the public gaze to instruct him. (This privacy will disappear when, in Acts 19, Paul does not take the powerful men aside to correct them; he does so publicly to their shame.) It is not so much that he falls but that she, as his teacher, rises above him. He, in turn, will catch up with her after she instructs him. Only one-half of the falling and rising theme is present. Her situation, therefore, is a less than adequate representation of the theme.[64]

Urban Crowds.   Jerusalem Converts (Acts 5:14). In an urban amalgam (πλήθη ἀνδρῶν τε καὶ γυναικῶν, *plēthē andrōn te kai gynaikōn*), the crowd of women are paired with the crowd of men. The majority

---

[62] Paul depended on the offerings of Christians if he wanted leisure time to preach and study the Scripture.

[63] Josephus, *Life* 429, LCL 1.157–59; Dio Chrysostom, *Or.* 46.5–7, LCL 4.231–33; "Sacred Tales," in Aristides, *Or.* 50.105–6, Behr 2.339.

[64] Aquila accompanies Prisca in order to instruct Apollos, thereby detracting from the female/male dichotomy between Prisca and Apollos. But this may be counterbalanced by the fact that Prisca is mentioned before Aquila in the teaching context. This would be a minor point if Luke had not introduced the couple with Aquila taking the lead in the context of working at a trade (18:2–3). When it comes to teaching, Prisca's name is first. Furthermore, Luke, one more time (v. 18), and Paul, one of two times (Rom 16:3; cf. 1 Cor 16:9), mention Prisca before Aquila. This may indicate her higher status (Meeks, *First Urban*, 59). If this is so, if status means wealth, and if wealth can buy education, then it may be conjectured that Prisca was educated well enough to instruct Apollos. This would be another factor weighing against her clear rise over Apollos, since the social gap between them would be narrowed. But her status, wealth, and education are sheer guesswork. Luke certainly does not spell this out.

probably are common laborers or from approximately the same class (category 2). Neither the men or women are exalted at the expense of the other; both convert equally.

Tyrian Disciples (Acts 21:5). Just before Paul and his team leave Tyre to board a cargo ship, the Christian men, women, and children accompany them to the shore to bid farewell and pray. As with the Jerusalem crowds, it is impossible to know the occupations of these disciples; but it may be assumed that they reflect urban society. They are placed, therefore, among the urban crowds. In an age when, according to certain modern scholarship, women were supposed to be segregated, these women disciples march in public with their husbands and children. This setting is less formal than Chariton's theater, in which crowds of women assembled with men to conduct an investigation or hearing about the trials of Chaereas and Callirhoe,[65] but the Christian women participate nonetheless. When the Syracusans voted to send out an expedition to search for Callirhoe, men, women, and children hurried to the harbor to see the members of the small fleet off.[66] This more closely resembles the scene in Luke–Acts. In Luke–Acts, this public participation accomplishes three feats: it elevates Christian women to parity with pagan women; Christian women are also allowed in public; and this in turn elevates, to some degree at least, Christian women to parity with Christian men. Though paired with men, neither group is exalted at the expense of the other. They conform, then, to category 2.

Peasants.   Peasants were in no way part of the upper classes because most lived at the knife's edge of poverty and depended on the whims of the powerful and of the weather. But neither were they among the unclean and degraded or the expendables because, in the aggregate, peasants are productive, contributing members of society.

Mary, Mother of James (Luke 24:10). It is impossible to discover who James was with absolute certainty, but he was a leader in the early church.[67] As the mother of a leader, Mary would have received honor among the Christians once the church got under way. Since most people in advanced agrarian societies came from the peasantry, she is placed accordingly; but this is sheer guesswork. Like Joanna

---

[65] Chariton 3.4, *CAGN* 56; 8.7, *CAGN* 121. See ch. 2, "Governing Orders and Urban Elite," p. 30. When I use Chariton's novel in comparison with Acts, I am not endorsing the theory that Acts is a novel; I am only searching for social conventions.

[66] Ibid., 3.5, *CAGN* 58.

[67] Plummer, *Luke,* 549; Marshall, *Luke,* 887–88; and Fitzmyer, *Luke,* 2.1546–77, do not know with certainty who Mary or James was.

and the other women from Galilee, with whom she goes out in public, she has the honor of believing in the resurrection before the doubting twelve (now eleven) believe. She is elevated over them, and by their unbelief they are temporarily demoted (category 4). The only mitigating circumstance is that she is identified as the mother of James. This augments her prestige beyond the multitude of peasants. Nevertheless, the message is clear: although the twelve (eleven) occupy a special place, women who obey the principles of the kingdom can excel even them.[68] And her case is appropriate: the social mobility of peasants—if she is one—was usually downward to the expendables, but the kingdom of God raises her up.

Other Women (Luke 13:21; 15:8–10; 17:35). These women fit into category 2. The baker hiding leaven (13:21) is compared with a man planting a mustard seed (13:19), and both keep their social standing. A woman with a lost coin (15:8–10) is paired with a man with lost sheep (15:1–7), and both keep their social standing.[69] Two women grinding flour (17:35) are compared with two men sleeping (17:34), though only one from each couple is favored by the kingdom; these two also keep their social standing. In each story, then, no one is exalted at the expense of men.

SUMMARY

Category 1 does not pair women with men, and it includes the prominent Thessalonians, Elizabeth, the four daughters of Philip, Mary and Martha, Mary (mother of John Mark), and Lydia, making a total of nine, if the Thessalonians are taken as a collective. Since a man, over against whom they might have risen, is not present in their stories, the women do not have the opportunity to act out the falling and rising theme in Luke 2:34.

Category 2 pairs women with men from approximately the same social level and includes the prominent Bereans, Timothy's mother (Eunice), Damaris, Mary (mother of Jesus), Peter's mother-in-law, Jerusalem converts, Tyrian disciples, a baker hiding leaven, a woman

---

[68] This is echoed in Paul's rebuke of Peter (Gal 2:7–16). Peter was reputed to be a pillar in the church; but when he showed preference for Jewish Christians over Gentile ones, Paul rebuked him. One who obeys the principles of the kingdom can receive honor over anyone who does not obey them.

[69] There is some debate over the status of shepherds in the ancient world. See Jeremias, *Jerusalem*, 312; and Sanders, *Judaism*, 461–64. In either case, the woman is not exalted at the expense of the man. Jesus is shown here as honoring the two from an equal level, poverty (category 2).

who loses her coins, and a woman grinding flour. This totals ten, if the Bereans, Jerusalem converts, and Tyrian disciples are counted as collectives. The women either keep their social standing or receive some measure of elevation over the men. It is unclear whether the men are explicitly demoted. The exception is Zacharias, who falls while Mary, the mother of Jesus, is promoted in the kingdom, but this vertical movement is flattened out because they come from the same social level and the same family, and mitigating circumstances arise later in Mary's case. Otherwise, none of the other stories about the women fulfills Luke 2:34; the missing element is the fall of men.

Category 3 pairs women with men (or women) from a lower class and includes the queen of the South, prominent Pisidian-Antiochenes, Joanna, Susanna (possibly), Jairus's daughter, and Tabitha. This totals six, if the Antiochenes are taken as a collective. (The Antiochenes are not, however, favored by the kingdom. They are mentioned here only as an illustration of powerful women oppressing lowly men; this argues in favor of dividing persons in Luke–Acts into classes.) The social gap becomes ambiguous (Joanna [and Susanna] vs. the twelve); or one criterion for socially locating a person is highlighted over another (the queen's ethnicity vs. the Chosen People); or powerful unbelievers are defeated by God's representatives (the Pisidian-Antiochenes vs. Paul and his team); or neither the man nor the woman is exalted at the expense of the other (the daughter of Jairus and Jairus himself vs. the hemorrhaging woman; Tabitha and Aeneas, who may be equals and would fit in category 2). Thus, Luke is preserving his theme spelled out in Luke 2:34, that only the rejects in society are raised up in the kingdom and the proud and mighty fall—not vice versa—even if the rich and powerful are women.

Category 4 offers the greatest opportunity for the theme in Luke 2:34 to be acted out because women from a lower level are paired with men from an upper level. And if the women are exalted while the men are demoted, the rising and falling movement should become evident. Only two women fit into this category: Prisca and Mary, mother of James. Prisca's story, however, is very ambiguous because her promotion over Apollos is private. Also, Apollos does not fall but is raised up to her level. Thus, only one-half of the falling and rising is evident. Mary, who is possibly a peasant, is esteemed for believing in the resurrection, while the faith of the twelve (eleven) fails them. But when she is identified as the mother of James, her prestige is elevated, narrowing the social gap between her and them. That only two persons are in category 4 is very revealing. Prisca's and Mary's stories beg the question whether there are more and whether the social bifurcation between the women and men could have been wider.

Therefore, the hypothesis stated at the beginning of this study is confirmed. Women in these levels of society do not have the honor of rising at the expense of powerful, prestigious, and wealthy men. And when there is the possibility of this, their rise and the men's fall become shortened or ambiguous. This honor is carefully reserved for women among the slaves, the unclean and degraded, and the expendables.

In conclusion, Luke does not depict most of these women as oppressed. But if they are, the oppression is not uniform. Although they do not ideally fulfill the theme in Luke 2:34, none suffer demotion, as they are favored by the kingdom or converted to the Jesus movement. Some even receive a promotion, such as Elizabeth, who is rid of the shame of barrenness. This shows that women are welcome in the kingdom. Some are elevated over men, even though the men may not be demoted. This is significant because women in Greco-Roman culture were still behind the men in the same class. The kingdom of God raises them up. After women convert, they are not shown to be socially inferior to men, and some women are shown to be superior. Even though the women in this chapter do not fulfill the theme in Luke 2:34, Luke still honors them. Thus, he artfully maintains his theme by exalting only the destitute, and at the same time he honors all women, regardless of their station in life. This would have been attractive to women who were looking for a religion to follow. It may be conjectured that at least for these social reasons (among others) women joined the Christian community or converted.

Father of orphans and protector of
widows is God in his holy habitation.
God gives the desolate a home to live;
he leads out the prisoners to prosperity,
but the rebellious live in a parched
land. (Ps 68:5–6)

5

THE FALL OF MEN AND THE RISE OF WOMEN

Since the women in the previous chapter who were wealthy, powerful, and privileged or who were at least productive, contributing
members of society do not adequately fulfill the theme of rising while
men fall, Luke reserves this honor for the slaves, the unclean and
degraded, and the expendables as they are paired with men who are
wealthy, powerful, and privileged. Representing the last of the four
groups—the target group—the following women fit into these classes:

I. SLAVES
    A. Beaten slaves (in story) (Luke 12:45)
    B. Servant accusing Peter (Luke 22:55–62)
    C. Rhoda (Acts 12:13–15)
    D. Pythoness (Acts 16:16–24)

II. UNCLEAN AND DEGRADED
    A. Sick
        1. Peter's mother-in-law (Luke 4:38–39)
        2. Healed crowd (Luke 8:2)
        3. Hemorrhaging woman (Luke 8:43–48)
        4. Daughter of Jairus (Luke 8:41–42, 49–56)
        5. Woman bent double (Luke 13:10–17)

    B. Demonized
            1. Mary Magdalene (Luke 8:2; 24:10)
            2. Delivered crowd (Luke 8:2)
            3. Woman bent double (Luke 13:10–17)
            4. Pythoness (Acts 16:16–24)
    C. Prostitutes
            1. "Sinful" woman (Luke 7:36–50)
            2. In parable of Prodigal Son (Luke 15:30)
    D. Ethnic
            1. Zarephathian widow (in story) (Luke 4:25–26)
            2. Samaritan converts (Acts 8:12)

III. EXPENDABLES
    A. Widows
            1. Anna (Luke 2:36–38)
            2. Zarephathian (in story) (Luke 4:25–26)
            3. Bereft of only son (Luke 7:11–17)
            4. Persistent widow (in story) (Luke 18:1–8)
            5. Widows with houses "devoured" (in story) (Luke 20:47)
            6. Poor-generous (Luke 21:1–4)
            7. Hellenistic and Hebrew (Acts 6:1–7)
            8. Mourners (Acts 9:36–41)
    B. Persecuted
            1. Οἶκος divided (Luke 12:52–53; 14:26; 18:29; 21:16)
            2. By Saul (Acts 8:3; 9:2–3; 22:4)

Not all of these women act out the theme of Luke 2:34 in the way
proposed in this chapter. For them Luke has other purposes that exceed
the scope of this study, since the focus here is on six women who most
dramatically fulfill this theme. It can be pointed out here, however,
that some fit into category 1 (women who are not paired with men) and
category 2 (women who are paired with men from approximately the
same class). Category 3 may be eliminated, since it assumes women
from higher classes. But except for the six women listed below, the
status of the remaining women in category 4 (women who are paired with
men from a higher class), which holds the greatest potential of fulfilling
Luke 2:34, is ambiguous or unclear. (A discussion of the roles can be
found in the appendix.) Still, there are six women for whom category 4
can be simplified because they fulfill more clearly than all other women
in Luke–Acts the theme of rising as men fall. Category 4 can now read,

> Unclean and degraded and expendable women paired with men from
> the upper classes shall rise and the men shall fall as they both confront
> the kingdom of God.

Culled out of the above outline, only those who conform to this
category are the subject of analysis in this chapter:

Prostitute: "sinful" woman (Luke 7:36–50)
Demonized: Mary Magdalene (Luke 8:2–3)
Sick: woman bent double (Luke 13:10–17)
Widow: poor-generous (Luke 21:1–4)
Ethnic: Samaritan converts (Acts 8:5–25)
Persecuted: by Saul (Acts 8:3; 9:2–3; 22:4)

THE CHARACTERIZATION GRAPH

The specific narratological method used is here called the *characterization graph*.[1] It measures or tracks the rising and falling motion. It is made of two axes, one horizontal, the other vertical. The horizontal axis is thematic because a theme is slowly unveiled (or worked out if it was announced beforehand) in a linear manner as the story progresses. Hence, this axis is called the *thematic axis.* In our case, the theme is the kingdom of God, a major one in Luke–Acts. It marches forward tirelessly and inexorably, making itself felt as it overarches the plot within each pericope. This agrees with Luke 2:34, in which it is Jesus who causes the fall and rise of many. Jesus is the perfect representative of the kingdom, and it is his teaching that sets in motion the fall and rise. Often his disciples, acting as agents for him and the kingdom, are representatives too. Jesus, his kingdom, and his agents always provoke a reaction in people. When a poor widow and a rich man, or an unclean woman and an exalted religious man, are confronted with the kingdom in the same pericope, how does Luke cause them to rise or fall?

Rising and falling are vertical movements. The vertical axis characterizes people as they confront the kingdom by measuring their positive or negative reaction. Hence, it is called the *characterization axis.* The words "positive" and "negative" are broad enough to encompass a wide range of reactions: on the positive side, someone

---

[1] J. D. Crossan, *The Dark Interval: Towards a Theology of Story* (Niles, Ill: Argus Communications, 1975) 63–66, also has a graph that measures the rising and falling movements in parables. Ours differs from his in three important aspects. First, his theme around which characters rise or fall varies from story to story; ours uses the kingdom of God as a unified theme in Luke–Acts. Second, his is based on A. J. Greimas's "actantial" model (and R. Barthes's adaptation of it) in all its complex interrelations of "actants" and their roles, thereby forcing the stories into conformity with the actants and models; ours reduces the number of characters and roles significantly and depends on the story to offer us its characters and roles, not on a preconceived, rigid structure. Finally, his separates audience expectations off from the graph, whereas ours incorporates them by the dotted or broken lines and by placing the men and women on the positive and negative sides of the kingdom.

might kneel and weep before Jesus, follow him, or receive praise or affirmation from him or his disciples; on the negative side, someone might walk away from Jesus, receive a rebuke from him, or get knocked off his high horse on the road to Damascus. In Luke's view, there is no middle ground.[2] One either embraces or resists the kingdom and its emissaries. The characterization graph can be dia-grammed as in figure 2.

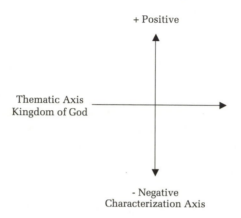

Fig. 2. Characterization Graph

The story of the sinful woman and Simon the Pharisee in Luke 7:36–50 can clarify how the graph works. Simon views himself on the positive side of the kingdom, and the religion, politics, and culture of the day would place him on that side. Literarily, the dominant person should also be placed on top because it is not until the true interpre-tation of the kingdom intervenes that the characters understand their position in it. Nevertheless, since Simon's viewpoint will prove to be false, it will be represented with a dotted or broken line (fig. 3).[3]

On the other hand, the degraded or sinful woman who "crashes the party" should be placed on the negative side of the kingdom or at the bottom according to that same religious, political, and cultural standard and the same literary strategy. But in vv. 40–43, when the kingdom of God breaks in as Jesus explains it, Simon is poised to fall off the precipice and does so in vv. 44–48 when Jesus compares Simon's neglect with the woman's extraordinary show of gratitude. In

---

[2] J. A. Darr, *On Character Building: The Reader and the Rhetoric of Characterization in Luke–Acts* (Louisville: Westminster/John Knox, 1992) 41–42.

[3] Some discussion has taken place over whether the woman was forgiven before she entered Simon's house. See Fitzmyer, *Luke*, 1.686–87. If she was, then her line on the negative side of the kingdom should also be broken or dotted.

vv. 44–48 the sinful woman begins to rise rapidly toward the positive side of the kingdom. For those who embrace it, the kingdom of God elevates the status of women of the unclean and degraded class. Only inside the kingdom are all past defects, sins, and status deficiencies wiped clean. In the new group that Jesus is forming, the unclean woman must receive honor. Therefore, the theme announced in Luke 2:34 is acted out and fulfilled. The woman rises, while the man falls.[4] Figure 3 depicts these movements.

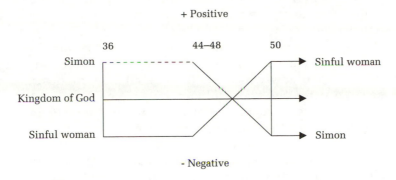

Fig. 3: The Sinful Woman and Simon the Pharisee

It should be pointed out, finally, that the characterization graph is not intended to have an exhaustive capacity for doing an analysis of all stories. Nor is it an exercise in reductionism. Instead, it is merely intended to illustrate visually the goal that Luke spells out verbally.

SHAME, CLASS, AND GENDER

Recently, in the wake of NT sociology, anthropology has been influencing NT studies, notably the anthropology of the Mediterranean

---

[4] York, *Last*, 42, calls this an implicit bipolar reversal. "Bipolar" means that the good becomes bad and the bad becomes good. "Implicit" means that the examples of reversals "function inductively, encouraging the reader to draw conclusions that are not explicit in the story itself" (p. 94). That is, explicit examples of reversals are usually accompanied by aphorisms; implicit ones are not. All of our stories in this chapter are what York considers implicit bipolar reversals, with two exceptions: the twelve and Saul, as we shall see, are restored after their fall. But in any case, though his treatment of reversals is thorough and perceptive, there is no need to adopt his methodology or terminology because, as stated, all of our stories are uniformly implicit and bipolar. My analysis does not take into account other literary forms in Luke–Acts, as York's does.

with its emphasis on honor and shame. These two values are linked with gender, and, I would argue, with class hierarchy.[5] Understanding them will help clarify the impact of the six stories, far removed from us in time and cultural mores.

Despite the remarkable gains women were making in the first century, they still lived by at least one cultural value that differed from that of men. A sense of shame was absolutely appropriate for, and indeed required of, women. It was tied to modesty, restraint, discretion, and purity, all of which are inward qualities. Shamelessness spelled ruin for women. In fairness, however, this cultural value of shame was not always the same for the wealthy and powerful and for the poor and weak. Powerful women were not required to show deference to every man, as slaves or peasants were. But one thing is certain: poor and lowly women (and men) had to defer in the presence of wealthy and powerful men (and women).

A man's sense of shame was also tied to his public honor in the public arena. For him to be shamed publicly meant loss of honor among his peers. His problem was compounded if a woman from a lower class than his played a role in his losing face. He risked irreparable social damage not only in the eyes of his peers but also in the steady gaze of those over whom he had wielded power and respect.

When Jesus heals the woman bent double (Luke 13:10–17), the synagogue official indignantly objects. Jesus counters with an argument that humiliates or shames (καταισχύνει, *kataischynei*) the official and other opponents (v. 17). Two dynamics that support the above thesis about shame are at work in this story: class distinction and gender distinction. The man is part of the local power structure, whereas the woman belongs to the unclean and degraded class; yet Jesus exalts this woman to humiliate the man.[6]

---

[5] See B. J. Malina and J. H. Neyrey, "Honor and Shame in Luke–Acts: Pivotal Values of the Mediterranean World," in *The Social World of Luke–Acts: Models for Interpretation* (ed. J. H. Neyrey; Peabody, Mass: Hendrickson, 1991) 25–65, for a recent and thorough discussion of honor and shame, though they do not emphasize class hierarchy often enough (except for group leaders) and they overemphasize that a woman's sense of shame was tied to the domestic and private spheres. To cite an example from another source, Malina and Rohrbaugh, *Social-Science Commentary,* 287, exaggerate when they claim that a Jewish newly wed woman was considered a "stranger" in her own house. They offer no ancient references and wisely put the word "stranger" in quotation marks. After my own survey of the anthropology scholarship on which Malina, Neyrey, Rohrbaugh, and others base their conclusions, I am not persuaded to incorporate as much of it as they do. So in the brief synopsis that follows, I include only the essentials.

[6] Of course, the larger picture is Jesus vs. the synagogue official. They are competing for honor or acceptance among the public. But if Jesus can

Though class and gender were bound together, class distinctions took slight priority over gender. This can be shown by a hypothetical example. If a woman from Herod's family had been healed, the official would not have objected, at least not in her presence. If he had, one would expect the more powerful woman to take "permanent action" against him. Rather, he would have shown great deference and humility before her. Social hierarchy must be considered as an even stronger factor than gender.

But in a patriarchal age, gender had a role to play. Although women were gaining ground in every area of life, men still controlled most of the financial, reputational, and political resources within their own class. When Jesus uses women to humble his proud male opponents, the humiliation or dishonor smarts that much more sharply than if he had used another man. Thus, in our example, the official is being threatened with potentially irreversible social demotion. Jesus literally and socially raises a woman at the official's expense. The official suffers a double defeat: Jesus, who comes from the official's own social level only in the sense that he is a religious leader, humbles him in front of the crowd. And a woman from a lower class, the official is likely to believe, should not exceed a man from a higher class in the public arena but remain modest and discreet. In the society that Jesus is creating, poor and sick women may receive more honor than rich and powerful men.

COMMENTARY

This commentary follows six lines of analysis: (1) Whenever Mark or Matthew has the same pericope, a brief comparison with Luke's version is made so that his unique strategies can come to the foreground.[7] (2) The context of the pericope is considered. The context

---

enhance his argument by showing how an unclean woman receives more honor than a wealthy and religious man, Jesus' acceptance by the crowd and the official's defeat are much more visible and permanent.

[7] This is not to say that I consider Matthew as a source for Luke. But a comparison can still be drawn between the three so that Luke's strategy can become clear. I do not use source criticism in a sociological analysis because I am assuming that Luke had control over his material, though the debate over precisely how much control he exerted over it vs. how much it controlled him can never be resolved. Luke develops his theme of rising and falling in the process of compiling his material. But more than this, his theme is distributed evenly throughout the narrative, regardless of the source and regardless of the literary genre (though I will focus on six stories in Luke–Acts). It is found not

may include the passages surrounding the pericope, or some parallel traditions, such as those about the Samaritans in Luke–Acts. (3) An outline of the pericope is presented in order to facilitate exegesis. (4) The politics of space is examined: according to the territory or setting of the pericope (a house, a synagogue, or the temple), one can determine who holds power and prestige. This determination enhances the reversals when the powerful men fall and the humble women rise. (5) The exegesis is limited to those elements that elucidate the rising and falling movement in the story. (6) A characterization graph concludes the analysis.

The Sinful Woman and Simon the Pharisee, Luke 7:36–50.   It is impossible to determine whether Luke uses Mark 14:3–9 as a source for 7:36–50.[8] If he does, then for our purposes three differences may be noted in Mark: Simon is a leper, not a Pharisee; "some," not Simon, object to her action (Matt 21:8 has the disciples); and the cost of the perfume is mentioned, whereas Luke omits it.[9]

Luke eliminates any confusion about who is unclean, Simon or the woman. If Simon were a leper, then both would be unclean, and questions of purity would never surface. When Simon the Pharisee, not "some" (nor the disciples, as in Matthew), objects to her behavior, he is portrayed as the villain. And the omission of the perfume's

---

only in the distinctive Lukan material but also in redactional changes Luke has made as he has taken over material from Mark, the assumed primary source for his Gospel. It is found in miracle stories, in chreiae, and in prophetic utterances. It occurs in the sayings attributed to Jesus and in the speeches attributed to the apostles in Acts. To my mind, this wide distribution of material calls for some accounting, and there is no other way of doing so than by seeing this theme as a conscious, deliberate organizing principle of Luke's redaction. For a convincing discussion of this wide distribution, see York, *Last,* 39–163, though he limits himself to the Gospel and has only one story about a woman, that of the sinful woman and Simon the Pharisee (Luke 7:36–50).

[8] For a discussion see Fitzmyer, *Luke,* 1.684–86; Marshall, *Luke,* 305–8; Whitney, "Women in Luke," 161; A. Feuillet, "Les deux onctions faites sur Jésus, et Marie-Madeleine," *RThom* 75 (1975) 357–94; R. Holst, "The One Anointing of Jesus: Another Application of the Form-Critical Method," *JBL* 95 (1976) 435–46; and J. Delobel, "L'onction par la pécheresse: La composition littéraire de Lc. VII, 36–50," *ETL* 42 (1966) 415–75.

[9] Schüssler Fiorenza, *In Memory,* 153, says that "Luke no longer understands this powerful story as the story of a woman prophet [cf. Mark 14:3–9], and replaces it with a 'repentant sinner.'" In my opinion, however, by the time this story is connected to others about rising and falling, Luke expands the vision of just one woman anointing Jesus into all the poor and needy who may anoint Jesus. Luke is only being consistent with his larger theme of the poor vs. the rich and powerful. He is not attempting to suppress women.

value keeps the financial gap between the two as wide as possible, or at least out of the foreground of the story. If Luke borrows from Mark, then his deft omissions and additions, coupled with the background stories in Luke 5–6, reveal how profoundly he understands social hierarchy and how he may manipulate it to illustrate his theology. As noted, Luke's sociology undergirds his literary strategy; his literary strategy assumes his sociology.

The context of Luke 7:36–50 is rich in prolepses, conflicts, and comparisons.[10] In Luke 5–6 Jesus confronts religious leaders four times over legal interpretations about proper behavior (5:17–26; 5:27–39; 6:1–5; 6:6–11). His interpretation prevails. In 5:17–26 and 6:6–11, Jesus heals two men with bodily afflictions and esteems them at the expense of Pharisees and scribes. (The two men could fit into category 4 if it were gender-inclusive.) Twice Jesus defends his befriending of tax gatherers and sinners (5:30–31; 7:34). All of these stories parallel the story of the sinful woman and Simon the Pharisee, but Luke provides a yet more striking comparison.

In 3:12 John baptized tax gatherers (retainers with questionable status). Jesus goes even further: he chooses a tax gatherer, Levi, to be one of his disciples (5:27–39). After Jesus selects him, the Pharisees and scribes question Jesus' associating with "tax-gatherers and sinners" (v. 30). He replies with great irony, "I have not come to call the righteous but sinners to repentance" (v. 32).

This exchange echoes another controversy just before the story of the sinful woman and Simon (7:24–35). Jesus announces that those born of women do not surpass John the Baptist, but he who is least in the kingdom is greater than John (v. 28). For this good word, the people and tax gatherers acknowledge God's justice because they were "baptized with the baptism of John" (v. 29). In contrast, the Pharisees and lawyers, says Luke, reject the purpose of God because they were not baptized by John. Jesus finishes his assessment of John, the people, and the religious leaders by repeating the phrase about himself, "a friend of tax-gatherers and sinners" (v. 34).

This epithet is important because Luke is building a background for the episode of the woman and Simon. Jesus carries on John's ministry to tax collectors by commanding Levi to follow him (5:27–28). He is also a friend of sinners, but he has yet to demonstrate this claim with a "sinner."[11] It is true that Jesus has healed a paralyzed man

---

[10] See D. A. S. Ravens, "The Setting of Luke's Account of the Anointing: Luke 7:2–8:3," *NTS* 34 (1988) 282–92.

[11] See Corley, *Private Women*, 89–93, for a discussion on the historical background of the word "sinner." She conjectures that the woman may have been "a lower-class working woman or freedwoman who may have earned her

whose affliction was linked with sin. But this comes before the religious leaders' accusation of Jesus that he was the friend of sinners. The paralyzed man's case is proleptic; the woman's will be a fulfillment. Besides, the women in Luke's audience may ask, Is Jesus a friend of sinful women?[12] Jesus' announcement in 7:34 that he is a friend of tax collectors and sinners informs the story of the woman and Simon and effectively pairs Levi the wealthy tax collector with the village ἁμαρτωλός, *hamartōlos* (sinner). But the woman still exceeds Levi in that her rise in the kingdom is more dramatic because it is set against Simon's fall, whereas Levi's rise is not directly set against anyone's fall. Both Levi, the wealthy and powerful male retainer with questionable status, and the unnamed village ἁμαρτωλός, a female, are esteemed in the kingdom, but her esteem is to the detriment of a prestigious male.

The outline of the pericope falls into eight parts determined by the interaction of the characters:

1. Simon invites Jesus to dinner (7:36)
2. Woman intrudes (vv. 37–38)
3. Simon inwardly doubts Jesus (v. 39)
4. Jesus, reading his thoughts, replies (vv. 40–48)
    a. The parable (vv. 41–43)
5. Woman exalted; Simon rebuked (vv. 44–47)
6. Woman forgiven (v. 48)
7. Guests question Jesus (v. 49)
8. Jesus dismisses woman in peace (v. 50)

Out of his own initiative, Simon invites Jesus to dinner. The battleground, then, is Simon's house, where he has even more power and prestige than in public. In there he is autocratic. But even in this private sphere the public is found. Jesus and probably Simon's peers (v. 49) are the invited guests. The coalescing of public and private is important because Luke invests Simon with extraordinary authority in his own house yet makes an audience witness his fall. Into this foreign and hostile house the woman intrudes (vv. 37–38) where she

---

freedom by prostituting herself" (p. 124). Corley does, however, say that "Luke intends for his readers to identify her as a prostitute" (ibid.). I prefer the latter option, given the lack of evidence for the former.

[12] For women reading differently from men, see Schüssler Fiorenza, "Luke 13:10–17: Interpretation," 306, who, for support, cites C. Belsey, "Constructing the Subject: Deconstructing the Text," in *Feminist Criticism and Social Change: Sex, Class, and Race in Literature and Culture* (ed. J. Newton and D. Rosenfelt; New York: Methuen, 1985) 50. See also K. M. Craig and M. A. Kristjansson, "Women Reading as Men/Women Reading as Women: A Structural Analysis for the Historical Project," *Semeia* 51 (1990) 119–36.

has no power or status. But it is in Simon's domain that she will receive honor at his expense. Thus, the atmosphere is charged with a sense of drama and impending irony because Luke's audience knows in advance that the Pharisees—and Simon is one—have rejected the purposes of God.

Simon's questioning of Jesus' lack of concern for purity shows that he holds some reservations about the itinerant preacher. Beforehand, Simon may have entertained the idea that Jesus might be a prophet and decided to invite him to dinner for closer inspection. Clearly, Simon sets himself up higher than Jesus. He sees himself sitting in the position of power, especially in his own house. This condescending skepticism may explain the puzzle why he did not offer Jesus tokens of hospitality (vv. 44–46). But when he sees Jesus allowing an unclean woman to touch him, the idea that Jesus is a prophet vanishes. Jesus fails inspection. But the tables are about to turn. It is Simon who is about to receive a close inspection and come up wanting, while the degraded woman will pass muster. Jesus will in fact read Simon's thought, thereby making Jesus the prophet for whom Simon was searching. The atmosphere is becoming charged with more irony.

As Nathan the prophet did to king David when David had sinned with Bathsheba (2 Sam 11:1–12:25), Jesus gives Simon an examination by a parable (vv. 41–43). The parable serves as a transition between Simon's high position—according to his self-view—and his fall, on the one hand, and the woman's lowly position and her rise, on the other. Jesus is teaching on the kingdom, on his new society. He is introducing new values into Simon's theology. Like Nathan's parable, Jesus' ends with a question designed to trap the respondent. Simon is made to set in motion his own downward slide and the woman's upward climb. The poetic justice and irony are now unleashed and could not be more powerful.

Jesus turns to the woman and verbally switches back and forth between Simon and her in order to draw a contrast (vv. 44–48). In these verses, the falling and rising motion begins. Jesus uses the adjective ταύτην, *tautēn*, as he refers to the woman; this denotes that he is pointing at her: "Do you see *this* woman?" Beginning the contrast, Jesus does not use a pronoun for Simon; instead, he depends on the second person singular inflection of the verb. For the woman, however, Luke has Jesus continue with the feminine pronoun αὕτη, *hautē*, three times because he is still pointing at her as the example to follow: Simon neglected to show hospitality by not using water to wash Jesus' feet, but *she* goes far beyond expectations by washing them with her tears and drying them with her hair; he neglected to greet Jesus with a kiss, but *she* does not cease from kissing his feet; he did not anoint Jesus' head, but *she* anoints his feet.

His neglect versus her gratitude betray an inner attitude. There-fore, she receives forgiveness but he does not. Jesus exalts the woman and lowers the Pharisee according to the new standards of the kingdom.[13] And the contrast between the powerful Pharisee falling in his own house—yet witnessed by a public—and the sinful woman rising in a foreign and hostile environment is very, very sharp and fills the story with a bitter reversal for the man and a sweet one for the woman.

When Jesus extends forgiveness to the woman (v. 48) and the dinner guests question his authority to do so (v. 49), the reader is reminded of the paralyzed man whose sins Jesus forgave (5:17–26). In that passage some Pharisees and teachers of the law also questioned his authority. Jesus took time to demonstrate it, first by announcing it, then by healing the man. In the present pericope, however, Jesus ignores their doubts and dismisses the woman in peace. He does not bother to clarify his authority. From 5:17–26 Luke's audience (outside the story) knows that Jesus can forgive sins, but the guests do not. Jesus' silence on the matter in the present story signals to the audience how insignificant and petty the opinions of the guests are. For the audience outside Luke's story, Jesus' silence *is* the answer; it is a silence that shouts the answer. The woman leaves, and the story ends happily for her. The same cannot be said for Simon.

The characterization graph for this pericope is repeated here (see fig. 3) as a summary. It can capture the movement of the two characters whose lives pivot on Jesus' version of the kingdom, with the horizontal axis the fulcrum.

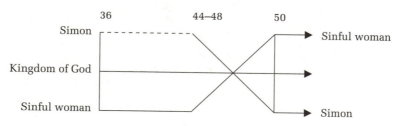

Fig. 4: The Sinful Woman and Simon the Pharisee

Mary Magdalene and the Twelve, Luke 8:1–3; 23:55–24:10.

The Gospel of Luke is the only one of the four to reveal that Mary was delivered from seven demons. Unfortunately, the only other reference

---

erington, *Women in Ministry*, 56, sees the reversal in a sinner vs. but not in class distinction.

to her condition is found in the troubled ending in Mark 16:9. If that ending is considered unreliable, then the missing characterization in the other three Gospel writers makes Luke's description stand out because of his ensuing story about her.

The placement of her former affliction and that of the other women in their context makes the afflictions also stand out. The placement has a multilayered purpose: they are so grateful to Jesus that they δικόνουν (serve) him and the twelve from their possessions;[14] powerful women can also be disciples; they who were unclean are still worthy of being disciples; and so forth. But for our purpose the key ingredient in this passage is the social hierarchy not only between Joanna, the wife of the powerful and wealthy retainer, and the others but between Mary and the twelve, mentioned one right after the other. This juxtaposition foreshadows two others.

In order to understand Mary's story vis-à-vis that of the twelve, it has to be compressed and interwoven with theirs by two kingdom principles: servanthood and consistent faith. These principles are chosen because in the few times that Mary appears in Luke, she excels in them:

1. Mary delivered from seven demons (8:2); twelve formally called (6:12–16)
2. Mary serves (8:2); they arrogate (22:24–27)
3. Mary believes (23:55–24:10); they doubt (24:11)

At first glance, the two references to Mary may call into question the importance of her role as compared with that of the twelve. But against this, two arguments may be made. First, "the twelve" are mentioned as such for the first time in precisely the same context in which Mary is first mentioned along with the female corps of disciples. The apposition seems deliberate. Second, Mary serves as a representative of the other women who were helped out of their condition by Jesus.[15] She (they) reappears in the resurrection and

---

[14] Malina and Rohrbaugh, *Social-Science Commentary,* 334, say that the women are paying off a debt incurred by their healings. I prefer the motive of gratitude. But their opinion on this matter is better than the idea that the women are patrons of Jesus and the twelve, as if Jesus and the twelve depended on them. Jesus and the twelve have a special place in the kingdom; it is not likely that they would be depicted as permanently depending on anyone—male or female—but God.

[15] Joanna and Susanna have already been discussed in ch. 4, "Retainers." There it was also argued that the "many" were peasants as Mary was. In my opinion, the Greek syntax in 8:2–3 indicates that the "many" were also part of those who were healed and delivered. Thus, their status before joining the Jesus movement was ambiguous.

Easter narratives also in apposition to the eleven. Therefore, an accounting must be made for their role as a corps of disciples.

Mary took her name after the rural town of Magdala[16] and was therefore probably no more than a village peasant. It is never said that Mary was a prostitute, *pace* tradition.[17] Be this as it may, her uncleanness comes through the demonization.[18] As stated, with strategic timing Luke mentions that Mary had seven demons driven out, just after he uses the designation "the twelve" (οἱ δώδεκα, *hoi dōdeka*) for the first time. The social bifurcation is deliberate because it sets up the rise and fall. Though she is delivered, the words δαιμόνια ἑπτά, *daimonia hepta* (seven demons) characterizes Mary as having started from a low or ambiguous status, whereas the epithet οἱ δώδεκα puts an august, almost elite aura around the men. But upon her deliverance in an unspecified past, she begins her rise in the kingdom.

The literary backdrop to Mary's condition and deliverance is found in 6:12–16, where the calling of the twelve is narrated. Jesus institutes a special place for them unlike that for any other male or female disciples.[19] In the politics of space, the twelve gather their authority and power from their proximity to Jesus. They make up the primary corps of disciples. After they are established, Luke, significantly, does not list other male disciples by name. Instead, he cites by name a group of women who make up the secondary corps. (This is why 6:12–16 should be considered the background to Mary's condition and deliverance.) In no way could Luke ever permanently overturn or reverse this two-tiered hierarchy—if he had even wanted to—because the tradition was deeply and ineradicably embedded in the Jesus movement.[20] The twelve, after all, are destined to judge the twelve tribes of Israel (22:30). But he can insert this passage about women disciples as a mirror to the twelve. And he can play with the hierarchy by honoring the principles of the kingdom over the twelve or anyone else who might violate them. The twelve do not have to be

---

[16] Plummer, *Luke,* 215; and Fitzmyer, *Luke,* 1.697.

[17] K. Corley, "Were the Women around Jesus Really Prostitutes? Women in the Context of Greco-Roman Meals," SBLSP 28 (1989) 487–521. Schüssler Fiorenza, "Word, Spirit, and Power," 52–55, has a history of Mary in later patristic writings.

[18] Malina and Rohrbaugh, *Social-Science Commentary,* 182–83, discuss how demonization makes a person unclean. I briefly discussed this in ch. 3, "Unclean and Degraded."

[19] Schüssler Fiorenza, "Les douze dans la communauté des disciples égaux: Contradiction ou malentendu?" *FoiVie* 88 (1989) 13–24, rightly says that the twelve do not limit the gender or function of other apostles.

[20] Whitney, "Women in Luke," 204–6, incorrectly believes that the twelve do not have higher status because of their call.

permanently dethroned for a fall to occur. Jesus and his teaching on the kingdom serve as a knife that opens up the inner workings of Mary and the twelve.[21]

One of the foremost principles in the kingdom is servanthood. Without lengthy teachings from Jesus, Mary is one of the women who serve (διηκόνουν)[22] (8:3), which counterbalances the two words describing her demonic oppression (8:2). Of the ten other times this verb is used, the three most significant occasions occur in 22:26–27. The twelve have just ignited a dispute over who would win prominence, when Jesus has to interrupt them. The verb in its participial inflection is piled up: "but let the greatest among you become as the youngest, and the leader as the servant (ὁ διακονῶν). For who is greater, the one reclining at table or the one serving (ὁ διακονῶν)? But I am among you as the one who serves (ὁ διακονῶν)." Mary has beaten the twelve to the punch because she was already among them as ἡ διακονοῦσα, hē diakonousa.[23] According to this kingdom principle, the woman who used to have δαιμόνια ἑπτά rises, while οἱ δώδεκα fall.

Mary and the contingent from Galilee begin to prepare spices for the burial, but they are characterized as having enough devotion to rest on the Sabbath (23:56). They not only stood at a distance from the cross, but they also followed Joseph of Arimathea to see where Jesus was buried. Of course, οἱ ἕνδεκα (hoi hendeka; reduced by one because of Judas's absence) are conspicuously absent from the drama in the Easter narrative.[24] Later, when the women enter the tomb, they do not find the body. Instead, two men in dazzling apparel, identified as angels (24:23), stand close to them. Like the prophets of old who

---

[21] It should be noted only in passing that Mark never juxtaposes a female corps of disciples to a male corps. The Lucan strategy is related to the social bifurcation we have been discussing.

[22] E. J. Via, "Women, the Discipleship of Service, and the Early Christian Ritual Meal in the Gospel of Luke," StLukeJ 29 (1985) 38, points out that this occurrence of the verb is not an explicit "metaphor" for discipleship. It is not, however, necessary to limit this verb, especially when Jesus uses it in the context of waiting on tables and then transforms it into discipleship (22:26–27). Likewise, in 8:3 διακονέω, diakoneō, can be expanded beyond just giving out of their means. It always speaks of a servant's heart.

[23] Of course, I have feminized the participle, and it does not occur in the text. Corley, Private Women, 120–21, unnecessarily limits 22:26–27 to Jesus and the twelve. While it is true that Jesus is addressing them, it is difficult to believe that Luke would not intend a larger audience to adopt a servant's posture in precisely the same way that Jesus delineates in these two verses. This is the nature of gospel stories.

[24] The men are present at the crucifixion (23:49) but sneak away into hiding during the Easter story.

saw visions and theophanies, the women are terrified and bow to the ground. The similarity of their response to that of the ancient and heroic men in Israel's rich history enhances the women's status because they are part of a new history—the very one Luke has undertaken to write. The least in the kingdom are greater than John the Baptist and the prophets of old. After hearing that Jesus has risen from the dead just as he had predicted in Galilee, they report these strange events to οἱ ἕνδεκα, (the eleven). "And this report appeared to them as nonsense [λῆρος, *lēros*], and they did not believe them" (24:11).[25] On their way to Emmaus, Cleopas and an unnamed disciple "saw" Jesus. With sad voices they recounted to him their dashed hope. They reveal, however, that it was women who surprised them about a resurrection. "Being at the tomb early in the morning and not finding his body, they came claiming to have seen a vision of angels who were saying that he is alive" (24:22–23, my translation).

Luke's first account of Mary, who used to have δαιμόνια ἑπτά, *shows* that she believed before οἱ ἕνδεκα and ignited their faith; in the second account put in the mouth of Cleopas and the other disciple, Luke *tells* the same story. Clearly this cause and effect are important to him, for it is only Peter who partially believes their message; it is only he who runs to the tomb immediately after hearing the report of the women (24:12). And after he returns home, he remains silent, unlike the women who boldly proclaimed what they had seen and heard. (Mark has the women frightened and silent [16:8]). Moreover, the women's faith is so childlike (a supreme quality in the kingdom) and strong that they believe after hearing the message of angels, not Jesus himself, whereas the two disciples on the road to Emmaus are so weak in faith and blinded that they do not recognize Jesus until he breaks bread late in the conversation. Eventually, Jesus has to appear to the male disciples to convince them, and even that takes a while (24:36–49). So it is the women who start the chain reaction of faith. Thus, when it first appeared that Luke was curtailing the women's role after the resurrection, he was actually interweaving their story with the men's and using rich irony to make the men ignorant (when they should have understood from the outset) and to make the women perceptive and faithful (when

---

[25] B. Metzger, *A Textual Commentary on the Greek New Testament* (3d ed.; New York: United Bible Societies, 1971) 184, gives v. 12, in which Peter runs to the tomb, a {D} rating but regards it as genuine. It seems to be an attempt to harmonize with 24:34. Also, the verse represents a quick change of mind from calling the women's words nonsense to then turning around to run to the tomb. But if it is reliable, then it is still at the insistence of the women that Peter runs to the tomb.

some in Greco-Roman society and perhaps even in the church would have expected the women to be ignorant and passive). Mary and other women are the true heroines of the resurrection narrative. Therefore, according to the kingdom principle of consistent faith, Mary rises and οἱ ἕνδεκα fall.

As noted earlier, the twelve occupy a unique position in the economy of God in Luke–Acts. But it is Mary and other women who help restore them to their institutionalized place of prominence after Peter partially believes them. If women (and other men) are barred from this unique position of power, then Luke can make sure that it is Mary and other women who reestablish the eleven, later the twelve (Acts 1:15–26). Significantly, Luke does not use lesser men to restore them. If he had wanted to restrict and suppress women, then he could have overlooked them altogether or made passing reference to them (if the tradition was too widely known) as he used other men to restore the twelve.[26]

To sum up, of all the followers of Jesus, the twelve should have been the first to serve and the first to believe in the resurrection. They occupy, after all, a politically privileged position close to Jesus. Mary, who experienced degradation in a way that the twelve never experienced, rises above them in these two kingdom principles. Thus, the thematic axis is made up of these principles (fig. 5). It is not a question of the men being outside the kingdom and Mary being inside. Her rise in the kingdom began sometime before 8:2 when she was delivered. She progresses upward along a straight line that peaks in 8:3 because this is where the word διακονέω, *diakoneō*, first appears. Her line then moves forward horizontally without breaking because of her consistent serving and believing. The line of the twelve is placed over Mary's because of their unique position in the Jesus movement and, later, the church. They also

---

[26] R. Brown, "Roles of Women in the Fourth Gospel," *TS* 36 (1975) 692–93, points out that John 20:11–18 has Mary see the risen Jesus first and that Luke is adhering to another tradition, possibly retained in 1 Cor 15:5, that has Peter seeing Jesus first. (Matthew 28:9–10 has Mary seeing Jesus first but does not contrast this with Peter.) He concludes that Mary's role is that of an *apostola apostolorum* because she conforms to the implicit criteria for being an apostle found in 1 Cor 9:1–2, 15:8–11; Gal 1:11–16: seeing Jesus and being sent to proclaim him. Thus, she sees Jesus and proclaims him to the apostles. It is my belief that because Peter has a dominant role in Acts, Luke has to preserve Peter's prominence. But Mary stills goes back to the eleven, ignites their faith, and helps in the restoration of their unique position. This picture is more powerful than that found in John because of the existence of Luke's second volume, Acts. It is a wonder that women, and not men, take on this restorative role in the first place.

move forward until they reach 22:24–27. When they arrogate authority, they begin their fall. Since time has been compressed and their
story has been interwoven with Mary's, their fall continues through
24:11, when they call Mary's and the women's report foolishness.
Afterwards, they are restored to their position of power through
Mary's proclamation. Even though the graph shows the twelve (or
eleven) ending up above Mary, one can still see their fall and her rise
and constant elevation. Indeed, because they even start above Mary
because of the hierarchy, their fall is all the more dramatic and
poignant—especially when their line on the way down intersects
with Mary's.

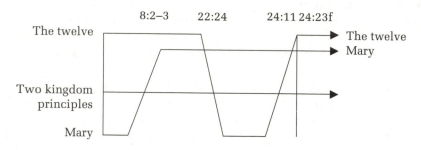

Fig. 5: Mary and the Twelve

A Daughter of Abraham and the Synagogue Ruler, Luke 13:10–17.
Of the five passages in the Synoptic Gospels about Jesus healing on
the Sabbath, Luke has three (6:6–11 [cf. Mark 3:1–6; Matt 12:9–14];
13:10–17; 14:1–6). Of these five, Luke alone includes the one about a
woman. This fact becomes significant when a comparison of the
responses of the religious leaders is made. In Luke 6:6–11 and its
parallels, after Jesus heals and explains his action, the opponents are
filled with rage and plot against him. This rage means they have
suffered a defeat but are able to recover to draw up plans against him.
In Luke 14:1–6, they are not able to make a reply; this silence also
means they suffer defeat.[27] Only in our present pericope (13:10–17),
however, does Luke explicitly use the word "shame," and in the
stronger compound form: κατησχύνοντο, *katēschynonto*. The difference between this passage and the other four is gender. Matching
with a powerful religious male leader a woman from the unclean and

---

[27] Malina and Rohrbaugh, *Social-Science Commentary,* 284–85, point
out that not responding or keeping silent is a sign of being shamed. But in
13:10–17, Luke explicitly uses the word "shame." Furthermore, the shame in
13:10–17 feeds into that in 14:1–6.

degraded class and defeating him through her drive home the point much more cogently than the two male-centered stories.[28]

In Luke 5–7, conflicts with the religious leaders are compacted together, and extended passages of healing and teaching are woven in between them. Similarly, when Jesus and the sinful woman soundly defeat Simon the Pharisee, a defeat that culminates Jesus' victory against all previous opponents, Luke allows the leaders a respite and moves on to other aspects of Jesus' ministry. But in 11:37–12:1, the bell sounds and another round of fighting begins.[29] Another dinner scene provides an opportunity for Jesus to pronounce a series of woes against overly scrupulous Pharisees and lawyers.[30] After this text, Jesus warns against fear of persecution (12:4–12), greed (vv. 13–21), and anxiety (vv. 22–34); admonishes all to be ready for the coming of the Son of Man (vv. 35–48); predicts familial strife because of him (vv. 49–53); again forewarns of persecution (vv. 54–59); concludes that the men living in Galilee are no better than the men whose blood Pilate mingled with a sacrifice (13:1–3) and that the men living in Jerusalem are no better than the eighteen debtors[31] on whom the tower of Siloam ominously fell (vv. 4–5); and tells the foreboding parable of the unproductive fig tree just one year away from getting cut down (vv. 6–9).[32] This long teaching is just as combative and cautionary as Jesus' rebuke of the Pharisees and lawyers.[33] With this

---

[28] Marshall, *Luke,* 559, points out that in the popular view of the day a long sickness was caused by sin in a person's life.

[29] In 11:14–27, it is not clear whether religious leaders or the people accuse Jesus of casting out demons by the ruler of demons. Matthew 12:22–30 and Mark 3:22–27 have the Pharisees and scribes, respectively. I think that Luke assumes and intends the religious leaders; in any case, this passage is confrontational.

[30] At first glance, Jesus' response may seem disproportionate to the crime. But Esler, *Community,* 71–109, 119–23, rightly points out that a larger strategy is at work. Luke is probably addressing the issues of table fellowship and the Torah between Jewish and Gentile Christians in his own time.

[31] The word "debtors" in Luke 13:4 is usually translated as "sinners." I prefer to keep both the financial and the social nuances. It is not utterly out of the question that eighteen debtors, frustrated with an oppressive system (oppressive to them at least), locked themselves in one of the many towers dotting the Palestinian landscape.

[32] J. B. Green, "Jesus and a Daughter of Abraham (Luke 13:10–17): A Test Case for a Lucan Perspective on Jesus' Miracles," *CBQ* 51 (1989) 651–52, conjectures that the tree with the care shown it "is the people represented by this neglected daughter of Abraham" (p. 652). This is another view of the close connection of this story with its context. I have highlighted the conflict between Jesus and his opponents, and the admonishments of his teaching.

[33] M. D. Hamm, "The Freeing of the Bent Woman and the Restoration of Israel: Luke 13:10–17 as Narrative Theology," *JSNT* 31 (1987) 30–31, sees a

background, the audience suspects that the moment Jesus heals the crippled woman on the Sabbath in front of religious leaders, sparks will fly.

The outline of the pericope is as follows:

1. Jesus teaches in synagogue on Sabbath (13:10)
2. A demonized and crippled woman is present (v. 11)
3. Jesus heals her (vv. 12–13)
4. Ἀρχισυνάγωγος objects (v. 14)
5. Jesus replies (vv. 15–16)
6. Opponents humiliated; people rejoice (v. 17)

It was not unusual for Jesus to teach in the synagogues on the Sabbath; he is following his custom (Luke 4:15–16, 44). The synagogue should not be an alien or hostile territory, though this is the last time he would enter one. Nor should the territory be hostile for the crippled woman. And the ἀρχισυνάγωγος does not protest their presence. In fact, he probably permitted Jesus to teach. In his own words he does not even protest against the healing of people on the other six days (v. 14). But when Jesus heals her on the Sabbath, he indignantly objects. As discussed in chapters 2 ("Retainers and Religionists," p. 50) and 4 ("Jairus's Daughter," pp. 134–35), synagogue rulers were wealthy and very likely contributed a lot of money for the building's construction and upkeep. Being no exception, this ἀρχισυνάγωγος therefore holds the most political power within the four walls.

The reason Luke offers for the objection of the leader is that he is exalting the letter of the law over the spirit of it (v. 15). As long as Jesus obeys the rules of the ἀρχισυνάγωγος in his territory, peace is maintained. But with anyone falling short of his interpretation of the Torah and, hence, of proper behavior, the ἀρχισυνάγωγος will seek to reclaim his authority by the only means at his disposal: a careful, intellectual interpretation of, and a practical observance of, tradition. He does not reclaim it by a counterhealing—or at least by a claim that he can heal as Jesus does (but not on the Sabbath).[34] Per contra, Jesus' authority is from God.

---

chiastic structure from 12:49–13:35, with this pericope serving as the centerpiece for the surrounding issues. It "illustrates both blessing and judgment" (p. 31) for Israel and anyone else who either receives or rejects the Messiah.

[34] So perhaps there was a second, broader, yet hidden reason for his vociferous protest. According to Luke, healing placed Jesus far above most spiritual leaders in the eyes of the people. Many healers, medicinal or otherwise, wandered through the countryside and villages of Palestine, but the three Gospel writers make it clear that Jesus' authority surpassed that of the healers (Mark 1:22–27; 2:10–12 par. Matt 9:2–8; Luke 5:18–26). Therefore, in

The leader turns to the multitude and teaches it about the tradition surrounding the Torah. If he can push the people to ratify or adhere to his rules, then Jesus will have lost his audience, the very people he was teaching about the kingdom. In reply Jesus calls them all hypocrites for even contemplating the issue of denying healing on the Sabbath. The plural ("hypocrites") faintly suggests that Jesus perceives that the people, and not only other religious leaders (v. 17), have been momentarily swayed by the ruler.[35] He uses the argument known as *a minori ad maius:* from the smaller fact to the larger fact. If people are permitted to loose animals to lead them to water, then why can he not loose this woman, a daughter of Abraham, he emphasizes, to drink living water (v. 15)? After citing an animal as worthy of kindness, Jesus refers to the woman as a daughter of the great patriarch Abraham. This far leap produces an incongruity that catches the audience's attention. Even though unclean by her physical condition and therefore expondable, the woman is still a daughter of Abraham. While the synagogue ruler and others like him favor animals in their scrupulous legal rulings, Jesus favors a lovely member of Abraham's offspring.

Jesus drives the point home by using wording similar to the ruler's. Ruler: δεῖ ἐργάζεσθαι, *dei ergazesthai* (v. 14); Jesus: ἔδει λυθῆναι, *edei lythēnai* (v. 16).[36] The better choice is obvious. The verb λύω, *lyō,* appears elsewhere in various forms. Jesus has already freed the woman by pronouncing over her an indicative statement in the perfect tense: "Woman, you have been loosed [ἀπολέλυσαι, *apolelysai*] from your infirmity" (v. 12). Each one of Jesus' opponents looses (λύει, *lyei*) his ox or ass from the manger, so it is urgent that the woman be loosed (λυθῆναι) from her chain. Jesus came to free people; they are here to loose animals and bind people. At this undeniable argument, the opponents are humiliated, and the people rejoice.

The rising and falling motions for the crippled woman and the ἀρχισυνάγωγος occur at different times (fig. 6). In vv. 11–13 Jesus

---

the aggregate, a competition for the approval of the people certainly arose between Jesus and certain leaders who exercised power in the villages and towns, though, as noted, this leader did not object to healings per se.

[35] Fitzmyer, *Luke,* 2.1011, observes that "the epithet is evoked by the subterfuge of the leader (sg.) who addresses his remarks, not to Jesus, but to the crowd. Jesus' accusation is not meant for them solely, apart from the leader. It characterizes the attitude of those who stand in need of timely reform."

[36] Ibid. According to Hamm, "Freeing," 27, with this wordplay Jesus is linking the Sabbath with re-creation, thereby drawing on the core teaching of the Torah on the Sabbath. Hamm bases his view on Schüssler Fiorenza's view (cf. *In Memory,* 126).

spiritually and physically raises the woman, who could not straighten up on her own. The leader would not have had to fall if he had accepted Jesus' act of freeing the daughter of Abraham. But, unfortunately, in v. 14 he lowers himself in God's kingdom, though the falling motion does not clearly begin until Jesus rebukes him in vv. 15–16. After Jesus explains the kingdom of God, the ruler's (and other opponents') falling motion ends in v. 17 with the word κατησχύνοντο. The final blow is delivered when the people reject the ruler's version of God's will and cheerfully accept Jesus' action as the divinely approved version. In his own territory the man goes away "bent double," or crippled socially vis-à-vis Jesus and the woman, whereas the woman stands upright by her social and physical restoration.

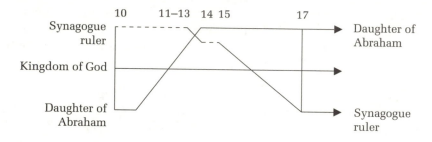

Fig. 6: The Daughter of Abraham and the Synagogue Ruler

The Poor-Generous Widow and the Rich, Luke 21:1–4.   The Gospel of Mark also records the incident of the poor-generous widow in the temple (12:41–44), but there are four notable differences between his version and Luke's. First, when Jesus watches the offerings, Mark uses a slightly rarer or more marked verb—ἐθεώρει, *etheōrei* ("perceived")—than Luke's commoner or less marked choice, εἶδεν, *eiden* ("saw").[37] Second, besides the widow and the rich, Mark has a whole multitude putting money into the treasury; Luke excludes the common masses and has only the widow and the rich.[38] Third, Mark has the rich putting in πολλά, *polla* (large sums), whereas Luke has them giving gifts out of their περισσεύοντος, *perisseuontos* (abundance). Fourth, Jesus in Mark points out the lesson of parsimony vs. generosity only to his disciples, but in Luke he announces his observation to his disciples and the crowd or to anyone who is listening (20:45).

---

[37] Marshall, *Luke,* 751.
[38] The word πλούσιος is masculine though, without further limitation, it can be inclusive.

Mark uses the stronger verb because Jesus has to watch carefully in order to keep track of the offerings of the masses if he wants to contrast them with the widow's. But the Lukan Jesus, since only the rich and the widow are contributing money at the time he looks up, does not need to exercise much discernment to distinguish between their offerings. That is, the contrast between the two classes in Luke leaps out at Jesus and is much more striking than the contrast between Mark's three classes. While Mark's three-tiered hierarchy fits nicely into the conclusions drawn from the descriptive survey of class structure in chapters 2 and 3 above (the upper classes, the masses, and the expendables), Luke widens the vertical social gap by omitting the masses. On the amount given by the rich, it is Luke's strategy to make them offer gifts out of their abundance so that they become stingier than meets the undiscerning eye. If they had given "much" (πολλά) as Mark depicts them, then Jesus' denunciation of them would not have been quite as strong. And the reason that the Lukan Jesus announces his observation to his disciples and the crowd can again be related to public honor and public shame. When the widow and the crowd, not guilty of stinginess, find out about the stinginess of the wealthy, the latter group is humbled publicly. Jesus is publicly on the side of the widow and the masses. In Mark only the disciples learn the lesson, so the rich and the crowd are barely humbled, if at all. Certainly the widow does not know that her generosity receives Jesus' praise.

The present pericope culminates Jesus' view on riches by the effective means of contrasting the rich, who are cited as such, with the poor in the same story. From the word πλούσιος and its cognates, previous stories include the parable of the Great Supper (14:12–24), the Rich Man and Lazarus (16:19–31), and the Ruler and the Disciples (18:18–30). In each, the poor are exalted and honored, while the wealthy disqualify themselves and fall out of favor with the new society, however much status they had in the old one. (Each story could fit into category 4 if the category were gender-inclusive.) The story of the poor-generous widow is the only one that explicitly contrasts a needy woman with the wealthy.

Stereotypically helpless in Luke's view, widows are mentioned just before the widow of 21:1–4. This earlier passage, 20:45–47, may be added to the three stories listed above. It, too, could fit into category 4, but the poor-generous widow represents this group of unknown widows. Jesus denounces the scribes for appearing religious yet devouring the houses of widows. This juxtaposes the powerful to the helpless. And not so coincidentally, right after Jesus makes this declaration, he looks up and happens to see the rich persons and the poor widow offering their gifts. Though Luke does not specify, it may be asked if the rich in 21:1 are religious leaders or experts in the Torah. The implication certainly is there. But whether just rich, or rich religious leaders, or rich legal experts, they will be condemned as were the scribes in 20:45–47. The textual atmosphere is now charged in such a way that Jesus can exalt a woman from among the expendables at the expense of the rich.

The temple was open to everyone because it was built from the taxes imposed on all the inhabitants of Palestine. Following religious restrictions, people from all walks of life could derive benefit from it. But this territory is not quite entirely neutral for the oncoming conflict in 21:1–4. The temple was the power base for the ruling elite.[39] The money that flowed into it from Jews all over the world[40] was controlled by the aristocracy. Immediately after our present passage Jesus predicts that it will be destroyed (21:5–6). Perhaps he believes, according to Luke, that it is a means for the rich to get richer and the powerful to gain more power and that it is alienating ordinary persons, the unclean and degraded, and the expendables, such as this lone widow.[41]

The brief episode in 21:1–4 falls into three phases:

1. Jesus sees the rich offering gifts (v. 1)
2. Jesus sees the widow offering two small coins (v. 2)
3. Jesus publicly draws his conclusions (vv. 3–4)

Literarily, the scene that Luke sets up in vv. 1–2 is the following: rich people dressed in fine clothing walk by the offering receptacle and visibly display how many coins they drop in; or they are silent enough for people to hear how many coins clink, hitting bottom. At a fortuitous moment, a single poor woman, dressed in a black, tattered garment, so to speak, approaches and drops in two λεπτά, *lepta*, the smallest coins in Palestine. Copper being light, the clink of her coins is barely audible. It is as if Luke has them all approach from different angles and in rapid succession. The speed of the action is seen from the close proximity of the aorist participle ἀναβλέψας, *anablepsas*, with the first aorist verb εἶδεν, to which is linked the second εἶδεν by the particle δέ: "After glancing up, Jesus saw . . . then he saw."

---

[39] Oakman, *Questions*, 205–18.

[40] Sanders, *Judaism*, 144.

[41] J. H. Elliott, "Temple versus Household in Luke–Acts: A Contrast in Social Institutions," in *Social World of Luke–Acts* (ed. Neyrey and Malina) 211–40, convincingly argues that in Luke–Acts the temple, the seat of power for the rich, is set in opposition to the household, the refuge for commoners and the poor. Certainly this is true of temples in the Greco-Roman world (see ch. 3, pp. 107–8).

This fast-moving action is designed to make Jesus' pronouncement easy and sure. The adverb ἀληθῶς, *alēthōs,* used only three
other times in Luke–Acts (Luke 9:27; 12:44; Acts 12:11), is the first
word Jesus speaks (v. 3): "Truly I say to you . . . " He wishes to make a
very significant point. In keeping with the previous four passages in
which the rich and poor are contrasted, Jesus exalts her and deflates
the rich. By comparing her giving with that of the rich, he values her
generosity and devalues their hypocritical, blind stinginess.[42] Until
Jesus' assessment, they have deceived themselves into believing they
are generous. But after he sizes up their total monetary worth, their
giving is measured against a new standard: a percentage that reveals
the heart. With strong rhetorical effect, two sets of two phrases mirror
each other. The rich, out of their surplus (ἐκ τοῦ περισσεύοντος
αὐτοῖς, *ek tou perisseuontos autois*), drop in gifts (τὰ δῶρα, *ta dōra*);
she, out of her poverty (ἐκ τοῦ ὑστερήματος αὐτῆς, *ek tou hysterēma-
tos autēs*), drops in her entire living (πάντα τὸν βίον, *panta ton bion*).
He sees through the external appearances and displays of the rich,
which often intimidated the poor in the ancient world.

To sum up, in vv. 1–2 life and its actors are passing by normally
and naturally. The rich can give much for their religion, the poor
little for theirs. In vv. 3–4, upon Jesus' apparently novel assessment,
life and its actors are turned upside down. The rich fall, and the poor
widow rises (fig. 7).

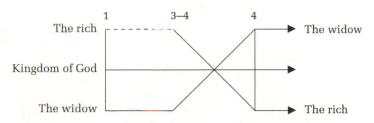

Fig. 7: The Poor-Generous Widow and the Rich

---

[42] A. G. Wright, "The Widow's Mites: Praise or Lament?—a Matter of
Context," *CBQ* 44 (1982) 256–65, sees Jesus' words as a lament because Jesus,
as we do, feels the pain of the widow who gives too much in a temple system
run amuck (pp. 256, 260–61). He bases this on the Markan "corban" passage
and the next pericope, in which Jesus says the temple will be destroyed
(260–61). Also, he claims that commentators who praise the "spirit of generosity" in the woman must read this into the text; nowhere does it use these
words. The "corban" passage is not, however, found in Luke. In my opinion,
it is possible for Jesus to praise this widow while denouncing the system. The
text does not need to have the words "spirit of generosity" in order to
communicate this message. After all, nowhere does the text say that this
widow was forced by specific religious leaders to give all her living.

Samaritan Women and Simon, Acts 8:5–25. In this passage the exaltation of women at the expense of a man may not seem as direct and obvious as the previous three pericopes; the fall and rise seem hidden behind other action in the story. But a careful reading proves otherwise. And although, admittedly, the juxtaposing of Samaritan women[43] and Simon and the exalting of the former over the latter may not be Luke's primary purpose,[44] the phenomenon nonetheless exists and must be noted, especially in light of Luke's other stories about Samaritans.

Far more than the other Synoptic authors, Luke portrays Jesus as having a special regard for the Samaritans (Luke 9:52–56; 10:25–37; 17:11–19; Acts 1:8; 8:5–25). Indeed, all these references fall within the so-called L material and Acts. Since Samaritans were considered by all levels of Jewish society to be ethnically unclean and degraded, Luke intends to exalt them in the society of the kingdom.

When the Samaritans discover that Jesus is journeying towards Jerusalem, they reject him, probably because they have felt for so long the full weight of religious exclusion from the leaders and people in Jerusalem (Luke 9:51–56).[45] To retaliate, the disciples want to pray down fire on them as Elijah did on others (2 Kgs 1:10–12; cf. Sodom and Gomorrah [Gen 19]). But Jesus is gracious in rejection and rebukes the disciples instead of the Samaritans. Identifying with them, he knows that he, too, will suffer rejection at the hands of the Jerusalemites. This is the only passage that is slightly ambiguous towards the Samaritans, but Jesus shows no opposition to them. On the contrary, he defends them.

---

[43] On the background of the Samaritans, Bruce, *Acts of the Apostles,* 216, notes that if the definite article for "the city" is retained, then the city was Hellenistic but "the impression given by the following narrative is of a mission to ethnic Samaritans." This impression is deliberate on Luke's part. It is unknown whether Simon was Jewish or Samaritan. Either way, in wealth, status, and power, he far exceeded the lame, paralyzed, and demonized women.

[44] It is probable that Luke's primary purpose in writing about Philip's campaign in Samaria includes demonstrating that the entire ethnically inferior Samaritan community is equal to Jews, Romans, and other Gentiles in the church. But the very fact that the phrase "both men and women" (ἄνδρες τε καὶ γυναῖκες) occurs only four other times in Acts (5:14; 8:3; 9:2; 22:4), turns the argument in favor of Luke's drawing attention to Samaritan women, as I hope to show. In any case, since men in the Bible have received the attention from scholarship and women have been marginalized or forgotten, I am reversing the hierarchy (as Luke is also doing).

[45] Fitzmyer, *Luke,* 1.824–26, discusses how this rejection fits into Luke's travel narrative. So it is not just a political reason.

Jesus' special regard for the Samaritans is revealed the most profoundly in the famous parable of the Good Samaritan (Luke 10:25–37). The Levite and the priest, probably not enjoying monetary and political power if they were typical, still have religious status in the villages and towns. The priest is going down (κατέβαινεν, *katebainen*) the road (v. 31), a verb which may indicate that he is leaving Jerusalem after performing his priestly tour of duty in the temple. The same may be true for the Levite (v. 32). They, however, circumvent the man lying on the road, beaten by robbers. If a priest and a Levite will not help the man, then who will? A commoner? For a moment Jesus leaves us in suspense. Whom will he choose to finish off the story? Placing the answer at the end gives the story its punch. He chooses the despised Samaritan who, out of the compassion that the religionists should have had, rescues the beaten. This surprises Jesus' audience. Jesus exalts a man from the unclean and degraded class at the expense of men from among the religionists (category 4).

A disease such as leprosy tends to narrow social gaps. This was seen in chapter 3 (pp. 107–8) among the sick or unclean and degraded who flocked together in temple precincts waiting for relief. The ten lepers (Luke 17:11–19) who meet Jesus in a village between Samaria and Galilee share a sad camaraderie, even though one is a Samaritan. But Luke may not bridge the social gap completely. When Jesus heals them all, only one returns to give thanks (v. 15). The sentence in v. 16, "And he was a Samaritan," is conspicuous by its placement. Only towards the end of his show of gratitude is his ethnic background revealed—while he is still prostrate before his healer. This also surprises Jesus' audience. Now it is incumbent upon the audience to assimilate the new twist in the story, which overturns their expectations, and to reinterpret the behavior of the unknown man—now a Samaritan—as even warmer and more remarkable than the audience was first led to believe. By virtue of Jesus' praise, the one who could not be cleansed of his ethnicity surpasses the higher-class Jews after both lose the trauma and stigma of their disease.[46]

On the surface, the truncated reference to women in Acts 8:12 appears as a slight. Why does Luke not spell out at the beginning of his report that the women are part of the action?[47] But at bottom, this seemingly last-minute postscript or addendum is conspicuous by its

---

[46] Jesus' last pronouncement, "Rise, and go on your way; your faith has made you well or saved you" (v. 19), strikes an ominous note for the other nine. Did their forgetful ingratitude cause them to miss a further blessing, such as salvation? Luke does not say outright. But if so, then the nine do not rise very high in the kingdom.

[47] See ch. 4 n. 15.

existence and placement, as with the thankful Samaritan in Luke 17:16.[48] The existence and location of the phrase ἄνδρες τε καὶ γυναῖκες, *andres te kai gynaikes,* draw more attention than they deflect. After all, Luke did not even have to mention women if he wrote about crowds. One could assume their presence. It may even be assumed that mentioning women draws more attention to them than to the men. One always assumes that men are in the crowd, especially with the ubiquitous and inclusive masculine πολλοί, *polloi,* and αὐτοί, *autoi.* Furthermore, by placing the phrase at the end of the defining action or change of character in vv. 6–8, and even at the end of the sentence in v. 12, Luke duplicates the location of the reference to the Samaritan in Luke 17:16 and thereby makes the women stand out all the more. As we had to do with the thankful Samaritan, we the readers are now required to go back over all the great signs, wonders, and blessings recorded in vv. 6–8 and understand that women took equal part.

But the action is not finished. Peter and John, sent by the other apostles, come from Jerusalem to ratify the results of Philip's preaching (v. 14). The women who were converted and baptized now receive the Holy Spirit. So the existence and placement of the phrase ἄνδρες τε καὶ γυναῖκες serve the purpose that was hoped for: Luke spells out the women's involvement forthrightly. As Luke identified the Samaritan in Luke 10:33 and afterwards described his merciful behavior (vv. 33–35), so Luke identifies the women in Acts 8:12 and afterwards describes the new course on which they embark with the arrival of Peter and John; they receive the Holy Spirit without hindrance or hesitation. Identifying them precedes describing them, and vice versa.[49]

If the discussion of the Samaritans in the Gospel and the Samaritan women in Acts has been extended, the reason is that the women are mentioned with deceptive brevity in Acts 8:12. The literary strategy in Luke 10:30–35 and 17:12–19 clarifies the strategy in Acts 8:5–17. It turns out that women fit nicely into the traditions about Samaritans in Luke–Acts. They do not sit on the periphery.

---

[48] Of course, with the Samaritan in 10:33, Luke could have delayed revealing who did this act of kindness until after the kindness was shown; but delaying this revelation after naming the priest and Levite was apparently adequate for creating some degree of suspense.

[49] Luke welds together the order of the appearance of the Samaritans in Luke 10:31–32, 33–35 with Acts 8:6–8, 14–17: (1) The good Samaritan appears (Luke 10:33) after the unmerciful priest and Levite (vv. 31–32). The women are mentioned (Acts 8:12) after Simon (vv. 9–11)—to whom they will be juxtaposed. (2) Now that the good Samaritan appears, his behavior is revealed (Luke 10:33–35). Now that the women have been identified, any further action with the two apostles must be interpreted as including them (Acts 8:14–17).

Therefore, for our purposes, the outline of the Samaritan campaign is as follows:

1. Crowds receive miracles through Philip (Acts 8:6–8)
2. Simon is introduced (vv. 9–11)
3. Women believe and are baptized (v. 12)
4. Simon believes and is baptized (v. 13)
5. Women receive Holy Spirit through Peter and John (vv. 14–17)
6. Simon falls out of favor (vv. 18–24)

The episodes about women who will rise are interwoven between those of Simon who will fall. This is as close as Luke can get to
the simultaneous action of two sets of characters. Clearly, this juxtaposing is deliberate on Luke's part; he wants to contrast the two sets.

In Acts 1:8 Jesus ordered his disciples to go into Samaria and
preach. When Philip, the emissary from Jerusalem, ejected because of
persecution (8:4–5), preaches about the Jewish Messiah, the Samaritan women immediately accept the message (vv. 5–8). Many of them
are paralyzed, lame, and held down by unclean spirits; their degradation, then, is not only ethnic. Luke does not specify the content of the
message that turned the despised Samaritans towards believing in the
Jewish Messiah, but miracles often play a deciding role in Luke's
soteriology (v. 7; cf. 2:43; 3:2–10; 4:16; 22; 30; 33; 5:12; 19:11; etc.).[50]
Experiencing a different kind of power from that offered by Simon,
they are set free of their physical uncleanness and so begin their rise
in the kingdom.

To political rulers in such cities as Rome and Jerusalem, magicians were expendable.[51] But to the ordinary people in the towns and
villages, they garnered great prestige and power to influence. They
were spokesmen and intermediaries for God or the gods. And in the
town of Samaria, Simon held sway over the "small and the great,"
who called him "the power [δύναμις] of God, which is called Great
[Μεγάλη, *Megalē*]" (v. 10). He used to amaze (ἐξεστακέναι, *exestak-
enai*) them with his magic. In the politics of space, it is clear from
Simon's power and prestige that Philip invades hostile territory. The
"small and the great"—another indicator of Luke's understanding of,
and emphasis on, social hierarchy—honor Simon, but Philip steals
the honor. With these descriptions of him, however, Simon is being

---

[50] Green, "Jesus," 643–54, has a relevant bibliography on the importance
of miracles in Luke–Acts.

[51] MacMullen, *Enemies,* 95–162. This may be only partially true, depending on the politician. In Lucian's "history" about Alexander the false
prophet (*Alexander,* LCL 4.175–253), Alexander holds sway over an entire
region and over the "smallest to the greatest," including a senatorial proconsul
(cf. Acts 13:6–12).

led into a trap. These words will be used against him when he begins his fall from power.

After the women accept Philip's message and help, their exaltation in the kingdom passes through the Lukan combination of "faith and baptism" (8:12; cf. 8:13; 10:43–47; 16:31–33; 18:8). Their exaltation travels on a smooth road from beginning to end.

When Simon observes Philip working "great miracles" (δυνάμεις μεγάλας, *dynameis megalas*) (v. 13), he too is amazed (ἐξίστατο, *existato*). The words that describe him in v. 10 now convert him in v. 13.[52] The powerful trapper is snared by a powerful trap. He is converted, or at least he believes, gets baptized, and attaches himself to Philip.[53] Rather than maintaining his position of "great power," he is now following someone more powerful than he; rather than following him, the Samaritan women, formerly lame, paralyzed, and demonized, are busy following Philip. Simon is standing on the precipice, poised for a crashing fall because he is losing his power base. Yet, because of his apparent conversion (v. 13), he still has to be placed on the positive side of the kingdom. Arguably, his dotted line on the characterization graph (fig. 8) turns solid at v. 13.

To create an atmosphere of immediacy, Luke condenses the time it would take for reports about the events in Samaria to get back to Jerusalem and for the apostles to reach Samaria in order to ratify Philip's efforts and fulfillment of Acts 1:8 (v. 14). Luke wants the Samaritans to receive quickly every aspect of his theology: miracles of health, faith, baptism, and the Holy Spirit from the apostles themselves. This receptivity shows that the women's inner motive is pure and humble.

On the other side, Simon is intrigued and offers the apostles money for the same authority to impart the Holy Spirit (vv. 18–19). In effect, he wants to win back his power to influence.[54] Peter is able to look into Simon's heart, which is "in the gall of bitterness and chain of unrighteousness" (v. 23). In v. 18 Simon begins his fall in earnest. He hits bottom when Peter denounces him (vv. 20–24).[55]

---

[52] Tannehill, *Narrative Unity*, 2.105.

[53] For my purposes it is unnecessary to engage in a debate over the problematic theology in Simon's apparent conversion. I will make my evaluation of his fall based on his obvious loss of power over, and prestige with, the people and on Peter's denouncement of him (vv. 20–23). It would exceed the limits of my analysis to delve into questions about when persons receive the Holy Spirit in Luke's theology.

[54] Tannehill, *Narrative Unity*, 2.107, proposes that Luke is drawing a larger lesson through Simon's life. Because Simon wants to buy power after he was baptized, Luke is warning church leaders not to allow money to corrupt them.

[55] Bruce, *Acts of the Apostles*, 223, notes that Justin (*First Apology* 26.6)

Since the episodes are interwoven, the graph presents the women's verses above Simon's. Beginning with their healing and deliverance (v. 7), the women are exalted without hindrance, while Simon's position of power has some ambiguity compared with not only the women but also the powerful men in the previous stories. But his fall is rapid.

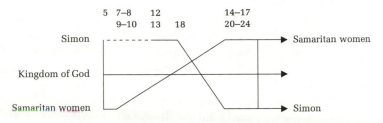

Fig. 8: The Samaritan Women and Simon

Persecuted Women and Saul, Acts 8:1–4; 9:1–22. Jesus predicted on four different occasions that his followers would be persecuted or have their households divided (Luke 12:52–53; 14:26; 18:29; 21:16). Unwittingly, Saul makes sure that Jesus' prediction finds its target. He goes from house to house dragging out men and women and putting them in prison (Acts 8:1). But this is irony. If Jesus predicts persecution and Saul fulfills it, then are not Jesus and his people vindicated? Saul is being set up for a fall.

In Acts 1:8, Jesus ordered the disciples to go forth into Samaria. Saul was a devout and zealous Jew interested in purity, so surely he must have despised the Samaritans. But it is Saul's persecution that scatters the disciples abroad (8:4) and launches Philip's campaign into the town of Samaria (vv. 5ff). Saul is an evangelist even when he attacks evangelist Christians. This is another example of Saul ironically fulfilling Jesus' words. Whomever Saul seeks to grab escapes into many directions. This foreshadows his fall when Jesus grabs him without a way of escape. But Luke's irony is extended and driven home even more forcefully.

In Acts 5:34–40 Saul's famous teacher, Gamaliel, stands up to offer his advice to the council on how to control the apostles. Luke makes sure that it is known that Gamaliel is honored (τίμιος, *timios*) by all the people. That is, his opinion is very significant. "If [ἐάν, *ean*] this plan or this action is [ἦ, *ē*] of man, it will be overthrown; if [εἰ, *ei*]

---

acknowledges that Simon and his followers were called Christians. Perhaps, but Luke does not report this.

it is [ἐστιν, *estin*] of God, you shall not be able to overthrow them. Never be found to be God-fighters" (5:38–39). The Greek construction is striking because Gamaliel starts off his proposal with a subjunctive conditional and ends it with an indicative conditional. The first alternative is more remote than the second. This implies that "Luke approves the second alternative, and therefore expresses it by means of a less remote construction."[56]

Gamaliel's famous pupil, Saul, neither exactly follows nor disobeys his teacher's counsel. Luke is very specific about Saul's fulfilling yet circumventing Gamaliel's counsel. If the sect is of God, the council shall not be able to overthrow "them" (αὐτούς, *autous*), meaning the apostles (5:39). Accordingly, Saul leaves them alone (8:1).[57] But this makes his fall and the poetic irony and justice all the more poignant. If Saul is humbled while persecuting ordinary women, then *a minori ad maius* he would have been humbled had he hunted down the popular, powerful, and miracle-working apostles. Again, bypassing the apostles and contrasting the women with Saul, Luke widens the social hierarchy. The irony culminates when Saul falls off his horse on the road to Damascus, thereby discovering that the new sect is in fact of God. Gamaliel's counsel was prophetic; Saul is a God-fighter. He is not at all able to overthrow the upstart sect. Better yet, its risen leader overthrows him—literally.

The outline is as follows:

1. Saul persecutes women (8:1–3)
2. Saul continues action (9:1–2)
3. Jesus intervenes (9:3–19)
4. Saul preaches gospel (9:20–22)

The territorial advantage belongs to Saul, not to the women. As he leaves Judea and Samaria, he receives permission from no one less than the high priest to carry out his policy in the synagogues (9:1).[58] As their now risen leader found out, the Christians are finding out that the synagogues are becoming hostile. Saul is now a very powerful religious retainer working with the full support and approval of

---

[56] Bruce, *Acts of the Apostles,* 178. He also points out that this subjunctive-indicative construction is Luke's Greek, not Gamaliel's Aramaic. This insight supports my claim that Luke intends Gamaliel's words to be used against his famous pupil, Saul.

[57] Tannehill, *Narrative Unity,* 2.102, emphasizes the apostolic courage and perseverance to stay in Jerusalem. But Saul does not even bother to approach them.

[58] F. J. Foakes Jackson and K. Lake, eds., *The Beginnings of Christianity* (5 vols.; London: Macmillan, 1920–33) 4.99, state that the high priest had the authority from Rome to bring Jewish malefactors back to Jerusalem.

the most powerful men in the whole Jewish world. But boundaries are not a concern for the women's defender: the resurrected Jesus. He is more powerful than the men from the governing class.

The women are mentioned three times along with men in Luke's story about Saul's persecution of Christians: both men and women (τε ἄνδρες καὶ γυναῖκες; 8:3; 9:2; 22:4). As with the Samaritan women, the very fact that they are mentioned at all draws attention to them. One always assumes that men make up a crowd; but when the women appear three times in Luke's story line, the spotlight shines more brightly on them, even though they are placed in the background when Saul is converted (9:3–22). It is likely that they come from lower levels in society because, it should be remembered, the wealthy Mary remained in Jerusalem even in the face of persecution (12:1–12). But when Saul attacks lower-level women, he turns them into expendables according to the ruling elite's viewpoint because they suffer loss of living quarters, deprivation of goods, and imprisonment.

Saul's social behavior changes when the bright light flashes; he falls to the ground and is blinded (9:3–4). Jesus identifies himself with the women when he says, "Why are you persecuting me?" (v. 4). The man who once believed that he was seeing everything clearly now has to be led by the hand into Damascus (v. 8). He falls not only literally but spiritually and socially as well. In the time elapsed in vv. 8–16, he has to contemplate that he was a God-fighter, as Gamaliel had forewarned.

When Jesus sends Ananias to Saul, Saul is filled with the Holy Spirit, regains his sight, and is baptized. Thus, unlike the other wealthy, honorable, and powerful men, Saul undergoes a fall (vv. 3–8) and rise (vv. 17–18) that culminates in such a profound resocialization into the customs and beliefs of the new sect he had been persecuting that he preaches with great strength that Jesus is the Messiah and confounds his former allies (v. 22). This is calculated to show the power of his conversion and the subsequent authority of Luke's hero. For Luke, Saul's conversion and call are of utmost importance. He tells it two other times (Acts 22:3–21; 26:9–18).

From Saul's point of view the women he was persecuting were on the negative side of the kingdom. The audience knows that this is false, so the women's line is dotted or broken on the graph (fig. 9). They begin their rise (according to Saul) when he falls because his perspective is considerably altered (v. 3–4). It is not clear when this alteration happens during the three days (v. 9), so the line depicting his fall and rise takes the form of a (squared) V and ends at v. 17 when Ananias lays hands on him. Saul is now on the positive side of the kingdom; he discovers that the women were there all along.[59] And because Saul is Luke's hero, he ends up higher than the women (and men). But this is not a problem; Paul, de facto, may even surpass the twelve according to Luke. For a while, however, the women rose in the kingdom, and Saul fell. This happens to anyone who opposes the kingdom of God, regardless of his importance. Mary Magdalene and the twelve can attest to this.

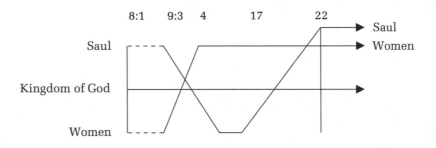

Fig. 9: Saul and Persecuted Women

SUMMARY

To fulfill the theme in Luke 2:34, Luke employed two overarching strategies. First, he bifurcated the social hierarchy between those who fell and those who rose before they confronted the kingdom of God. This agrees with the findings in chapters 2 and 3, in which it was observed that Greco-Roman society was also undergoing a bifurcation. But unlike society, Luke skillfully reversed the hierarchy. Second, Luke went out of his way to include women among those who were exalted. These two features stood out when a comparison was made between Luke's Gospel and Matthew's and Mark's Gospels. When Matthew and Mark were fuzzy about social hierarchy in parallel traditions, as, for example, with Simon the leper (not the Pharisee) vs. an ordinary woman who anoints Jesus' feet (not a sinful woman), Luke clarified matters by making the social gap wider. When Matthew and Mark did not mention women in parallel stories, as in the situation about doing good on the Sabbath, Luke included them.

---

[59] It may be objected that women are the silent background during Saul's conversion. This is true, but Saul is Luke's hero. He occupies a place of prominence over everyone except perhaps the twelve. As noted, the "Lukan silence," if extended to its logical conclusion, would include nearly every story Luke told. What happened to Barnabas when he and Paul split? What happened to the Ethiopian eunuch?—and so on.

The six women whom Luke chose to exalt at the expense of wealthy, powerful, and prestigious men came from the underside of society: a prostitute (Luke 7:36–50); Mary Magdalene, a peasant who was formerly demonized and who represented many other such women (Luke 8:1–3; 23:55–24:10); a woman bent over double, caused by a spirit (Luke 13:10–17); a poor widow (Luke 21:1–4) who represented other widows whose houses were devoured by scribes (Luke 20:45–47); ethnically inferior Samaritans, many of whom were unclean because of illness or demonization (Acts 8:5–25); and those made expendable because of Saul's persecution of them (Acts 8:1–4; 9:1–22). In all cases their rise came about as Jesus intervened to announce the true kingdom of God. The women, some of whom had not realized it, found themselves on the positive side of the kingdom when the announcement was finished. The men, on the other hand, believed that from the beginning they were on the positive side. They overestimated themselves and underestimated Jesus and his ways. The women's innocence and the men's presumption about the things of the kingdom made for dramatic and ironic reversals.

Men from the unclean and degraded and the expendable classes were also paired with wealthy and powerful men; but the reversals smarted that much more sharply for the upper-class men when women were so paired, because of male honor and female shame. Women from the underbelly of society should have deferred to the men or showed them a sense of shame. Honor, shame, and social hierarchy combined to make the fall and rise all the more poignant. This was especially true when the men held the reins of power in their own space, such as in the house of Simon the Pharisee (Luke 7:36–50) or in the synagogue of which the ἀρχισυνάγωγος was in charge (Luke 13:10–17). When Jesus invaded their power base, however, he was operating from a higher authority. He apparently showed little regard for spatial politics. Therefore, he exalted the women and humbled the men, as brought out in the characterization graphs, which catch the vertical movement that could otherwise get lost in a plethora of words.

When the Lacedaemonians came on,
the women were not dismayed at their
battle-cry, but stood their ground
and fought valiantly.[1]

6

CONCLUSION

Luke, who was no casual observer of society, noticed at least two facts of social life. First, society was undergoing a bifurcation between the haves and the have-nots. "Fewer have more,"[2] and, conversely, more have less. Second, women were behind men within their own social class. Women participated in this widening gulf on both sides, but they were a step behind the men in terms of wealth, status, and power. Casual observers, who made up the millions of inhabitants of the Mediterranean culture, would also have noticed these two realities, but they would have resigned themselves to them. (The men would have resigned themselves to the bifurcation, and the women to the bifurcation and their inferior status within their own class.)

But Luke did not resign himself. As an enthusiastic adherent of the new religion of Christianity, he absorbed the teachings of Jesus on the poor and the rich—to speak generically (as ultimately expressed

---

[1] Pausanius 20.9, trans. Jones, LCL 1.353–55, records this gem of a legend, which Pausanius and the ancients regarded as historical, occurring in 510 B.C.E. When the Lacedaemonians killed the Argive men, Telesilla the poetess mustered women of various strengths and weaknesses to fight them. Pausanius continues, "Then the Lacedaemonians, realizing that to destroy the women would be an invidious success while defeat would mean disaster, gave way before the women."

[2] MacMullen, *Roman Social Relations*, 38.

in Luke 1:52–53; 4:18; 6:20–26; 14:12–24; etc.), whether they were male or female. And beyond just an adherence, he set out to investigate the various accounts about Jesus and his claims and to compose one himself (Luke 1:1–4). As a Christian who was both aware of the distinctions in his society and imbued with Jesus' and the apostles' teaching, Luke wrote his account, including Acts, reflecting the economic and hierarchical bifurcation, and he remained true to their teaching on wealth and poverty.

One more consideration has to be factored into this dual strategy found in Luke–Acts. In biblical studies it is usually assumed that the NT texts were written for Christian communities.[3] Also, it is assumed that the issues in the documents reflect the concerns and problems in the communities, though the author of a text may be praising a community.[4] The problem of a social bifurcation between the prosperous Christians—who may or may not necessarily live in the highest levels in society—and the less prosperous members is found in Luke–Acts. Many women (and men) to whom the kingdom showed favor (e.g., healing) or who converted were not poor but well-off. Yet the narrative shows Jesus and the apostles often ministering to the unclean and degraded and the expendables. How could Luke honor such women without dishonoring prosperous women? Luke, then, had to consider how to blend three factors (among many) into his story—the social hierarchy of his culture, the teaching of Jesus and the apostles handed down to him through his research, and the relevance of this to the members in his own Christian community—without offending the godly rich and godly poor.[5]

---

[3] This is not always the case, however. See Esler, *Community,* 24–26, for a survey of those who believe that Luke–Acts was written for individuals. I agree with Esler's refutations of their arguments and his conclusion that Luke–Acts was written for a community. For the purposes of this chapter I am assuming there was only one, but there may have been more. Either way, my thesis is not altered.

[4] This is a debated point, and the two scholars who have been found in the center of the controversy are R. J. Karris, "The Lukan *Sitz im Leben:* Methodology and Prospects," SBLSP 10 (1976) 219–33, who favors that a text speaks to communities and their problems; and L. T. Johnson, "On Finding the Lukan Community: A Cautionary Essay," SBLSP 16 (1979) 87–100, who does not favor this. Not every pericope has to correspond to a community problem. For example, Luke's value for women may not reflect a community in trouble over this issue. On the contrary, Luke may be congratulating the community for honoring women (Karris, "Lukan *Sitz im Leben,*" 91).

[5] I am not arguing that this is the only strategy and purpose in Luke–Acts. It is misguided to find a single one to the exclusion of others. I am highlighting this strategy and purpose because it is the direction my own analysis took.

The last factor assumes that the stories about the upper classes, productive persons, and the unclean and degraded and the expendables in Luke–Acts reflect the prosopography of the Lukan community somewhere in the Greek East, though it would be wrong to assert that the details correspond in precise terms to the members in Luke's community (e.g., that the rich persons whom Jesus confronted in Palestine are exactly like later rich Christians, or that the sinful woman [Luke 7:36–50] represents a numerous group of prostitutes who converted). For our purposes it is only necessary to assume that this overlapping, three-tiered hierarchy was present in Luke's community and that he intended to convey to them values in his stories.[6] For example, when Luke constantly esteems women in Luke–Acts, and especially six from the unclean and degraded and the expendable classes at the expense of wealthy, powerful, and prestigious men, then he is transmitting a value about women to the Christian community, especially about poor women.[7]

---

[6] I said earlier that the culture of Luke's day was undergoing a social bifurcation, yet presently I am claiming that there are three tiers in society and in Luke–Acts. In Greco-Roman society, the bifurcation occurs between the aristocrats and the productive. By definition those at the very bottom were always deprived. But depending on the individual circumstances, Luke can play or manipulate those in the widest portion of the model (fig. 1) in our ch. 2 for his own ends. They may appear on either side of the two-way split, though they mostly appear in the upper one in Luke–Acts. After all, the model (fig. 1) in ch. 2 reflects a continuum of levels, not layers in a rigid geological sense. Some merchants were very prosperous, and some artisans who engaged in specialized crafts were well-off (Acts 19:25). Often, Luke's play or manipulation is calculated to enhance the rise of the unclean and degraded and the expendable women.

[7] Summarizing the best of scholarship, J. Camery-Hoggatt, *Irony in Mark's Gospel: Text and Subtext* (New York: Cambridge, 1992) 29–35, offers several functions of narratives in a community. "The very act of telling a story involves taking a point of view, a particular 'slant,' on the relative significance of, and the relationships between, its various elements" (p. 29). The elements left in and caused to interact as they do are important carriers of meaning and, hence, values. This selectivity informs the newcomer of what is important to the group: (1) The stories inform the listeners of proper behavior—what the heroes do, and how the enemies act. (2) One telling of a story may emerge as the official version. When this happens, the story can function to establish the group's legitimacy to exist the way it does; it may legitimate its institutions and structures. If a newcomer rejects the official version, then he or she is calling into question the existence of the group itself. (3) The stories create solidarity in a group. "Stories, like language in general, create the preconditions of group cohesiveness by providing the basis and understructure of a common life-world" (p. 30). (4) The stories establish the group's identity as the members hear and absorb the values in the stories. (5) The stories contain values that provide group solidarity. (6) The stories are transmitted to members in order to inculcate or reinforce the values contained in them.

As it turns out, this assumption of a three-tiered hierarchy in Luke's Christian community and of his intention to convey his values (as he understands the teaching of Jesus) is confirmed from an interesting source. Even so brief an epistle as that authored by James,[8] written mostly to churches in the Greek East, reflects this class structure and transmission of values. The class structure contains (1) the upper levels (the rich [1:10–11; 2:6; 5:1–3, 5]); (2) the productive (merchants and traders [4:13–16], farmers[9] [5:7], day laborers[10] [5:4]); and (3) the unclean and degraded (sick and suffering [5:13–15]) and the expendables (widows and orphans [1:27], the poor [1:9; 2:2–6]). As for the transmission of values, in each of these passages James sharply rebukes those who exploit or show favoritism, and gently encourages the exploited and weak.[11]

This epistle is relevant for three reasons. First, it independently confirms the assumption that the three levels found within Luke–Acts mirror the levels found in Luke's original community. Second,

---

[8] Whether James the brother of Jesus authored the epistle or someone else did, or whether the epistle was written a few decades before Luke–Acts or approximately at the same time, does not alter the main points of my discussion.

[9] James is using the farmer as an example of a man who is patient. It is not likely that a farmer was an intricate part of an urban Christian community.

[10] Overlapping with the third group, these day laborers are depicted in a rural setting because the land owned by the rich were in the outlying regions. I am assuming that they were part of the churches and corresponded to urban day laborers, since they travelled from the city to the country when harvest arrived. It would seem hard to believe that James would spend so much time encouraging or rebuking the persons he mentions by occupational title or access to wealth if they were not part of the church.

[11] The author of 1 Timothy also grapples with this social bifurcation. The less prosperous members he instructs,

> But those who want to be rich fall into temptation and are trapped by many senseless and harmful desires that plunge men into ruin and destruction. For the love of money [ἡ φιλαργυρία, *hē philargyria*] is the root of all kinds of evil. (1 Tim 6:9–10)

But those who already had wealth when they joined the church he exhorts differently:

> As for those who in the present age are rich, command them not to be haughty, or to set their hopes on the uncertainty of riches, but rather on God who richly provides us with everything for our enjoyment; they are to do good, to be rich in good works, generous, and ready to share, thus storing up for themselves the treasure of a good foundation for the future so that they may take hold of the life that really is life. (1 Tim 6:17–19)

since, according to James, Christians in the East were not above discriminating against the poor in favor of the rich, there was a need to bring correction. Luke had a motive to include as one of his major themes the honoring of the poor, even if at the expense of the rich. Third, this epistle could speak directly to the members of churches by their occupational title or their access to wealth, unlike stories in Luke–Acts, which, by their nature, could only assume or allude indirectly to such members. An epistle can transmit the values of its author with explicit rebukes or exhortations, such as, "Hey, now, you rich! Weep and wail over your miseries that are coming!" (Jas 5:1, my translation). Storytellers transmit the same value by crafting the elements, structure, plot, and so forth in their stories to lead the audience to discover on its own the intended value. Even if Luke the storyteller had a reliable character such as Jesus directly commanding his immediate listeners in Palestine to honor the needy, one still has to assume that members in Luke's intended audience needed to learn this lesson. Thus, the epistle of James and its explicitly mentioned audience serve as confirmation of this lesson for Luke–Acts and its audience.

Since most literary works known in Luke's days employed a preface or a prologue that revealed the main themes and characters, Luke also made use of two prefaces, one in each volume of Luke–Acts. Furthermore, he revealed throughout the first two chapters of his Gospel one of his major characters (Jesus) and themes (the fall of the rich and powerful and the rise of the poor and weak). This theme was especially foregrounded in the words of Simeon in 2:34, "This child is destined for the falling and the rising of many." That is, as various characters in Luke–Acts meet up with Jesus (and his emissaries), either they fall from their high social standing if they are arrogant, or they are elevated if they are needy and humble of heart. Faithful to Jesus' teaching on the poor versus the rich, Luke sought to overturn or reverse the social bifurcation that he observed overwhelming the Greco-Roman world. This bifurcation must not control or govern the Christian community so that the poor are discriminated against and dishonored.

In his narrative Luke was not satisfied with describing characters in vague terms, such as the weak versus the strong. He disclosed their social location with seemingly offhanded clues, by indicating they were a centurion, πρῶτος, synagogue ruler, Samaritan, retainers and artisans of various sorts, peasants, and so forth. But for Luke's first audience these titles or occupational adjectives were not offhand; they conveyed lively meaning necessary to understand Luke's stories to their fullest. Luke exploited the characters' social location to fulfill his literary theme. In Luke–Acts the social undergirds the literary, and the literary assumes the social.

This exploitation of Luke's theme meant exploiting the Mediterranean value of public honor and public shame. Women from the lower classes had to show a sense of shame to men in the upper classes. But when Luke showed Jesus humbling wealthy, powerful, and prestigious men by means of unclean and degraded, or expendable, women, then this humbling smarted that much more sharply for the men than if Luke had only used other unclean and degraded, or expendable, men (whom he did in fact also use). Luke's theme and treatment of honor and shame also meant exploiting the politics of space. When the men were shamed in the territory where they held the reins of power (e.g., Simon the Pharisee in his house), their fall from power gained an added poignancy.

Women who were among the upper classes or who were at least productive in society never suffered from a social demotion upon receiving favor from the kingdom or upon their conversion. Either they moved laterally into the Jesus movement or early church without losing their social standing, or they received some measure of elevation. For example, Lydia (Acts 16:14–15, 40) and the prominent Thessalonians (Acts 17:4) converted without losing their prosperity, while Elizabeth (Luke 1:5–7, 24–25, 39–80) was elevated with fertility and a celebrated son, thereby ridding her of the social shame of barrenness. The value or lesson in these stories is clear to women who had already joined the church or who were contemplating joining: the kingdom of God will never damage them socially. Wealth does not prima facie disqualify a person from conversion. It is a question of the heart.

Women who were paired with men from approximately the same social level underwent the same phenomena. Either their conversion made them receive a blessing equal to that of men, or their conversion elevated them above the men. This is significant because, as noted, women were a step behind men within their own class. In contrast to his own culture Luke was conveying the value that in the kingdom of God women can be made equal to men or even rise above them. Damaris and her male counterparts, Dionysius and a few others (Acts 17:34), converted equally, while Mary (mother of Jesus) (Luke 1:27–36; 2:41–51) was temporarily elevated over Zacharias. And even though Mary, the mother of the resurrected Jesus, received clarification about who really was Jesus' mother—anyone who hears and does the word (Luke 8:19–21)—the message in this passage rings clearly: women who hear and obey the word can be equal to the mother of Jesus. Jesus is forming a fictive family to which all women are invited and in which all women will receive honor upon accepting the invitation.

But Luke understood that women in the upper levels enjoyed more wealth, status, and power than men or women in the classes below them. Therefore, these upper-level women were never elevated at the expense of men or women in lower classes. Jairus the synagogue ruler and his daughter (Luke 8:41–42, 49–56) were paired with the hemorrhaging woman (8:43–48), and both received an equal blessing from Jesus because he never shows favoritism. Indeed, in order for the synagogue ruler to receive healing for his daughter, he fell prostrate before his healer (v. 41). If there was a possibility of upper-level women or men being exalted over lower-level men or women, then Luke made the social standing of upper-level men and women ambiguous or the rise and fall of both sets ambiguous, as in the case of Joanna and the twelve. Thus, Luke was preserving his theme spelled out in Luke 2:34 that only the rejects in society are raised up while the rich and powerful fall—not vice versa—even if the rich and powerful are women.

The ultimate fulfillment of Luke's theme occurred when he paired women from the unclean and degraded and the expendable classes with men who were wealthy, powerful, and had high status. These women rose in the kingdom, and the men fell. The six women whom Luke chose came from the depths of society: a prostitute (Luke 7:36–50); Mary Magdalene, a formerly demonized peasant who represented other such women (Luke 8:1–3; 23:55–24:10); a woman bent double caused by a spirit (Luke 13:10–17); a poor but generous widow (Luke 21:1–4) who represented widows whose houses were devoured by scribes (Luke 20:45–47); ethnically inferior Samaritans (Acts 8:5–25); and persecuted women (Acts 8:1–4; 9:1–22).

When a comparison was made between Luke's Gospel and Mark's and Matthew's Gospels, it became clear how deliberate Luke's strategy was. To cite only two instances, in the story of the poor-generous widow (Mark 12:41–44; Luke 21:1–4), Mark has a three-tiered hierarchy—the rich, the masses, and the widow—but Luke omits the masses and contrasts only the rich and the poor-generous widow. In the story about the woman who anoints Jesus' feet (Luke 7:36–50), Mark (14:3–9) and Matthew (26:6–13) portray Simon as a leper, whereas Luke has him as a Pharisee, the very person who was most concerned about purity; and Matthew and Mark portray the woman as ordinary, whereas Luke sees her as a "sinner," that is, a prostitute. Following his own culture, which was bifurcating into the haves and the have-nots, Luke also split the social gap between the two opposing sets of characters in his stories. But in contrast to his own culture, he skillfully overturned or reversed the hierarchy.

As noted, the values or lessons conveyed in these stories about women are profound for the women (and men) in Luke's community.

First, in general terms, Luke was agreeing with the overall message in the epistle of James: Christians should not discriminate against the poor in favor of the rich. It is almost as if the scene that James set up in his epistle could have occurred in Luke's community as well. In Jas 2:1–13 a rich man in beautiful clothing enters the assembly and is given the choice seat, while the poor man in dirty clothing is forced, as if out of embarrassment at his presence, to move to the back on the floor in deference to the rich man. At this tragic scene, James rains down a scathing rebuke on the church, as would Luke (cf. Luke 6:24–25).

Second, any women who were wealthy or only had modest means never suffered a social demotion upon entering the Christian community if they did not place their loyalties and trust in wealth but had humble hearts. Some may have even assumed a leadership role, as did evidently Lydia (Acts 16:14–15, 40) and Mary (Acts 12:12). Prisca the tentmaker, who was of modest means according to Luke, also ended up teaching the wealthy and learned Apollos (Acts 18:24–26), regardless of the mitigating circumstances.

Third, women who are unclean and degraded or expendable must receive honor and prestige in the church. If they have any physical need, they are to receive help as well (Acts 6:1–6; cf. Jas 1:27). Any leader who thinks that he is on the positive side of the kingdom and is walking fully in its precepts but despises these kinds of women is poised for a crashing fall. The twelve and Mary Magdalene could attest to this. A true follower of Jesus honors these women as Jesus did.

Though Luke's falling and rising theme crossed gender boundaries, women were chosen as the subject of this study because of the modern debate over their role in Luke–Acts. Most scholars have viewed Luke as favoring women, but in recent years some have questioned this assumption.[12] This study has sought to take a fresh look at Luke's reputed high view of women. It can be stated that Luke's high view was confirmed. If there was any evidence of a "suppression" of women's roles (and the evidence was to the contrary), then one must consider the social hierarchy of Luke's day and women's place in it. Not all oppression was created equal. Women who were unclean and degraded, or expendable, could attest to this.

---

[12] Schüssler Fiorenza, *In Memory*, 50, 145–46; she sees traces in Acts of women's involvement in leadership roles but claims that Luke ultimately suppresses more than he clarifies (pp. 160–99). S. Davies, "Women in the Third Gospel and the New Testament Apocrypha," in *"Women Like This"* (ed. Levine) 187, says, "I see no elevation of women's status in Luke." Corley, *Private Women*, 109, 144–46, claims Luke is conservative towards women because he upholds the traditional, submissive, and domestic roles in Greco-Roman society.

Do not be afraid, little flock,
for it is your Father's good
pleasure to give you the kingdom.
(Luke 12:32)

APPENDIX

Not all of the women in the slave, unclean and degraded, and expendable classes are adequate candidates for the falling and rising theme in Luke 2:34. They can be placed into categories 1 (women not paired with men), 2 (women paired with men from approximately the same class), and 4 (women paired with men from a higher class). Category 3 is eliminated because it assumes women from higher classes.

Category 1. *Prostitutes* (Luke 15:30). They are mentioned only in passing in the parable of the Prodigal Son and serve only to show the degradation of the errant son.

Mourners for Tabitha (Acts 9:36–41). When Tabitha dies, they weep in grief over her as they show Peter all the garments that she made. Perhaps the widows were her employees. They certainly know where to find Tabitha's products and have access to them. But the claim about their employment is only a guess.

Rhoda the Slave (Acts 12:13–15). Rhoda, though not paired explicitly with men, plays a role that has a curious resonance with the role played by the women in the Easter narrative: (1) Jesus is placed in the tomb by the Roman authorities; Peter is thrown into prison by the Roman authorities. (2) Jesus is resurrected ("released") with angels present; Peter is released by an angel. (3) At first, there are somewhat unclear tokens of Jesus' resurrection; Peter knocks on the door out of Rhoda's sight. (4) The women hurriedly run back to the eleven to announce Jesus' resurrection; Rhoda runs back to the prayer meeting in Mary's house to announce Peter's release. (5) The women's report is called foolish; Rhoda is called mad. (6) Peter runs to the tomb; the praying but unbelieving disciples go to the door where Peter is standing. (7) Jesus appears to the men; Peter "appears" to the praying disciples. (6) The women's and Rhoda's reports are now believed.[1]

Rhoda could fit into category 4 if it did not compare women with only men, since in her case it is possible that she has the lowest status of any of the men and women in the prayer meeting. She is the first to believe in Peter's release (although in her excitement she forgets to open the door for him), and the others are wrong to call her mad. Rhoda is vindicated (an exaltation); the rest are humorously shown to be unbelievers (a demotion) even though they are praying for Peter. She is not the very best example, however, of women in category 4 because, despite the possibility that she has the lowest status, it is unclear where the other believers at Mary's house are to be located socially.

But if Mary her mistress is isolated, then Rhoda can serve as an example that Luke differentiates between even women in the lower classes and women in the upper classes. After all, Rhoda's and Mary's names are brought to the foreground in the narrative, and they are identified as having a direct relationship as mistress-slave. If this pairing is so, then the claim that social hierarchy takes slight priority over gender is confirmed.[2] Luke is not afraid of exalting a slave woman at the expense of a wealthy, slave-owning woman.

Category 2.   *Anna* (Luke 2:36–48). A devout, elderly widow, she is paired with Simeon, yet it is impossible to know from which level in society Simeon comes. But clearly Luke is intending to highlight the devotion of both to God on an equal basis. Both are esteemed in the narrative.

Hebrew and Hellenistic Widows (Acts 6:1–7). It is unclear whether Luke intends to pair these widows with the seven deacons (category 4) or whether he pairs the Hebrew widows with the Hellenistic widows (category 2, if it were gender-neutral). I prefer the latter alternative for the simple reason that there is strife between the

---

[1] Tannehill, *Narrative Unity,* 2.152–53, sees this connection between Jesus' and Peter's arrest, but he does not emphasize Rhoda's role, as I do.
[2] For support of this claim, see ch. 5, "Shame, Class, and Gender" (pp. 155–57).

widows, and the seven, through the twelve, have to intervene. The widows cannot be candidates for the theme in Luke 2:34 because they come from approximately the same class and, though one group is exalted, the other is not demoted.

In favor of the first alternative, pairing the widows with the deacons, Witherington points out that men are consigned to serve tables for the poor widows, whereas women are not appointed for this "menial" task.[3] He states that such a consignment for men would have brought shame according to the mores of the Hellenistic world, but not in the Jewish world, so men's and women's roles are reversed.[4] His source for this conclusion is one reference from the Roman censor Cato (234–149 B.C.E.), a sentiment we would expect from a man of Cato's standing.[5] It would have been better had Witherington not appealed to the elite Cato in the Latin West.

But if the larger Greek East is brought into the analysis, then different conclusions may have been reached had Witherington reconsidered the language: διακονεῖν τραπέζαις, *diakonein trapezais* (to serve "tables"). The verb διακονέω does not always imply a menial task, especially when it comes to serving the poor—a special interest to Luke. In Luke 8:3 the women διηκόνουν αὐτοῖς ἐκ τῶν ὑπαρχόντων αὐταῖς, *diēkonoun autois ek tōn hyparchontōn autais* ("served them [Jesus and the twelve] out of their possessions [or means]"). Furthermore, from the Hellenistic to the Greco-Roman periods, temples were associated with banking and money changing; and by coincidence the word used for this financial institution is τραπέζα, *trapeza* (bank), the word usually translated as "tables" in Acts 6:2.[6] It is likely that Luke's audience in Greco-Roman Asia Minor or Syria would have thought that the seven have an important task instead of a menial one because of the temple environment in which they carry out their assignment. In Acts 4:35 the twelve were in charge of the community funds for the needy, and now they are turning the responsibility over to the seven. The very fact that the apostles sanction the task and call for men with high spiritual qualifications indicate that it is more than menial, that it is an ongoing ministry exercising a powerful control

---

[3] Witherington, *Women in Earliest Churches,* 145.

[4] Ibid.

[5] Cato, *Agr.* 143, LCL 125.

[6] See Broughton, "Roman Asia Minor," 888; and M. Rostovtzeff, *The Social and Economic History of the Hellenistic World* (2d ed.; 3 vols.; New York: Clarendon) 2.1280–81. In Mark 11:15 and Matthew 21:12 Jesus overturns "tables," but the tables are in the context of banking or money changing. Undoubtedly, the literal table, as is true for metaphors, was quickly associated semantically with the business that was transacted on the table: banking, money changing, and other financial dealings.

over the flow of resources. Tannehill is correct when he observes that "the appointment of the seven in 6:1–6 resembles a group of Septuagint stories about appointing to authority a person or persons who have wisdom and Spirit."[7]

Therefore, as noted, the widows should not be paired opposite to the seven. Rather, the seven act as arbiters under the direct authority of the twelve to settle the dispute between two groups of widows. The two groups are paired with each other and cannot adequately fulfill Luke 2:34.

Category 4. *Widow Bereft of Only Son* (Luke 7:2–17). Unique to Luke, this widow's story has her paired with a very wealthy and honored (vv. 4–5) Gentile centurion. She and the ethnically inferior centurion (in terms of his slave) receive benefit from Jesus. If the superior ethnicity of the widow were to counterbalance the centurion's wealth and honor, then they might have been placed in category 2. In any case, neither one is exalted or demoted at the expense of the other. Indeed, the woman is treated equally, though an expendable; and the centurion (with his slave) is treated equally, though a Gentile.

Beaten Slave Women (Luke 12:41–48). These women are paired with a male slave who is promoted to being a retainer. In this position of power he begins to mistreat the female slaves. When the master returns, the slave is punished with a gruesome death (the ultimate fall) that protects the slave women (a rise of sorts). The vertical movement is flattened out, however, for two reasons: (1) As slaves, his and the women's legal status are the same. (2) It is not clear how the women are promoted after the retainer falls other than by receiving protection from their master. Thus, this story does not adequately fulfill Luke 2:34.

Persistent Widow (Luke 18:1–8). Pairing this widow with a judge, Jesus uses her as a positive example in his parable. But the judge, even though he is characterized as not fearing God and as ὁ κριτὴς τῆς ἀδικίας, *ho kritēs tēs adikias* (the unrighteous or unjust judge), cannot be said to be demoted socially. Indeed, he still has enough power to favor the widow. Nevertheless, even though the judge does not fall, this story is a reminder that Jesus will honor an expendable female in the face of a powerful man.

Pythoness Slave Girl (Acts 16:16–24). By having Paul cast a demon out of this slave girl, Luke indicates that she receives benefit from the kingdom of God. This signals Luke's audience, which has

---

[7] Tannehill, *Narrative Unity*, 2.83–84.

progressed far enough into Luke–Acts, that demon expulsion is a benefit, that she is spiritually free, and that she is now presumably a part of, and protected by, the Christian community in Philippi. (The owners, however, would still have legal rights over her.) But Luke's message is clear: because of her deliverance from a demon, she can no longer be exploited as a fortune-teller. Unfortunately, Luke quickly leaves her behind to focus on Paul and his team, who are persecuted by her owners.

The owners are on the brink of a fall because they lose a large amount of revenue. But they retain enough power to drag Paul and Silas before the magistrates. Luke is portraying the owners as so wicked and exploitative that they care nothing about the life of another human, the woman, but only about their loss of profits. Luke then leaves the slaveowners out of the picture, so their fall is never enacted. His narrative is turned towards the authorities. Paul and Silas, however, ultimately triumph over them as a jailer converts and the magistrates personally escort them out of jail with apologies. Before leaving Philippi, they freely and without fear return to Lydia's house and encourage the disciples meeting there (v. 40).

BIBLIOGRAPHY

ANCIENT AUTHORS AND TEXTS

"The Apocryphal/Deuterocanonical Books." New Revised Standard Version 1989. In *The HarperCollins Study Bible*. Ed. W. Meeks. New York: HarperCollins, 1993.

Aristides, Aelius. *The Complete Works: Orations*. 2 vols. Trans. C. Behr. Leiden: Brill, 1981–86.

Cato. *De agri cultura*. Trans. W. D. Hooper. Rev. H. B. Ash. LCL. Cambridge: Harvard, 1967.

Chariton. *Chaereas and Callirhoe*. Trans. B. Reardon. In *Collected Ancient Greek Novels*. Ed. B. Reardon. Los Angeles: University of California, 1989. Greek Text: Ed. W. E. Blake. Oxford Classical Texts. New York: Oxford, 1938.

Cicero. *The Verrine Orations*. 2 vols. Trans. L. Greenwood. LCL. Cambridge: Harvard, 1928–35.

_____. *Pro Flacco*. Trans. C. MacDonald. LCL. Cambridge: Harvard, 1976.

Columella. *De re rustica*. 3 vols. Trans. H. Ash, E. Forster, and E. Heffner. LCL. Cambridge: Harvard, 1941–55.

Dio Chrysostom. *Discourses*. 5 vols. Trans. J. Cohoon and H. Crosby. LCL. Cambridge: Harvard, 1932–51.

The Documents from the Bar Kokhba Period in the Cave of the Letters. Ed. N. Lewis, Y. Yadin, and J. Greenfield. Jerusalem: Israel Exploration Society and Hebrew University of Jerusalem, 1989.

Epigraphica: Texts on the Social History of the Greek World. Vol 2. Ed. H. W. Pleket. Leiden: Brill, 1969.

Josephus. *The Life*. Trans. H. St. J. Thackeray. LCL. Cambridge: Harvard, 1926.

_____. *Jewish War.* 2 vols. Trans. H. St. J. Thackeray. LCL. Cambridge: Harvard, 1927–28.

_____. *Jewish Antiquities.* 6 vols. Trans. H. St. J. Thackeray et al. LCL. Cambridge: Harvard, 1930–65.

Longus. *Daphnis and Chloe.* Trans. C. Gill. In *Collected Ancient Greek Novels.* Ed. B. Reardon. Los Angeles: University of California, 1989.

Lucian. *Lucian.* 8 vols. Trans. A Harmon and M. Macleod. LCL. Cambridge: Harvard, 1913–61.

The Mishnah. Trans. H. Danby. London: Oxford, 1933.

The Mishnah. Trans. J. Neusner. New Haven: Yale, 1988.

Old Testament Pseudepigrapha. Ed. J. H. Charlesworth. New York: Doubleday, 1983.

Pausanius. *Description of Greece.* 5 vols. Trans. W. Jones. LCL. Cambridge: Harvard, 1918–35.

Phaedrus. *Fables.* Trans. B. Perry. LCL. Cambridge: Harvard, 1965.

Plutarch, *Moralia.* Trans. F. C. Babbitt et al. 15 vols. LCL. Cambridge: Harvard, 1927–69.

Septuaginta. Ed. A. Rahlfs. Stuttgart: Deutsche Bibelgesellschaft, 1979.

Strabo. *Geography.* 8 vols. Trans. H. Jones. LCL. Cambridge: Harvard, 1941–55.

The Tosephta. Trans. J. Neusner et al. New York: Ktav, 1977–86.

Varro. *De re rustica.* In Cato, *De agri cultura.* Trans. W. D. Hooper. Rev. H. B. Ash. LCL. Cambridge: Harvard, 1938.

SOCIOLOGY AND HISTORY

Akurgal, E. *Ancient Civilizations and Ruins of Turkey.* 6th ed. Trans. J. Whybrow and M. Emre. Istanbul: Haset Kitabevi, 1985.

Akurgal, E., R. Merkelbach, et al., eds. "Inschriften von Perge." In *Epigraphica Anatolica.* Pages 122–27, 133, 138–40, 146, 149, 152, 160. Bonn: R. Habelt, 1988.

Alföldy, G. *Die römische Gesellschaft.* Wiesbaden: Steiner, 1986.

Allardt, E. "Theories about Social Stratification." In *Social Stratification.* Ed. J. A. Jackson. Pages 14–24. New York: Cambridge, 1968.

Amaru Halpern, B. "Portraits of Biblical Women in Josephus' *Antiquities.*" JJS 39 (1988) 143–70.

Applebaum, S. "Economic Life in Palestine." In *The Jewish People in the First Century.* 2 vols. Ed. S. Safrai and M. Stern. Vol. 2, pages 631–700. CRINT. Philadelphia: Fortress, 1976.

_____. "The Social and Economic Status of Jews in the Diaspora." In *The Jewish People in the First Century.* 2 vols. Ed. S. Safrai and M. Stern. Vol. 2, pages 701–27. CRINT. Philadelphia: Fortress, 1976.

Archer, L. J. *Her Price Is beyond Rubies The Jewish Woman in Greco-Roman Palestine.* JSOTSup 60; Sheffield: Sheffield Academic, 1990.

Archer, L. J. et al., eds. *Women in Ancient Societies.* New York: Routledge, 1994.

Avigad, N. "How the Wealthy Lived in Herodian Jerusalem." *BARev* 2 (1976) 1, 23–45.

Avi-Yonah, M. *The World History of the Jewish People: Volume 7, The Herodian Period.* 1st series. New Brunswick, N.J.: Rutgers, 1975.

Barber, B. *Social Stratification: A Comparative Analysis of Structure and Process.* New York: Harcourt, Brace & World, 1957.

_____. "Introduction to 'Social Stratification.'" *IESS.* 15.288–96.

Barrow, R. H. 1928. *Slavery in the Roman Empire.* Reprint. New York: Barnes & Noble, 1968.

Bartchy, S. S. Μᾶλλον Χρῆσαι: *First-Century Slavery and the Interpretation of 1 Corinthians 7:21.* SBLDS 11. Missoula, Mont: Scholars, 1973.

Beebe, H. K. "Domestic Architecture and the New Testament." *BA* 38 (1975) 89–104.

Bendix, R., and S. M. Lipset. *Class, Status, and Power.* 2d ed. New York: Free Press, 1966.

Berger, P. L. *The Sacred Canopy: Elements of a Sociological Theory of Religion.* Garden City, N.Y.: Doubleday, 1969.

Berger, P. L., and Thomas Luckmann. *The Social Construction of Reality: A Treatise in the Sociology of Knowledge.* Garden City, N.Y.: Doubleday, 1966.

Best, T. "The Sociological Study of the New Testament: Promise and Peril of a New Discipline." *SJT* 36 (1983) 181–94.

Blasi, A. J. "Role Structures in the Early Hellenistic Church." *Sociological Analysis* 47 (1986) 226–48.

Boatwright, M. T. "Plancia Magna of Perge: Women's Roles and Status in Roman Asia Minor." In *Women's History and Ancient History.* Ed. Sarah Pomeroy. Pages 249–72. Chapel Hill: University of North Carolina, 1991.

Bouchier, E. S. *Syria as a Roman Province.* Oxford: Basil Blackwell, 1916.

Bradley, K. R. *Slaves and Masters in the Roman Empire.* Reprint 1984. New York: Oxford, 1987.

Braunstein, O. *Die politische Wirksmankeit der griechischen Frau.* Leipzig: August Hoffman, 1911.

Briant, P. "Village et communautés villageoises d'Asie achéménide et hellénistique." *JESHO* 18 (1975) 165–88.

Brooten, B. J. *Women Leaders in the Ancient Synagogue.* BJS 36. Chico, Calif: Scholars, 1982.

Broughton, T. R. S. "Roman Landholding in Asia Minor." *TAPA* 65 (1934) 207–39.

_____. "Roman Asia Minor." In *An Economic Survey of Ancient Rome*. Ed. F. Tenney. Vol. 4, pages 499–916. Baltimore: John Hopkins, 1938. Reprint. Paterson, N.J.: Pagent Books, 1959.

Brunt, P. *Social Conflicts in the Roman Republic*. London: Chatto & Windus, 1971.

_____. "Aspects of the Social Thought of Dio Chrysostom and of the Stoics." In *Studies in Greek History and Thought*. Pages 210–44. New York: Clarendon, 1993.

Burford, A. *Craftsmen in Greek and Roman Society*. London: Thames & Hudson, 1972.

Cairns, D. "The Thought of Peter Berger." *SJT* 27 (1974) 181–97.

Cameron, A. " 'Neither Male nor Female'." *GR* 27 (1980) 60–68.

Cameron, A., and A. Kuhrt, eds. *Images of Women in Antiquity*. Detroit: Wayne State University, 1983.

Cantarella, E. *Pandora's Daughter*. Trans. Maureen B. Fant. Baltimore: Johns Hopkins, 1981.

Carney, E. " 'What's in a Name?': The Emergence of a Title for Royal Women in the Hellenistic Period." In *Women's History and Ancient History*. Ed. Sarah Pomeroy. Pages 154–72. Chapel Hill: University of North Carolina, 1991.

Casey, R. "Simon Magus." In *The Beginnings of Christianity*. 5 vols. Ed. F. J. F. Jackson and K. Lake. Vol. 5, pages 151–63. London: Macmillan, 1933.

Chapot, V. *La Province romaine proconsulaire d'Asie depuis ses origines jusqu'à la fin du Haut-Empire*. 1904. Reprint. Rome: "L'Erma" di Bretschneider, 1968.

Charlesworth, M. P. *The Roman Empire*. New York: Oxford, 1968.

Chastagnol, A. "Les homines novi entrés au sénat sous le règne de Domitien." In *Studien zur antiken Sozialgeschichte*. Ed. W. Eck, H. Galsterer, and H. Wolff. Cologne and Vienna: Böhlau, 1980.

Corbo, V. *The House of St. Peter of Capharnaum*. Trans. S. Saller. Jerusalem: Franciscan, 1969.

Countryman, L. W. "Welfare in the Churches of Asia Minor under the Early Roman Empire." In SBLSP 16. Pages 131–46. 2 vols. Chico, Calif.: Scholars, 1979.

Crossan, J. D. *The Historical Jesus: The Life of a Mediterranean Jewish Peasant*. San Francisco: Harper, 1991.

Dar, S., and S. Appelbaum. *Landscape and Pattern: An Archeological Survey of Samaria, 800 B.C.E.–636 C.E.* 2 vols. Oxford: Biblical Archeology Review, 1986.

Dareste, R., B. Haussoulier, and T. Reinach, eds. *Recueil des inscriptions juridiques grecques: texte, traduction, commentaire.* 2 vols. Rome: "L'Erma" di Bretschneider, 1965.

Debord, P. *Aspects sociaux et économiques de la vie religieuse dans l'Anatolie gréco-romaine.* Etudes Préliminaires aux Religions Orientales dans l'Empire Romain 48. Leiden: Brill, 1982.

Deissmann, A. "The Excavations in Ephesus." *Biblical Review* 15 (1930) 332–46.

Dickey, S. "Some Economic and Social Conditions of Asia Minor Affecting the Expansion of Christianity." In *Studies in Early Christianity.* Ed. S. J. Case. Pages 393–416. New York: Century, 1928.

Dobson, B. "The Centuriate and Social Mobility during the Principate." In *Recherches sur les structures sociales dans l'antiquité classique.* Ed. C. Nicolet. Pages 99–117. Paris: Editions du Centre National de la Recherche Scientifique, 1970.

Dodge, H. "Brick Construction in Roman Greece and Asia Minor." In *Roman Architecture in the Greek World.* Ed. S. Macready and F. Thompson. London: Society of Antiquaries of London, 1987.

Donaldson, J. *Woman: Her Position and Influence in Ancient Greece and Rome, and among Early Christians.* London: Longman, Green & Co, 1907.

Dumont, L. "A Modified View of Our Origins: The Christian Beginnings of Modern Individualism." *Religion* 12 (1982) 1–27.

Eck, W. "Die Präsenz senatorischer Familien in den Städten des Imperium romanum bis zum späten 3. Jahrhundert." In *Studien zur antiken Sozialgeschichte.* Ed. W. Eck, H. Galsterer, and H. Wolff. Pages 283–322. Cologne and Vienna: Böhlau, 1980.

Edwards, O. C., Jr. "Sociology as a Tool for Interpreting the New Testament." *ATR* 65 (1983) 431–48.

Eisenstadt, S. N. "Prestige, Participation, and Strata Formation." In *Social Stratification.* Ed. J. A. Jackson. Pages 62–103. New York: Cambridge, 1968.

Eisenstadt, S. N., and L. Roniger. *Patrons, Clients, and Friends.* New York: Cambridge, 1984.

Elliot, J. H. *A Home for the Homeless: A Sociological Exegesis of 1 Peter, Its Situation and Strategy.* Philadelphia: Fortress, 1981.

——. "Social-Scientific Criticism of the New Testament: More on Methods and Models." *Semeia* 35 (1986) 1–33.

Etienne, R., and G. Fabre. "Démographie et classe sociale." In *Recherches sur les structures sociales dans l'antiquité classique.* Ed. C. Nicolet. Pages 81–98. Paris: Editions du Centre National de la Recherche Scientifique, 1970.

Falk, Z. W. "Private Law: Jewish Private Law." In *The Jewish People in the First Century.* 2 vols. Ed. S. Safrai and M. Stern. Vol. 1, pages 504–33. CRINT. Philadelphia: Fortress, 1976.

Fiensy, D. A. *The Social History of Palestine in the Herodian Period: The Land Is Mine.* Studies in Bible and Early Christianity 20. Lewiston, N.Y.: Edwin Mellen, 1991.

Filson, F. "The Significance of House Churches." *JBL* 58 (1939) 105–12.

Finley, M. I., ed. *Studies in Ancient Society.* Boston: Routledge & Kegan Paul, 1974.

_____. *The Ancient Economy.* 2d ed. London: Hogarth, 1985.

Foley, H. P., ed. *Reflections of Women in Antiquity.* New York: Gordon & Breach, 1981.

Frayne, J. M. *Subsistence Farming in Roman Italy.* London: Centaur, 1979.

Freyne, S. *Galilee from Alexander the Great to Hadrian: 323 B.C.E. to 135 C.E.* Notre Dame: Notre Dame, 1980.

_____. *Galilee, Jesus, and the Gospels.* Dublin: Gill & Macmillan, 1988.

Gagé, J. *Les classes sociales dans l'Empire romain.* 2d ed. Paris: Payot, 1971.

Gager, J. G. *Kingdom and Community: The Social World of Early Christianity.* Englewood Cliffs, N.J.: Prentice Hall, 1975.

_____. "Shall we Marry Our Enemies? Sociology and the New Testament." *Int* 36 (1982) 256–65.

_____. "Sociological Description and Sociological Analysis in the Study of Early Christianity: A Review Essay." In *The Bible as Liberation: Political and Sociological Hermeneutics.* Ed. N. K. Gottwald. Pages 428–40. Maryknoll, N.Y.: Orbis, 1983.

Garnsey, P. *Social Status and Legal Privilege in the Roman Empire.* Oxford: Clarendon, 1970.

_____. 1983. "Grain for Rome." In *Trade in the Ancient Economy.* Ed. P. Garnsey, K. Hopkins, and C. R. Whittaker. Pages 118–30. Los Angeles: University of California, 1983.

_____. "Non-slave Labour in the Roman World." *Non-slave Labour in the Greco-Roman World.* Ed. P. Garnsey; Cambridge: Cambridge Philological Society, 1980, 34–45.

Garnsey, P., K. Hopkins, and C. R. Whittaker, eds. *Trade in the Ancient Economy.* Berkeley: University of California, 1983.

Gaudemet, J. "Le statut de la femme dans l'Empire romain." *Recueils de la société Jean Bodin. La Femme* 1 (1959) 191–222.

Gill, R. "Berger's Plausibility Structures: A Response to Professor Cairns." *SJT* 27 (1974) 198–207.

Goodman, M. *The Ruling Class of Judaea.* New York: Cambridge, 1987.

Goodwater, L. *Women in Antiquity: An Annotated Bibliography.* Metuchen, N.J.: Scarecrow, 1974.

Gottwald, N. K., ed. *The Bible and Liberation: Political and Sociological Hermeneutics.* Maryknoll, N.Y.: Orbis, 1983.

____. "Social Class as an Analytical and Hermeneutical Category in Biblical Studies." *JBL* 112 (1993) 3–22.

Hamel, G. *Poverty and Charity in Roman Palestine, First Three Centuries C.E.* Los Angeles: University of California, 1990.

Hands, A. R. *Charities and Social Aid in Greece and Rome.* Ithaca: Cornell, 1968.

Hanfmann, G., L. Robert, and W. Mierse, ed. "The Hellenistic Period," in *Sardis: From Prehistoric to Roman Times.* Pages 109–38. Cambridge: Harvard, 1983.

Harmand, J. "Le soldat prolétarien et le barbare dans le Sénat à la fin de la République." In *Recherches sur les structures sociales dans l'antiquité classique.* Ed. C. Nicolet. Pages 117–32. Paris: Editions du Centre National de la Recherche Scientifique, 1970.

Harrington, D. J. "Sociological Concepts and the Early Church: A Decade of Research." *TS* 41 (1980) 181–90.

____. "Second Testament Exegesis and the Social Sciences: A Bibliography." *BTB* 18 (1988) 77–85.

Hatzfeld, J. *Les traficants italiens dans l'orient hellénique.* Paris: E. de Boccard, 1919.

Heichelheim, F. M. "Roman Syria." In *An Economic Survey of Ancient Rome.* Ed. F. Tenney. Vol. 4, pages 121–258. Baltimore: John Hopkins, 1938. Reprint. Paterson, N.J.: Pagent Books, 1959.

Hengel, M. *Judaism and Hellenism.* 2 vols. Trans. John Bowden. Philadelphia: Fortress, 1974.

Hock, R. F. "Paul's Tentmaking and the Problem of His Social Class." *JBL* 97 (1978) 555–64.

____. *The Social Context of Paul's Ministry.* Philadelphia: Fortress, 1980.

Holmberg, B. *Sociology and the New Testament: An Appraisal.* Philadelphia: Fortress, 1990.

Horsley, R. A., and J. S. Hanson. *Bandits, Prophets, and Messiahs.* Chicago: Winston, 1985.

Horsley, R. A. *Sociology and the Jesus Movement.* New York: Crossroad, 1989.

Ilan, T. *Jewish Women in Greco-Roman Palestine.* Peabody, Mass.: Hendrickson, 1995.

Jackson, J. A., ed. *Social Stratification.* New York: Cambridge, 1968.

____. "Social Stratification—Editorial Introduction." In *Social Stratification.* Pages 1–13. New York: Cambridge, 1968.

Jaczynowska, M. "Les organisations de Iuvenes et l'aristocratie munici-
    pale." In *Recherches sur les structures sociales dans l'antiquité
    classique.* Ed. C. Nicolet. Pages 265–74. Paris: Editions du Cen-
    tre National de la Recherche Scientifique, 1970.
Jameson, S. "Cornutus Tertullus and the Plancii of Perge." *JRS* 55
    (1965) 54–58.
Jastrow, M. *A Dictionary of the Targumim, the Talmud Babli and
    Yerushalmi, and the Midrashic Literature.* 2 vols. 1903. Reprint.
    New York: Judaica, 1950.
Jeremias, J. *Jerusalem in the Time of Jesus.* Trans. F. H. Cave and C. H.
    Cave. 3d ed. Philadelphia: Fortress, 1969.
Johnson, B. "Sociology and Religious Truth." *Sociological Analysis*
    38 (1977) 368–87.
Jones, A. H. M. *The Greek City.* New York: Oxford, 1940.
_____. "Prefects and Procurators in the Early Principate." In *Studies in
    Roman Government and Law.* Pages 115–25. New York: Basil
    Blackwell, 1960.
_____. *The Herods of Judaea.* Rev. ed. Oxford: Clarendon, 1967.
_____. *The Cities of the Eastern Roman Provinces.* 2d ed. Ed. Michael
    Avi-Yonahet et al. New York: Oxford, 1971.
_____. *The Roman Economy: Studies in Ancient Economic and Adminis-
    trative History.* Ed. P. A. Brunt. Oxford: Basil Blackwell, 1974.
Jones, C. P. "The Plancii of Perge and Diana Planciana." *Harvard
    Studies in Classical Philology* 80 (1976) 231–37.
Joshel, S. R. *Work, Identity, and Legal Status at Rome: A Study of the
    Occupational Inscriptions.* Norman: University of Oklahoma, 1992.
Judge, E. A. "The Social Identity of the First Christians: A Question of
    Method in Religious History." *JRH* 11 (1980) 201–17.
Kaufman, M. *The Woman in Jewish Law and Tradition.* Northvale,
    N.J.: Jason Aronson, 1993.
Kearsley, R. A. 1986. "Asiarchs, *Archiereis,* and the *Archiereiai* of
    Asia." *GRBS* 27: 183–92.
Kee, H. C. *Christian Origins in Sociological Perspective.* Philadel-
    phia: Fortress, 1980.
_____. *Miracle in the Early Christian World.* New Haven: Yale, 1982.
_____. *Medicine, Miracle, and Magic in New Testament Times.* New
    York: Cambridge, 1986.
_____. *Knowing the Truth: A Sociological Approach to New Testament
    Interpretation.* Philadelphia: Fortress, 1989.
King, U. *Women in the World's Religions: Past and Present.* New
    York: Paragon House, 1987.
Klausner, J. "Queen Salome Alexandra." In *The World History of the
    Jewish People. Volume 6, The Hellenistic Age.* Ed. A. Schalit.
    Pages 242–54. New Brunswick, N.J.: Rutgers, 1972.

Kraemer, R. S. *Maenads, Martyrs, Matrons, Monastics: A Sourcebook on Women's Religions in the Greco-Roman World.* Philadelphia: Fortress, 1988.

_____. *Her Share of the Blessings: Women's Religions among Pagans, Jews, and Christians in the Greco-Roman World.* New York: Oxford, 1992.

Kreissig, H. *Wirtschaft und Gesellschaft im Seleukidenreich.* Berlin: Akademie, 1978.

Kreitzer, L. J. "A Numismatic Clue to Acts 19:23–41, the Ephesian Cistophori of Claudius and Agrippina." *JSNT* 30 (1987) 59–70.

Kyrtatas, D. J. *The Social Structure of the Early Christian Communities.* New York: Verso, 1987.

Lefkowitz, M. R. "Influential Women." In *Images of Women in Antiquity.* Ed. A. Cameron and A. Kuhrt. Pages 49–64. Detroit: Wayne State University, 1983.

Lefkowitz, M. R., and M. B. Fant. *Women in Greece and Rome.* Toronto: Samuel-Stevens, 1977.

_____. *Women's Life in Greece and Rome.* London: Duckworth, 1982.

Le Gall, J. "Un critère de différenciation sociale: La situation de la femme." In *Recherches sur les structures sociales dans l'antiquité classique.* Ed. C. Nicolet. Pages 275–86. Paris: Editions du Centre National de la Recherche Scientifique, 1970.

Lenski, G. E. *Power and Prestige: A Theory of Social Stratification.* New York: McGraw-Hill, 1966.

Lenski, G. E., and J. Lenski. *Human Societies: An Introduction.* 5th ed. New York: McGraw-Hill, 1987.

Levick, B. *Roman Colonies in Southern Asia Minor.* Oxford: Clarendon, 1967.

Lévy, I. "Etudes sur la vie municipale de l'Asie Mineure sous les Antonins." *REG* 8 (1895) 203–50; 11 (1899) 255–89; 14 (1901) 350–71.

Lipset, S. M. "Social Class." *IESS.* 15.296–316.

Littlejohn, J. *Social Stratification.* London: George Allen & Unwin, 1972.

Loewe, R. *The Position of Women in Judaism.* London: SPCK, 1966.

Love, S. L. "Women's Role in Certain Second Testament Passages: A Macrosociological View." *BTB* 17 (1987) 50–59.

MacDonald, D. "Virgins, Widows and Paul in Second Century Asia Minor." In SBLSP 16. Pages 169–84. 2 vols. Chico, Calif.: Scholars, 1979.

MacMullen, R. *Enemies of the Roman Order: Treason, Unrest, and Alienation in the Empire.* Cambridge: Harvard, 1966.

_____. *Roman Social Relations: 50 B.C. to A.D. 284.* New Haven: Yale, 1974.

_____. "Woman in Public in the Roman Empire." *Historia* 29 (1980) 208–18.

Macurdie, G. *Hellenistic Queens: A Study in Woman-Power in Macedonia, Seleucid Syria, Ptolemaic Egypt.* Johns Hopkins University Studies in Archaeology 14. Baltimore: Johns Hopkins, 1932. Reprint. New York: AMS, 1967.

_____. *Vassal-Queens and Some Contemporary Women in the Roman Empire.* Johns Hopkins University Studies in Archaeology 22. Baltimore: Johns Hopkins, 1937.

Magie, D. *Roman Rule in Asia Minor to the End of the Third Century after Christ.* 2 vols. Princeton: Princeton, 1950.

Makal, M. *A Village in Anatolia.* Trans. W. Deedes. London: Vallentine & Mitchell, 1954.

Malherbe, A. J. *Social Aspects of Early Christianity.* 2d ed. Philadelphia: Fortress, 1983.

Malina, B. J. *The New Testament World: Insights from Cultural Anthropology.* Atlanta: John Knox, 1981.

_____. "The Social Sciences and Biblical Interpretation." In *The Bible and Liberation: Political and Social Hermeneutics.* Ed. N. K. Gottwald. Pages 11–25. Maryknoll, N.Y.: Orbis, 1983.

_____. *Christian Origins and Cultural Anthropology: Practical Models for Biblical Interpretation.* Atlanta: John Knox, 1986.

_____. "Dealing with Biblical (Mediterranean) Characters: A Guide for U.S. Consumers." *BTB* 19 (1989) 127–41.

Malina, B. J., and R. L. Rohrbaugh. *Social-Science Commentary on the Synoptic Gospels.* Minneapolis: Fortress, 1992.

Mansel, A. M. "Villes mortes d'Asie Mineure occidentale." In *Corsi di Cultura sull'arte Ravennate e Bizantina.* Pages 520–39. Ravenna: Edizioni Dante, 1965.

Marshall, A. J. "Roman Women and the Provinces." *Ancient Society* 6 (1975) 109–27.

Mason, H. J. *Greek Terms for Roman Institutions.* American Studies in Papyrology 13. Toronto: Hakkert, 1974.

McCown, C. C. "ὁ τέκτων." In *Studies in Early Christianity.* Ed. S. J. Case. Pages 173–89. New York: Century, 1928.

McKay, A. *Houses, Villas, and Palaces in the Roman World.* London: Thames & Hudson, 1975.

McLaren, J. S. *Power and Politics in Palestine.* JSOTSup 63. Sheffield: Sheffield Academic, 1991.

Meeks, W. A. *The First Urban Christians: The Social World of the Apostle Paul.* New Haven: Yale, 1983.

Millar, F. *The Roman Near East, 31 B.C.–A.D. 337.* Cambridge: Harvard, 1993.

Mitchell, S. "The Plancii in Asia Minor." *JRS* 64 (1974) 27–39.

____. *Anatolia: Land, Men, and Gods in Asia Minor.* 2 vols. New York: Oxford, 1993.

Moore, G. F. *Judaism in the First Centuries of the Christian Era: The Age of the Tannaim.* 3 vols. Cambridge: Harvard, 1954.

Moxnes, H. "Sociology and the New Testament." In *Religion as a Social Phenomenon: Theologians and Sociologists Sharing Research Interests.* Ed. Erik Karlsaune. Pages 143–59. Trondheim: Tapir, 1988.

Murphy, F. J. *The Religious World of Jesus.* Nashville: Abingdon, 1991.

Neusner, J. *A History of the Mishnaic Law of Women.* 5 vols. Leiden: Brill, 1980.

____. *A History of the Mishnaic Law of Damages.* 5 vols. Leiden: Brill, 1985.

Nouoner, J., et al., eds. *The Social World of Formative Christianity and Judaism.* Philadelphia: Fortress, 1988.

Nicolet, C. *Recherches sur les structures sociales dans l'antiquité classique.* Paris: Editions du Centre National de la Recherche Scientifique, 1970.

Osiek, C. *What Are They Saying about the Social Setting of the New Testament?* New York: Paulist, 1984.

Packer, J. E. "Housing and Population in Imperial Ostia and Rome." *JRS* 57 (1967) 77–95.

____. *The Insulae of Imperial Ostia.* Rome: American Academy, 1971.

Paris, P. *Quatenus Feminae Res Publicas in Asia Minore, Romanis Imperantibus, Attigerint.* Paris: Ernest Thorin, 1891.

Peradotto, J., and J. P. Sullivan, eds. *Women in the Ancient World: The Arethusa Papers.* Albany: State University of New York, 1984.

Pflaum, H. G. "Titulaire et rang social durant le Haut-Empire." In *Recherches sur les structures sociales dans l'antiquité classique.* Ed. C. Nicolet. Pages 159–86. Paris: Editions du Centre National de la Recherche Scientifique, 1970.

Pilch, J. J. "Understanding Healing in the Social World of Early Christianity." *BTB* 22 (1992) 26–33.

Pleket, H. W. "Urban Elites and Business in the Greek Part of the Roman Empire." In *Trade in the Ancient Economy.* Ed. P. Garnsey, K. Hopkins, and C. R. Whittaker. Pages 131–44. Los Angeles: University of California, 1983.

Poloma, M. M. "Toward a Christian Sociological Perspective: Religious Values, Theory and Methodology." *Sociological Analysis* 43 (1982) 95–108.

Pomeroy, S. B. *Goddesses, Whores, Wives, and Slaves: Women in Classical Antiquity.* New York: Schocken, 1975.

_____. *Women in Hellenistic Egypt.* New York: Schocken, 1984.

_____, ed. *Women's History and Ancient History.* Chapel Hill: University of North Carolina, 1991.

Préaux, C. "Le statut de la femme à l'époque hellénistique, principalement en Egypt." *Recueils de la société Jean Bodin. La Femme* 11 (1959) 127–75.

Raepsaet-Charlier, M.-T. "Epouses et familles de magistrats dans les provinces romaines aux deux premiers siècles de l'Empire." *Historia* 31 (1982) 56–67.

_____. *Prosopographie des femmes de l'ordre sénatorial (Ier–IIe siècles).* 2 vols. Louvain: Peeters, 1987.

Ramsay, W. M. *The Cities of St. Paul: Their Influence on His Thought and Life.* London: Hodder & Stoughton, 1907.

_____. *The Social Basis of Roman Power in Asia Minor.* Ed. J. G. C. Anderson. Aberdeen: Aberdeen University, 1941.

Reumann, J. " 'Stewards of God'—Pre-Christian Religious Application of the *Oikonomos* in Greek." *JBL* 77 (1958) 339–49.

Richter, P. J. "Recent Sociological Approaches to the Study of the New Testament." *Religion* 14 (1984) 77–90.

Robert, J., and L. Robert. "Bulletin épigraphique." *REG* 80 (1967) 548–49.

Robert, L. *Etudes anatoliennes.* Paris: E. de Boccard, 1937. Reprint. Amsterdam: A. M. Hakkert, 1970.

Rodd, C. S. "On Applying a Sociological Theory to Biblical Studies." *JSOT* 30 (1981) 95–106.

Rodman, H. "The Structure of Stratification Systems." *IESS.* 15: 325–37.

Rohrbaugh, R. L. "Methodological Considerations in the Debate over the Social Class Status of Early Christians." *JAAR* 52 (1983) 519–46.

_____. " 'Social Location of Thought' as a Heuristic Construct in New Testament Study." *JSNT* 30 (1987) 103–19.

Rostovtzeff, M. *The Social and Economic History of the Hellenistic World.* 2d ed. 3 vols. New York: Clarendon, 1953.

_____. *The Social and Economic History of the Roman Empire.* 2d ed. 2 vols. Ed. P. M. Fraser. New York: Clarendon, 1957.

Rowland, C. "Reading the New Testament Sociologically: An Introduction." *Theology* 88 (1985) 358–64.

Runcimann, W. G. "Class, Status, and Power." In *Social Stratification.* Ed. J. A. Jackson. Pages 25–61. New York: Cambridge, 1968.

Safrai, S. "Home and Family." In *The Jewish People in the First Century.* 2 vols. Ed. S. Safrai and M. Stern. Vol. 2, pages 728–92. CRINT. Philadelphia: Fortress, 1976.

Safrai, S., and M. Stern, eds. *The Jewish People in the First Century.* 2 vols. CRINT. Philadelphia: Fortress, 1976.

Saldarini, A. J. *Pharisees, Scribes, and Sadducees in Palestinian Society: A Sociological Approach.* Wilmington, Del: Michael Glazier, 1988.

Sanders, E. P. *Judaism: Practice and Belief, 63 BCE–66 CE.* Philadelphia: Trinity, 1992.

Schaps, D. M. *Economic Rights of Women in Ancient Greece.* Edinburgh: Edinburgh University, 1979.

Schottroff, W., and W. Stegemann, eds. *The God of the Lowly: Social-Historical Interpretations of the Bible.* Maryknoll, N.Y.: Orbis, 1984.

Schürer, E. *The History of the Jewish People in the Age of Jesus Christ (175 B.C.–A.D. 135).* 3 vols. Ed. and enl. G. Vermes, F. Millar, and M. Black. Edinburgh: T. & T. Clark, 1979.

Schütz, J. H. Introduction. In *The Social Setting of Pauline Christianity: Essays on Corinth* by Gerd Theissen. Trans. Ed. J. H. Schütz. Pages 1–23. Philadelphia: Fortress, 1982.

Scroggs, R. "The Earliest Christian Communities as Sectarian Movement." In *Christianity, Judaism, and Other Greco-Roman Cults.* Vol. 2. Pages 1–23. Ed. J. Neusner. 4 vols. Leiden: Brill, 1975.

_____. "The Sociological Interpretation of the New Testament: The Present State of Research." *NTS* 26 (1980) 164–79.

Sherwin-White, A. N. *Roman Society and Roman Law in the New Testament.* New York: Clarendon, 1963.

Sjoberg, G. *The Preindustrial City Past and Present.* Glencoe, Ill: Free Press, 1960.

Skinner, M. B. *Rescuing Creusa: New Methodological Approaches to Women in Antiquity.* Helios 13. Lubbock, Tex.: Texas Tech, 987.

Smallwood, E. M. *The Jews under Roman Rule.* Leiden: Brill, 1981.

Smith, J. Z. "The Social Description of Early Christianity." *Religious Studies Review* 1 (1975) 19–25.

Smith, R. H. "Were the Early Christians Middle-Class? A Sociological Analysis of the New Testament." In *The Bible and Liberation: Political and Sociological Hermeneutics.* Ed. N. K. Gottwald. Pages 441–57. Maryknoll, N.Y.: Orbis, 1983.

Sperber, D. "Cost of Living in Roman Palestine." *JESHO* 8 (1965) 248–71.

Stambaugh, J. E., and D. L. Balch. *The New Testament in Its Social Environment.* Library of Early Christianity 2. Philadelphia: Westminster, 1986.

Stark, R. "The Class Basis of Early Christianity: Inferences from a Sociological Model." *Sociological Analysis* 47 (1987): 216–25.

Ste. Croix, G. E. M. de. "Early Christian Attitudes to Property and Slavery." In *Church, Society, and Politics*. Ed. D. Baker. Pages 1–38. New York: Oxford, 1975.

_____. *The Class Struggle in the Ancient Greek World*. 2d ed. Ithaca: Cornell, 1989.

Stern, M. "Aspects of Jewish Society: The Priesthood and Other Classes. In *The Jewish People in the First Century*. 2 vols. Ed. S. Safrai and M. Stern. Vol. 2, pages 561–630. CRINT. Philadelphia: Fortress, 1976.

Stowers, S. K. "The Social Sciences and the Study of Early Christianity." Pages 149–81. In *Approaches to Ancient Judaism*. Ed. W. S. Green. Missoula, Mont.: Scholars, 1978.

Svencickaja, I. S. "Some Problems of Agrarian Relations in the Province of Asia." *Eirene* 15 (1977) 27–54.

Tenney, F., ed. *An Economic Survey of Ancient Rome*. Vol. 4. Baltimore: John Hopkins, 1938. Reprint. Paterson, N.J.: Pagent Books, 1959.

Theissen, G. *Sociology of Early Palestinian Christianity*. Trans. John Bowden. Philadelphia: Fortress, 1978.

_____. *The Social Setting of Pauline Christianity: Essays on Corinth*. Trans. and ed. J. H. Schütz. Philadelphia: Fortress, 1982.

_____. "The Sociological Interpretation of Religious Traditions: Its Methodological Problems as Exemplified in Early Christianity." In *The Bible and Liberation: Political and Sociological Hermeneutics*. Ed. N. K. Gottwald. Pages 38–58. Maryknoll, N.Y.: Orbis, 1983.

_____. "Vers une théorie de l'histoire sociale du christianisme primitif." *ETR* 63 (1988) 199–225.

Thompson Crawford, D. J. "Nile Grain Transport under the Ptolemies." In *Trade in the Ancient Economy*. Ed. P. Garnsey, K. Hopkins, and C. R. Whittaker. Pages 64–75. Los Angeles: University of California, 1983.

Tidball, D. *An Introduction to the Sociology of the New Testament*. Grand Rapids, Mich: Zondervan, 1983.

_____. *The Social Context of the New Testament*. Grand Rapids, Mich.: Zondervan, 1984.

Trebilco, P. *Jewish Communities in Asia Minor*. New York: Cambridge, 1991.

Van Bremen, R. "Women and Wealth." In *Images of Women in Antiquity*. Ed. A. Cameron and A. Kuhrt. Pages 223–42. Detroit: Wayne State University, 1983.

Vatin, C. *Recherches sur le mariage et la condition de la femme mariée à l'époque hellénistique*. Paris: E. de Boccard, 1970.

Vidal-Naquet, P. "Esclavage et gynécratie." In *Recherches sur les structures sociales dans l'antiquité classique.* Ed. C. Nicolet. Pages 63–80. Paris: Editions du Centre National de la Recherche Scientifique, 1970.

Verner, D. C. *The Household of God: The Social World of the Pastoral Epistles.* Chico, Calif: Scholars, 1983.

Vetters, H. "Die Insulabauten in Ephesos." In *Wohnungsbau im Altertum.* Berlin: Deutschen Archäologischen Instituts, 1978.

Veyne, P. *Bread and Circuses.* Abridged O. Murray. Translated Brian Pearce. London: Penguin, 1990.

Waltzing, J.-P. *Les corporations professionelles chez les Romains.* 4 vols. 1895–1900. Reprint. Rome: "L'Erma" di Bretschneider, 1968.

Weaver, P. R. C. "Social Mobility in the Early Roman Empire: The Evidence of the Imperial Freedmen and Slaves." In *Studies in Ancient Society.* Ed. M. I. Finley. Pages 121–40. Boston: Routledge & Kegan Paul, 1974.

Wegner, J. R. *Chattel or Person? The Status of Women in the Mishnah.* New York: Oxford, 1988.

Westermann, W. *The Slave Systems of Greek and Roman Antiquity.* Memoirs of the American Philosophical Society 40. Philadelphia: American Philosophical Society, 1955.

White, K. D. *Roman Farming.* London: Thames & Hudson, 1970.

White, L. M.. "Sociological Analysis of Early Christian Groups: A Social Historian's Response." *Sociological Analysis* 47 (1986) 249–66.

Zeitlin, S. *The Rise and Fall of the Judaean State: A Political, Social and Religious History of the Second Commonwealth.* 2d ed. Philadelphia: Jewish Publication Society of America, 1969.

GENERAL NT STUDIES

Alter, R. *The Art of Biblical Narrative.* New York: Basic Books, 1981.

Aune, D. E. *The New Testament in Its Literary Environment.* Library of Early Christianity 8. Philadelphia: Westminster, 1987.

Beasley-Murray, G. R. *Jesus and the Kingdom of God.* Grand Rapids, Mich: Eerdmans, 1986.

Camery-Hoggatt, J. *Irony in the Mark's Gospel: Text and Subtext.* New York: Cambridge, 1992.

Crossan, J. D. *The Dark Interval: Towards a Theology of Story.* Niles, Ill: Argus Communications, 1975.

Donahue, J. R. "Tax Collectors and Sinners: An Attempt at Identification." *CBQ* 33 (1971) 39–61.

Duling, D. C. "Matthew's Plurisignificant 'Son of David' in Social Science Perspective: Kinship, Kingship, Magic, and Miracle." *BTB* 22 (1992) 99–116.

_____. "The Kingdom of God." *ABD*. 4.49–69.

Freedman, D., et al., eds. *The Anchor Bible Dictionary*. 6 vols. New York: Doubleday, 1992.

Jeremias, J. *The Parables of Jesus*. New York: Scribners, 1963.

Lohfink, G. *Jesus and Community*. Trans. J. P. Galvin. Philadelphia: Fortress, 1984.

Love, S. L. "The Household: A Major Component for Gender Analysis in the Gospel of Matthew." *BTB* 23 (1993) 21–31.

Oakman, D. E. *Jesus and the Economic Questions of His Day*. Lewiston, N.Y.: Edwin Mellen, 1986.

Schmidt, T. E. *Hostility to Wealth in the Synoptic Gospels*. JSNTSup 17; Sheffield: JSOT, 1987.

Scobie, C. H. H. "The Origins and Development of Samaritan Christianity." *NTS* 19 (1973) 390–414.

Walker, W. O. "Jesus and the Tax Collectors." *JBL* 97 (1978) 221–38.

COMMENTARIES AND GENERAL STUDIES IN LUKE–ACTS

Baltzer, K. "The Meaning of the Temple in the Lukan Writings." *HTR* 58 (1965) 263–77.

Bartchy, S. S. "Community of Goods in Acts: Idealization or Social Reality?" In *The Future of Christianity*. Ed. B. Pearson. Minneapolis: Fortress, 1991.

Brawley, R. L. *Luke–Acts and the Jews: Conflict, Apology, and Conciliation*. Atlanta: Scholars, 1987.

_____. *Centering on God: Method and Message in Luke–Acts*. Louisville: Westminster/John Knox, 1990.

Bruce, F. F. *The Acts of the Apostles: The Greek Text with Introduction and Commentary*. 3d enl. ed. Grand Rapids, Mich: Eerdmans, 1990.

Cadbury, H. J. *The Making of Luke–Acts*. 2d ed. Rev. and enl. London: SPCK, 1961.

Caird, G. B. *Saint Luke*. Philadelphia: Westminster, 1963.

Chance, J. B.. *Jerusalem, the Temple, and the New Age in Luke–Acts*. Macon, Ga.: Mercer, 1988.

Conzelmann, H. *The Theology of St. Luke*. Trans. Geoffrey Buswell. Philadelphia: Fortress, 1961.

_____. *Acts of the Apostles*. Ed. E. Epp and C. Matthews. Trans. J. Limburg, A. Kraabel, and D. Juel. Philadelphia: Fortress, 1987.

Danker, F. W. *Jesus and the New Age: A Commentary on St. Luke's Gospel.* Rev. ed. Philadelphia: Fortress, 1988.

Darr, J. A. *On Character-Building: The Reader and the Rhetoric of Characterization in Luke–Acts.* Louisville: Westminster/John Knox, 1992.

Dawsey, J. M. *The Lukan Voice: Confusion and Irony in the Gospel of Luke.* Macon, Ga.: Mercer, 1986.

_____. "The Origin of Luke's Positive Perception of the Temple." *Perspectives in Religious Studies* 18 (1991) 5–22.

Dibelius, M. *Studies in the Acts of the Apostles.* Ed. H. Greeven. Trans. Mary Ling. London: SCM, 1956.

Elliott, J. H. "Household and Meals vs. Temple Purity Replication Patterns in Luke–Acts." *BTB* 21 (1991) 102–8.

_____. "Temple versus Household in Luke–Acts." In *The Social World of Luke-Acts: Models for Interpretation.* Ed. J. H. Neyrey. Pages 211–39. Peabody, Mass: Hendrickson, 1991.

Elliot, J. K. "Jerusalem in Acts and the Gospels." *NTS* 23 (1077) 462–69.

Esler, P. F. *Community and Gospel in Luke–Acts: The Social and Political Motivations of Lucan Theology.* New York: Cambridge, 1987.

_____. "Glossalalia and the Admission of Gentiles into the Early Christian Community." *BTB* 22 (1992) 136–42.

Fitzmyer, J. A. *The Gospel according to Luke.* 2 vols. AB 28, 28a. New York: Doubleday, 1981–85.

Foakes Jackson, F. J., and K. Lake, eds. *The Beginnings of Christianity.* 5 vols. London: Macmillan, 1920–33.

Garrett, S. R. *The Demise of the Devil: Magic and the Demonic in Luke's Writings.* Minneapolis: Augsburg/Fortress, 1991.

Gasque, W. W. *A History of Interpretation of the Acts of the Apostles.* Reprint. Peabody, Mass: Hendrickson, 1989.

Grassi, J. A. *God Makes Me Laugh: A New Approach to Luke.* Wilmington, Del: Michael Glazier, 1986.

Haenchen, E. *The Acts of the Apostles: A Commentary.* Trans. R. McL. Wilson. Philadelphia: Westminster, 1971.

Hardon, J. A. "The Miracle Narratives in the Acts of the Apostles." *CBQ* 16 (1954) 303–18.

Hemer, C. J. *The Book of Acts in the Setting of Hellenistic History.* Ed. Conrad H. Gempf. Tübingen: J. C. B. Mohr (Paul Siebeck), 1989.

Hubbard, B. J. "Luke, Josephus, and Rome: A Comparative Approach to the Lukan *Sitz im Leben.*" In SBLSP 16. Pages 59–68. 2 vols. Chico, Calif.: Scholars, 1979.

Jervell, J. "The Lost Sheep of the House of Israel: The Understanding of the Samaritans in Luke–Acts." In *Luke and the People of God:*

    A New Look at Luke–Acts. Pages 113–32. Minneapolis: Augsburg, 1972.

Johnson, L. T. *The Literary Function of Possessions in Luke–Acts.* SBLDS 39. Missoula, Mont: Scholars, 1977.

_____. "On Finding the Lukan Community: A Cautious Cautionary Essay." In SBLSP 16. Pages 87–100. 2 vols. Chico, Calif.: Scholars, 1979.

_____. *Luke–Acts: A Story of Prophet and People.* Chicago: Franciscan Herald, 1981.

_____. *Sharing Possessions.* Philadelphia: Fortress, 1981.

Karris, R. J. "The Lukan *Sitz im Leben:* Methodology and Prospects." In SBLSP 10. Pages 219–33. Missoula, Mont.: Scholars, 1973.

_____. "Missionary Communities: New Paradigms for the Study of Luke–Acts." *CBQ* 41 (1979) 80–97.

_____. "Windows and Mirrors: Literary Criticism and Luke's *Sitz im Leben.*" In SBLSP 16. Pages 47–58. 2 vols. Chico, Calif.: Scholars, 1979.

Keck, L. E., and J. L. Martyn, eds. *Studies in Luke–Acts.* Philadelphia: Fortress, 1980.

Kraybill, D., and D. M. Sweetland. "Possessions in Luke–Acts." *Perspectives in Religious Studies* 10 (1983) 215–39.

Kurz, W. S. *Reading Luke–Acts: Dynamics of Biblical Narrative.* Louisville: Westminster/John Knox, 1993.

Maddox, R. L. *The Purpose of Luke–Acts.* Ed. John Riches. Edinburgh: T. & T. Clark, 1982.

Malina, B. J., and J. H. Neyrey. "Honor and Shame in Luke–Acts: Pivotal Values of the Mediterranean World." In *The Social World of Luke–Acts: Models for Interpretation.* Ed. J. H. Neyrey. Pages 25–65. Peabody, Mass: Hendrickson, 1991.

_____. "Reading Theory Perspective: Reading Luke–Acts." In *The Social World of Luke–Acts: Models for Interpretation.* Ed. J. H. Neyrey. Pages 3–24. Peabody, Mass: Hendrickson, 1991.

Marshall, I. H. *The Gospel of St. Luke: A Commentary on the Greek Text.* Exeter: Paternoster, 1978.

Mattill, A. J., ed. *A Classified Bibliography of Literature on the Acts of the Apostles.* Leiden: Brill, 1966.

Mills, W. E., ed. *A Bibliography of the Periodical Literature on the Acts of the Apostles.* NovTSup 58. Leiden: Brill, 1986.

Morris, L. *The Gospel according to St. Luke.* Grand Rapids, Mich: Eerdmans, 1974.

Moscato, M. A. "Current Theories Regarding the Audience of Luke–Acts." *CurTM* 3 (1976) 355–61.

Moxnes, H. *The Economy of the Kingdom: Social Conflict and Economic Relations in Luke's Gospel.* Philadelphia: Fortress, 1988.

Munck, J. *The Acts of the Apostles.* Rev. W. Albright and C. Mann. AB 31. Garden City, N.Y.: Doubleday, 1967.

Neyrey, J. H., ed. *The Social World of Luke–Acts: Models for Interpretation.* Peabody, Mass: Hendrickson, 1991.

Oakman, D. E. "Was Jesus a Peasant? Implication for Reading the Samaritan Story (Luke 10:30–35)." *BTB* 22 (1992) 117–25.

O'Toole, R. F. "Activity of the Risen Jesus in Luke–Acts." *Bib* 62 (1981) 471–98.

Packer, J. W. *Acts of the Apostles.* New York: Cambridge, 1966.

Pervo, R. I. *Profit with Delight: The Literary Genre of the Acts of the Apostles.* Philadelphia: Fortress, 1987.

Pilch, J. J. "Sickness and Healing in Luke–Acts." *TBT* 27 (1989) 21–28.

Pilgrim, W. *Good News to the Poor: Wealth and Poverty in Luke–Acts.* Minneapolis: Augsburg, 1981.

Plummer, A. *A Critical and Exegetical Commentary on the Gospel according to S. Luke.* 5th ed. ICC. Edinburgh: T. & T. Clark, 1922.

Powell, M. A. "The Religious Leaders in Luke: A Literary-Critical Study." *JBL* 109 (1990) 93–110.

Reese, Thomas. "The Political Theology of Luke–Acts." *Biblical Theology* 22 (1972) 62–65.

Robbins, Vernon K. "The Social Location of the Implied Author of Luke–Acts." In *The Social World of Luke–Acts: Models for Interpretation.* Ed. J. H. Neyrey. Pages 305–32. Peabody, Mass: Hendrickson, 1991.

Seccombe, D. P. *Possessions and the Poor in Luke–Acts.* Linz: Studien zum Neuen Testament und seiner Umwelt, 1983.

Segbroeck, F. *The Gospel of Luke: A Cumulative Bibliography, 1973–88.* Louvain: Leuvin, 1989.

Smith, D. E. "Table Fellowship as a Literary Motif in the Gospel of Luke." *JBL* 106 (1987) 613–38.

Sternberg, M. *The Poetics of Biblical Narrative.* Bloomingtom: Indiana University, 1987.

Talbert, C. H. *Literary Patterns, Theological Themes, and the Genre of Luke–Acts.* SBLMS 20. Missoula, Mont: Scholars, 1975.

_____, ed. *Luke–Acts: New Perspectives from the Society of Biblical Literature Seminar.* New York: Crossroad, 1984.

_____. *Reading Luke: A Literary and Theological Commentary on the Third Gospel.* New York: Crossroad, 1988.

Tannehill, R. C. *The Narrative Unity of Luke–Acts.* 2 vols. Philadelphia: Fortress, 1986–90.

Tiede, D. L. *Prophecy and History in Luke–Acts.* Philadelphia: Fortress, 1980.

Wagner, G., ed. *An Exegetical Bibliography of the New Testament: Luke and Acts*. Macon, Ga.: Mercer, 1985.

Webber, R. C. " 'Why Were the Heathen So Arrogant?' The Socio-rhetorical Strategy of Acts 3–4." *BTB* 22 (1992) 19–25.

Weinert, F. D. "The Meaning of the Temple in Luke–Acts." *BTB* 11 (1981) 85–89.

_____. "Luke, the Temple, and Jesus' Saying about Jerusalem's Abandoned House." *CBQ* 44 (1982) 68–76.

_____. "Luke, Stephen, and the Temple in Luke–Acts." *BTB* 17 (1987) 88–90.

Wilson, S. G. *The Gentiles and the Gentile Mission in Luke–Acts*. New York: Cambridge, 1973.

York, J. O. *The Last Shall Be First: The Rhetoric of Reversal in Luke*. JSNTSup 46; Sheffield: JSOT, 1991.

WOMEN

Abrahamsen, V. "Women at Philippi: The Pagan and Christian Evidence." *JFSR* 3 (1987) 17–30.

Alexander, L. "Sisters in Adversity: Retelling Martha's Story." In *Women in the Biblical Tradition*. Ed. G. J. Brooke. Pages 167–86. Studies in Women and Religion 31. Lewiston, N.Y.: Edwin Mellen, 1992.

Bailey, K. E. "The Song of Mary: Vision of a New Exodus (Lk. 1:46–55)." *Near Eastern School of Theology* 2 (1979) 29–35.

Bass, D. C. "Women's Studies and Biblical Studies: An Historical Perspective." *JSOT* 22 (1982) 6–12.

Beauduin, A. "The Infancy Narratives, a Confession of Faith: Texts from Lk. 1." *Lumen Vitae* 39 (1984) 167–77.

Benoit, P. "Et toi-même, un glaive te transpercera l'âme. (Lc. 2, 35)." *CBQ* 25 (1963) 251–61.

Berger, K. "Das Canticum Simeonis (Lk. 2: 29–32)." *NovT* 27 (1985) 27–39.

Beydon, F. "Luc et 'ces dames de la haute société.' " *ETR* 61 (1986) 331–41.

_____. "A temps nouveau, nouvelles questions: Luc 10:38–42." *FoiVie* 88 (1989) 25–32.

Blank, J. "Frauen in den Jesusüberlieferungen." Pages 9–91. In *Die Frau im Urchristentum*. Ed. G. Dautzenberg et al. QD 95. Freiburg i.B.: Herder, 1983.

Bode, E. L. *The First Easter Morning: The Gospel Accounts of the Women's Visit to the Tomb of Jesus*. Rome: Biblical Institute, 1970.

Boucher, M. I. "Women and Apostolic Community." In *Women Priests*. Ed. A. Swidler and L. Swidler. Pages 152–55. New York: Paulist, 1977.

Bouwman, G. "La pécheresse hospitalière (Lc. VII, 36–50)." *NTS* 45 (1969) 172–79.

Braumann, G. "Die Schuldner und die Sünderin Luk. vii. 36–50." *NTS* 10 (1964) 487–93.

Brennan, I. "Women in the Gospels." *New Blackfriars.* 52 (1971) 291–99.

Brooke, G. J. *Women in the Biblical Tradition.* Studies in Women and Religion 31. Lewiston, N.Y.: Edwin Mellen, 1992.

Brooten, B. "Feminist Perspectives on New Testament Exegesis." In *Conflicting Ways of Interpreting the Bible.* Ed. H. Küng. Pages 55–61. Consilium Religion in the Eighties 138. New York: Seabury, 1980.

_____. "Early Christian Women and their Cultural Context." Pages 66–91. In *Feminist Perspectives on Biblical Scholarship.* Ed. A. Yarbro Collins. 1985.

Brown, P. *The Body and Society: Men, Women, and Sexual Renunciation in Early Christianity.* New York: Columbia, 1988.

Brown, R. E. "The Presentation of Jesus (Luke 2:22–40)." *Worship* 51 (1977) 2–11.

_____. *The Birth of the Messiah.* Garden City, N.Y.: Doubleday, 1979.

_____. "Roles of Women in the Fourth Gospel." *TS* 36 (1975) 692–93.

Brown, R. E., et al., eds. *Mary in the New Testament.* Philadelphia: Fortress, 1978.

Brutscheck, J. "Lukanische Anliegen in der Maria-Marta-Erzählung: Zu Lk. 10:38–42." *Geist und Leben* 62 (1989) 84–96.

Busman, C. "Gibt es christologische Begründungen für Unterordnung der Frau im Neuen Testament?" Pages 254–62. In *Die Frau im Urchristentum.* Ed. G. Dautzenberg et al. QD 95. Freiburg i.B.: Herder, 1983.

Carmignac, J. "The Meaning of *PARTHENOS* in Luke 1:27—a Reply to C. H. Dodd." *BT* 28 (1977) 327–30.

Carmody, D. L. *Biblical Women.* New York: Crossroad, 1988.

Cassidy, R. J., and P. J. Scharper, eds. *Political Issues in Luke–Acts.* Maryknoll, N.Y.: Orbis, 1983.

Castelli, E. "Virginity and Its Meaning for Women's Sexuality in Early Christianity." *JFSR* 2 (1986) 74–78.

Chafins, T. L. "Women and Angels . . . When They Speak It's Time to Listen! A Study of the Structure of Luke 23:50–24:12." *Ashland Theological Bulletin* 21 (1990) 11–17.

Christ, C. P., and J. Plaskow, eds. *Womanspirit Rising: A Feminist Reader in Religion.* San Francisco: Harper & Row, 1979.

Clark, S. B. *Man and Woman in Christ: An Examination of the Roles of Men and Women in Light of Scriptures and the Social Sciences.* Ann Arbor, Mich: Servant Books, 1980.

Collins, A. "The Ministry of Women in the Apostolic Generation." In *Women Priests.* Ed. A. Swidler and L. Swidler. Pages 159–66. New York: Paulist, 1977.

_____, ed. *Feminist Perspectives on Biblical Scholarship.* Chico, Calif.: Scholars, 1985.

Corley, K. "Were the Women around Jesus Really Prostitutes? Women in the Context of Greco-Roman Meals." In SBLSP 28. Pages 487–521. Atlanta: Scholars, 1989.

_____. *Private Women, Public Meals: Social Conflict in the Synoptic Tradition.* Peabody, Mass: Hendrickson, 1993.

Craig, K. M., and M. A. Kristjansson. "Women Reading as Men/Women Reading as Women: A Structural Analysis for the Historical Project." *Semeia* 51 (1990) 119–36.

Creach, J. F. *The Nature of Marian Discipleship in Luke–Acts: A Test of Feminist Theological Reconstruction (Fiorenza).* Thesis, Southern Baptist Seminary. Ann Arbor, Mich: University Microfilms International, 1989.

D'Angelo, M. R. "Beyond Father and Son." In *Justice as Mission: An Agenda for the Church.* Ed. T. Brown and C. Lind. Pages 107–18. Ontario: Trinity, 1985.

_____. "Images of Jesus and the Christian Call in the Gospels of Luke and John." *Spirituality Today* 37 (1985) 196–212.

_____. "Women in Luke–Acts: A Redactional View." *JBL* 109 (1990) 441–61.

_____. "Women Partners in the New Testament." *JFSR* 6 (1990) 65–86.

Daniélou, J. *The Ministry of Women in the Early Church.* Trans. Bishop of Llandaff. London: Faith, 1961.

Dautzenberg, G., et al., eds. *Die Frau im Urchristentum.* QD 95. Freiburg i.B.: Herder, 1983.

Davies, S. "Women in the Third Gospel and the New Testament Apocrypha." In *"Women Like This": New Perspectives on Jewish Women in the Greco-Roman World.* Ed. A.-J. Levine. Pages 185–98. Society of Biblical Literature. Atlanta: Scholars, 1991.

de Jonge, H. J. "Sonship, Wisdom, and Infancy: Luke 2:41–51a." *NTS* 24 (1978) 317–54.

de la Potterie, I. "Κεχαριτωμένη en Lc. 1:28: Etude exégétique et théologique." *Bib* 68 (1987) 357–82.

_____. "Κεχαριτωμένη en Lc. 1:28: Etude philologique." *Bib* 68 (1987) 480–508.

Delobel, J. "L'onction par la pécheresse: La composition littéraire de Lc. VII, 36–50." *ETL* 42 (1966) 415–75.

_____. "Encore la pécheresse: Quelques réflexions critiques." *ETL* 45 (1969) 180–83.

_____. "Le monde, la logique, et le sens du Magnificat." *Sémiotique biblique* 53 (1989) 1–17.

Demel, S. "Jesu Umgang mit Frauen nach dem Lukasevangelium." *BN* 57 (1991) 41–95.

Derrett, J. D. M. "Further Light on the Narratives of the Nativity." *NovT* 17 (1975) 81–108.

_____. "Ananias, Sapphira, and the Right of Property." In *Studies in the New Testament.* Pages 193–201. Leiden: Brill, 1977.

_____. " 'Eating up the Widows Houses': Jesus's Comment on Lawyers?" In *Studies in the New Testament.* Pages 118–27. Leiden: Brill, 1977.

_____. "Law in the New Testament: The Parable of the Unjust Judge." In *Studies in the New Testament.* Pages 32–47. Leiden: Brill, 1977.

_____. "Law in the New Testament: The Syrophoenician Woman and the Centurion of Capernaum." In *Studies in the New Testament.* Pages 143–69. Leiden: Brill, 1977.

Donohue, J. J. "The Penitent Woman and the Pharisee: Luke 7:36–50." *AER* 142 (1960) 414–21.

Drexler, H. "Die grosse Süderin Lucas 7:36–50." *ZNW* 59 (1968) 159–73.

Dupont, J. "Jésus et la pécheresse (Luc 7:36–50)." *Communautés et Liturgies* 65 (1983) 11–17.

Durber, S. "The Female Reader of the Parables of the Lost." In Pages 187–207. *Women in the Biblical Tradition.* Ed. G. J. Brooke. Studies in Women and Religion 31. Lewiston, N.Y.: Edwin Mellen, 1992.

Elliot, J. K. "Anna's Age (Luke 2:36–37)." *NovT* 30 (1988) 100–102.

Epstein, L. *The Jewish Marriage Contract: A Study in the Status of the Woman in Jewish Law.* New York: Arno, 1973.

Evans, M. J. *Woman in the Bible.* Exeter: Paternoster, 1983.

Faxon, A. C. *Women and Jesus.* Philadelphia: Pilgrim, 1973.

Ferry, B.-M. "La pécheresse pardonnée (Lc. 7:36–50): Pourquoi verse-t-elle des pleurs?" *Esprit et Vie* 99 (1989) 174–76.

Feuillet, A. "Les deux onctions faites sur Jésus, et Marie-Madeleine." *RThom* 75 (1975) 357–94.

_____. "Le Sauveur et sa mère dans les récits de l'enfance de Saint Matthieu et de Saint Luc: Deuxième partie." *Divinitas* 34 (1990) 103–50.

Figueras, P. "Symeon et Anne, ou le témoinage de la loi et des prophètes." *NovT* 20 (1978) 84–99.

Fiorenza, E. Schüssler. "Interpreting Patriarchal Traditions." In *The Liberating Word.* Ed. L. Russell. Pages 39–61. Philadelphia: Westminster, 1976.

————. "The Apostleship of Women in Early Christianity." In *Women Priests.* Ed. A. Swidler and L. Swidler. Pages 135–40. New York: Paulist, 1977.

————. "The Twelve." In *Women Priests.* Ed. A. Swidler and L. Swidler. Pages 114–22. New York: Paulist, 1977.

————. "The Study of Women in Early Christianity: Some Methodological Considerations." In *Critical History and Biblical Faith: New Testament Perspectives.* Ed. J. T. Ryan. Pages 30–58. Villanova: Catholic Theology Society, 1979.

————. "Word, Spirit, and Power: Women in Early Christian Communities." In *Women of Spirit.* Ed. R. R. Ruether and E. C. McLaughlin. Pages 29–70. New York: Simon & Schuster, 1979.

————. "Toward a Feminist Biblical Hermeneutic: Biblical Interpretation and Liberation Theology." In *The Challenge of Liberation Theology.* Ed. B. Mahan and L. Richesin. Pages 91–112. Maryknoll, N.Y.: Orbis, 1981.

————. "Feminist Theology and New Testament Interpretation." *JSOT* 22 (1982) 32–46.

————. *In Memory of Her: A Feminist Theological Reconstruction of Christian Origins.* New York: Crossroad, 1983.

————. " 'You Are Not to Be Called Father': Early Christian History in Feminist Perspective." In *The Bible and Liberation: Political and Sociological Hermeneutics.* Ed. N. K. Gottwald. Pages 394–417. Maryknoll, N.Y.: Orbis, 1983.

————. *Bread Not Stone: The Challenge of Feminist Biblical Interpretation.* Boston: Beacon, 1984.

————. "A Feminist Critical Interpretation for Liberation: Martha and Mary—Luke 10:38–42." *Religion and Intellectual Life* 3 (1986) 21–36.

————. "Theological Criteria and Historical Reconstruction: Martha and Mary—Luke 10:38–42." *Center for Hermeneutical Studies Protocol Series* 53 (1987) 1–12.

————. "Les douze dans la communauté des disciples égaux: Contradiction ou malentendu?" *FoiVie* 88 (1989) 13–24.

————. "Lk. 13:10–17: Interpretation for Liberation and Transformation." *TD* 36 (1989) 303–19.

Flanagan, N. M. "The Position of Women in the Writings of St. Luke." *Marianum* 40 (1978) 288–304.

Foley, H. *Reflections on Women in Antiquity.* New York: Gordon & Beach, 1981.

Ford, M. J. " 'The Permanent Value of Jesus and the Apostles.' " In *Women Priests.* Ed. A. Swidler and L. Swidler. Pages 183–90. New York: Paulist, 1977.

_____. "Women Leaders in the New Testament." In *Women Priests*. Ed. A. Swidler and L. Swidler. Pages 132–34. New York: Paulist, 1977.

Geiger, R.. "Die Stellung der geschiedenen Frau in der Umwelt des Neuen Testamentes." Pages 134–57. In *Die Frau im Urchristentum*. Ed. G. Dautzenberg et al. QD 95. Freiburg i.B.: Herder, 1983.

Getty, M. A. "God's Fellow Worker and Apostleship." In *Women Priests*. Ed. A. Swidler and L. Swidler. Pages 176–82. New York: Paulist, 1977.

Goodman, P. "The Mother of Jesus: Thoughts on Her Role." *TBT* 87 (1976) 1006–9.

Grassi, J. A. "Luke, Theologian of Grace, and Mary, Mother of Jesus." *TBT* 51 (1970) 148–54.

_____. *The Hidden Heroes of the Gospels: Female Counterparts of Jesus*. Collegeville, Minn: Liturgical, 1989.

Green, J. B. "Jesus and a Daughter of Abraham (Luke 13:10–17): A Test Case for a Lucan Perspective on Jesus' Miracles." *CBQ* 51 (1989) 643–54.

Gryson, R. *The Ministry of Women in the Early Church*. Collegeville, Minn: Liturgical, 1976.

Gubler, M.-L. "Selig, die geglaubt hat—das Marienbild des Lukas: Überlegungen aus der Perspektiv einer Frau." *TPQ* 136 (1988) 130–39.

Hamel, E. "Le Magnificat et le renversement des situations: Réflexions théologiques-bibliques." *Greg* 60 (1979): 55–84.

Hamerton-Kelly, R. *God the Father: Theology and Patriarchy in the Teaching of Jesus*. Philadelphia: Fortress, 1979.

Hamm, M. D. "The Freeing of the Bent Woman and the Restoration of Israel: Luke 13:10–17 as Narrative Theology." *JSNT* 31 (1987) 23–44.

Heine, S. *Women and Early Christianity*. Trans. John Bowden. 2d ed. Minneapolis: Augsburg, 1988.

Hengel, M. "Maria Magdalena und die Frauen als Zeugen." In *Abraham unser Vater*. Ed. Paul Schmidt. Pages 243–56. Leiden: Brill, 1963.

Holst, R. "The One Anointing of Jesus: Another Application of the Form-Critical Method." *JBL* 95 (1976) 435–46.

Humenay, R. L. "The Place of Mary in Luke: A Look at Modern Biblical Criticism." *AER* 168 (1974) 291–303.

Hurley, J. B. *Man and Woman in Biblical Perspective*. Grand Rapids, Mich: Academie, 1981.

Imbach, J. "Die Türe nicht zuschlagen: Eine Jesusbegegnung als Lehrstück für zwischenmenschliche Beziehungen." *Geist und Leben* 64 (1991) 7–16.

Isaacs, M. E. "Mary in the Infancy Narrative." *Way,* Supplement (1975) 80–95.

Jacquemin, P.-E. "L'accueil de la parole de Dieu: Lc. 11:27–28." *Assemblée du Seigneur* 66 (1973) 10–19.

_____. "Le Magnificat: Lc. 1:46–55." *Assemblée du Seigneur* 66 (1973) 28–40.

Jervell, J. "The Daughters of Jacob." In *The Unknown Paul: Essays on Luke–Acts and Early Christian History.* Trans. R. A. Harrison. Pages 146–57. Minneapolis: Augsburg, 1984.

Karris, R. J. "Mary's *Magnificat* and Recent Study." *Review for Religious* 42 (1983) 903–8.

Ketter, P. *Christ and Womankind.* Trans. Isabel McHugh. 2d ed. Westminster, Md.: Newman, 1952.

Kilgallen, J. J. "John the Baptist, the Sinful Woman, and the Pharisee." *JBL* 104 (1985) 675–79.

_____. "A Proposal for Interpreting Luke 7,36–50." *Bib* 72 (1991) 305–30.

Kirchschlager, W. "Beobachtungen zur Struktur der lukanische Vorgeschichten Lk. 1–2." *BLit* 57 (1984) 244–51.

Kopas, J. "Jesus and Women: Luke's Gospel." *TT* 43 (1986) 192–202.

Küng, H. *Conflicting Ways of Interpreting the Bible.* Consilium Religion in the Eighties 138. New York: Seabury, 1980.

LaLand, E. "Die Martha-Maria Perikope in Lukas 10:38–42. *ST* 13 (1959) 70–85.

LaMarche, P. "La guérison de la belle-mère de Pierre et le genre littéraire des Evangiles." *NRT* 87 (1965) 515–26.

LaVerdière, E. "No Room for Them in the Inn." *Emmanuel* 91 (1985) 552–57.

_____. "The Virgin's Name Was Mary." *Emmanuel* 92 (1986) 185–89.

Legaré, C. "Jésus et la pécheresse: Analyse sémiotique d'un fragment de l'Evangile de Luc 7:36–50. *Sémiotique biblique* 29 (1983) 19–45.

Léon-Dufour, X. "La guérison de la belle-mère de Simon Pierre." *EstBib* 24 (1965) 193–216.

Levine, A.-J. *"Women Like This": New Perspectives on Jewish Women in the Greco-Roman World.* Society of Biblical Literature. Atlanta: Scholars, 1991.

Lohfink, G. "Weibliche Diakone im Neuen Testament." Pages 320–38. In *Die Frau im Urchristentum.* Ed. G. Dautzenberg et al. QD 95. Freiburg i.B.: Herder, 1983.

MacHaffie, B. J. *Her Story: Women in Christian Tradition.* Philadelphia: Fortress, 1986.

Maly, E. H. "Women and the Gospel of Luke." *BTB* 10 (1980) 99–104.

Martin, F. "Le geôlier et la marchande de pourpre: Actes des Apôtres 16:6–40 (première partie)." *Sémiotique et Bible* 59 (1990) 9–29.

Massey, L. F. *Women in the New Testament.* Jefferson, N.C.: McFarland, 1989.

McArthur, H. K. "Son of Mary." *NovT* 15 (1973) 38–58.

McHugh, J. *The Mother of Jesus in the New Testament.* London: Dartman, Longman & Todd, 1975.

Meeks, W. A. "The Myth of the Androgyne: Some Uses of Symbols in Earlier Christianity." *History of Religions* 13 (1974) 165–208.

Mickelsen, A., ed. *Women, Authority, and the Bible.* Downers Grove, Ill: Intervarsity, 1986.

Middleton, D. F. "The Story of Mary: Luke's Version." *New Blackfriar* 70 (1989) 555–64.

Milot, L. "Guérison d'une femme infirme un jour de sabbat (Luc 13:10–17): L'importance d'une comparaison." *Sémiotique biblique* 39 (1985) 23–33.

Minear, P. S. "Luke's Use of the Birth Stories." In *Studies in Luke–Acts.* Ed. L. E. Keck and J. L. Martyn. Pages 111–30. Philadelphia: Fortress, 1980.

Mollenkott, V. *Women, Men, and the Bible.* Nashville: Abingdon, 1977.

Moltmann-Wendel, E. *The Women around Jesus.* New York: Crossroad, 1982.

Nelson, R. D. "David: A Model for Mary in Luke?" *BTB* 18 (1988) 138–42.

Neyrey, J. H. "Jesus' Address to the Women of Jerusalem (Lk. 23:27–31)—a Prophetic Judgment Oracle." *NTS* 29 (1983) 74–86.

Oliver, H. H. "The Lucan Birth Stories and the Purpose of Luke–Acts." *NTS* 10 (1964) 202–26.

Parvey, C. F. "The Theology and Leadership of Women in the New Testament." Pages 117–49. In *Religion and Sexism.* Ed. R. R. Ruether. New York: Simon and Schuster, 1974.

Perkins, P. "Peter's Pentecost Sermon: A Limitation on Who May Minister . . . ?" In *Women Priests.* Ed. A. Swidler and L. Swidler. Pages 156–58. New York: Paulist, 1977.

Pesch, R. "Jairus (Mk. 5, 22/Lk. 8,41)." *BZ* 14 (1970) 252–56.

Plaskow, J., and J. A. Romero, eds. *Women and Religion, Proceedings of the American Academy of Religion, 1972–1973.* Rev. ed. Missoula, Mont: Scholars, 1974.

Pomeroy, S. B., R. Kraemer, and N. Kampen. "Selected Bibliography on Women in Classical Antiquity." In *Women in the Ancient World: The Arethusa Papers.* Ed. J. Peradotto and J. P. Sullivan. Pages 317–72. Albany: State University of New York, 1984.

Portefaix, L. *Sisters Rejoice: Paul's Letter to the Philippians and Luke–Acts as Seen by First-Century Philippian Women.* ConNT 20. Stockholm: Almquist & Wiksell, 1988.

Poucata, P. "Un couple au service de l'évangile: Aquilas et Prisca." *Spiritus* 28 (1987) 165–74.

Quesnell, Q. "The Women at Luke's Supper." In *Political Issues in Luke–Acts.* Ed. R. J. Cassidy and P. J. Scharper. Pages 59–79. Maryknoll, N.Y.: Orbis, 1983.

Ramaroson, L. "Simon et la pécheresse anonyme (Lc. 7:36–50)." *ScEs* 24 (1972) 379–83.

_____. "Le premier, c'est l'amour (Lc. 7:47a)." *ScEs* 39 (1987) 319–29.

Rausch, T. P. "Ordination and the Ministry Willed by Jesus." In *Women Priests.* Ed. A. Swidler and L. Swidler. Pages 123–31. New York: Paulist, 1977.

Ravens, D. A. S. "The Setting of Luke's Account of the Anointing: Luke 7:2–8:3." *NTS* 34 (1988) 282–92.

Reinhartz, A. "From Narrative to History: The Resurrection of Mary and Martha." In *"Women Like This": New Perspectives on Jewish Women in the Greco-Roman World.* Ed. A.-J. Levine. Pages 161–84. Society of Biblical Literature. Atlanta: Scholars, 1991.

Resseguie, J. L. "Automatization and Defamiliarization in Luke 7:36–50." *Literature and Theology* 5 (1991) 137–50.

Ritt, H. "Die Frau und die Osterbotschaft." Pages 117–33. In *Die Frau im Urchristentum.* Ed. G. Dautzenberg et al. QD 95. 1983.

Robbins, V. K. "The Woman Who Touched Jesus' Garment: Socio-rhetorical Analysis of the Synoptic Accounts." *NTS* 33 (1987) 502–15.

Rossmiller, C. J. "Prophets and Discipleship in Luke's Infancy Narratives." *TBT* 22 (1984) 361–65.

Ruether, R. R. *Religion and Sexism.* New York: Simon & Schuster, 1974.

Ruether, R. R., and E. C. McLaughlin, eds. *Women of Spirit.* New York: Simon & Schuster, 1979.

_____. "Women's Leadership in the Jewish and Christian Traditions: Continuity and Change." In *Women of Spirit.* Pages 16–27. New York: Simon & Schuster, 1979.

Russell, L. M., ed. *Feminist Interpretation of the Bible.* Philadelphia: Westminster, 1985.

_____., ed. *The Liberating Word.* Philadelphia: Westminster, 1976.

Ryan, R. "Lydia, a Dealer in Purple Goods." *TBT* 22 (1984) 285–89.

"The Women from Galilee and Discipleship in Luke." *BTB* 15 (1985) 56–59.

Saiving, V. "Androcentrism in Religious Studies." *JR* 56 (1976) 330–45.

Schmidt, P. "Maria in der Sicht des Magnifikat." *Geist und Leben* 46 (1973) 417–30.

____. "Maria und das Magnificat: Maria im Heilshandeln Gottes im Alten und Neuen Gottesvolk." *Catholica* 29 (1975) 230–46.

Schneiders, S. M. "Feminist Ideology Criticism and Biblical Hermeneutics." *BTB* 19 (1989) 3–10.

Schottroff, L. "Maria Magdalena und die Frauen am Grabe Jesus." *EvT* 42 (1982) 3–25.

____. "Women Followers of Jesus in New Testament Times: An Exercise in Socio-historical Exegesis of the Bible." In *The Bible and Liberation: Political and Sociological Hermeneutics.* Ed. N. K. Gottwald. Pages 418–27. Maryknoll, N.Y.: Orbis, 1983.

Sim, D. C. "The Women Followers of Jesus: The Implication of Luke 8:1–3." *HeyJ* 30 (1989) 51–62.

Stagg, E., and F. Stagg. *Woman in the World of Jesus.* Philadelphia: Westminster, 1978.

Stendahl, K. *The Bible and the Role of Women.* Trans. E. T. Sander. Philadelphia: Fortress, 1966.

Stock, A. "Lydia and Prisca." *Emmanuel* 94, no. 9 (1988) 514–21, 25.

Stock, K. "Die Berufung Marias (Lk. 1:26–38)." *Bib* 61 (1980) 457–91.

____. "Von Gott berufen und von den Mensch seliggepreisen: Die Gestalt Marias in Lukas 1: 25–56." *Geist und Leben* 64 (1991) 52–63.

Swidler, A., and L. Swidler, eds. *Women Priests.* New York: Paulist, 1977.

Swidler, L. *Biblical Affirmations of Women.* Philadelphia: Westminster, 1979.

Swidler, L. *Women in Judaism: The Status of Women in Formative Judaism.* Metuchen, N.J.: Scarecrow, 1976.

Tannehill, R. C. "The Magnificat as Poem." *JBL* 93 (1974) 264–75.

Taussig, H. "The Sexual Politics of Luke's Mary and Martha Account: An Evaluation of the Historicity of Luke 10:38–42." *Forum* 7 (1991) 317–19.

Tetlow, E. *Women and Ministry in the New Testament.* New York: Paulist, 1980.

Thurston, B. B. *The Widows: A Women's Ministry in the Early Church.* Minneapolis: Fortress, 1989.

Tolbert, M. A., ed. *The Bible and Feminist Hermeneutics.* Semeia 28. Chico, Calif: Scholars, 1988.

Trible, P. "Depatriarchialization in Biblical Interpretation." *JAAR* 41 (1973) 30–49.

____. *God and the Rhetoric of Sexuality.* Philadelphia: Fortress, 1978.

____, ed. *Texts of Terror: Literary-Feminist Readings of Biblical Narratives.* Overtures to Biblical Theology 13. Philadelphia: Fortress, 1984.

Trudinger, L. P. " 'No Room at the Inn': A Note on Luke 2:27." *ExpT* 102 (1991) 172–73.

Tuckett, C. M. "Feminine Wisdom in Q?" In *Women in the Biblical Tradition.* Ed. G. J. Brooke. Pages 112–28. Studies in Women and Religion 31. Lewiston, N.Y.: Edwin Mellen, 1992.

Tyson, J. B. "The Birth Narratives and the Beginning of Luke's Gospel." *Semeia* 52 (1990) 103–20.

Venetz, H.-J. "Die Suche nach dem 'einem Notwendigen.' Beobachtungen und Verdächtigungen rund um die Marta-Maria-Perikope (Lk. 10:38–42)." *Orientierung* 54 (1990) 185–89.

Via, E. J. "Women, Discipleship of Service, and the Early Christian Ritual Meal in the Gospel of Luke." *StLukeJ* 29 (1985) 37–60.

_____. "Women in the Gospel of Luke." In *Women in the World's Religions: Past and Present.* Ed. U. King. Pages 38–55. New York: Paragon House, 1987.

Wall, R. W. "Martha and Mary (Luke 10:38–42) in the Context of a Christian Deuteronomy." *JSNT* 35 (1989) 19–35.

Wanbrough, H. "The Lowliness of Mary." *Way* 20 (1980) 176–83.

Weiser, A. "Die Rolle der Frau in der urchristlichen Mission." Pages 158–81. In *Die Frau im Urchristentum.* Ed. G. Dautzenberg et al. QD 95. Freiburg i.B.: Herder, 1983.

Wilkinson, J. "The Case of the Bent Woman in Luke 13:10–17." *EvQ* 49 (1977) 195–205.

Winandy, J. "Simon et la pécheresse (Luc 7:36–50)." *BVC* 47 (1962) 38–46.

_____. "La Prophétie de Syméon (Lc. 2:34–35). *RB* 72 (1965) 321–51.

Witherington, B. "On the Road with Mary Magdalene, Joanna, Susanna, and Other Disciples—Luke 8:1–3." *ZNW* 70 (1979) 243–48.

_____. *Women in the Ministry of Jesus.* New York: Cambridge, 1984.

_____. *Women in the Earliest Churches.* New York: Cambridge, 1988.

_____. *Women and the Genesis of Christianity.* Ed. A. Witherington. New York: Cambridge, 1990.

Whitney, W. V. *Women in Luke: An Application of a Reader-Response Hermeneutic.* Diss., Southern Baptist Seminary. Ann Arbor, Mich: University Microfilms International., 1990.

Wright, A. G. "The Widow's Mites: Praise or Lament?—A Matter of Context." *CBQ* 44 (1982) 256–65.

INDEX OF MODERN AUTHORS

INDEX OF ANCIENT SOURCES